Places to Go with Children

IN

MIAMI AND SOUTH FLORIDA

Cheryl Lani Juárez
Deborah Ann Johnson

Chronicle Books ▪ *San Francisco*

To our families, and especially our husbands,
Alfonso and Dwight

Copyright © 1990 by Cheryl Lani Juárez and Deborah Ann Johnson. All rights reserved. No
part of this book may be reproduced in any form without written permission from the
publisher.

Printed in the United States of America.

Library of Congress Cataloging in Publication Data
Juárez, Cheryl Lani.
　　Places to go with children in Miami and south Florida / Cheryl Lani Juárez,
Deborah Ann Johnson.
　　　　p.　　cm.
　　ISBN 0-87701-672-0
　　1. Miami (Fla.)—Description—Guide-books.　　2. Florida—Description and travel—
1981—Guide-books.　　3. Family recreation—Florida—Miami—Guide-books.　　4. Family
recreation—Florida—Guide-books.　　5. Children—Travel—Florida—Miami—Guide-
books.　　6. Children—Travel—Florida—Guide-books.
I. Johnson, Deborah Ann, 1958–　.　　II. Title.
F309.3.J83　　1990
917.5904′63—dc20
　　　　　　　　　　　　　　　　　　　　　　　　　　　　　　　　　　　　　　89-28780
　　　　　　　　　　　　　　　　　　　　　　　　　　　　　　　　　　　　　　CIP

Editing: Marcella Friel
Book design: Seventeenth Street Studios
Cover design: Brenda Eno
Cover photograph: Alfonso Juárez
Composition: Another Point, Inc.

10　9　8　7　6　5　4　3　2　1

Chronicle Books
275 Fifth Street
San Francisco, CA 94103

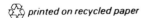 printed on recycled paper

Contents

Introduction

Tell me and I forget.
Teach me and I remember.
Involve me and I learn.

—Benjamin Franklin

Miami. Key West. Palm Beach. Fort Lauderdale. These cities conjure images of exotic vacation destinations for adults, retirement communities, and cruise-ship ports. We've discovered that the area stretching from Tequesta, in Palm Beach County, down to Fort Jefferson, in the Dry Tortugas (68 miles west of the southernmost point in the United States), and west to the Everglades, provides hundreds of places to go with children of all ages. This book aims to help families get out and explore this wonderful part of the world, and, in the process, enjoy spending time together.

As we searched for new settings for our family adventures, we discovered that standard travel guides often neglect children's needs and interests, so it was difficult to find destinations beyond our own neighborhoods. Through informal meetings in playgroups, chats in waiting rooms and school parking lots, and other gatherings where parents share their concerns, we knew that we weren't alone in our dilemma. So we started keeping track of our discoveries (a playground found by making a wrong turn, a restaurant mentioned by a friend of a friend, a store described in an old guidebook), shared them with our network of desperate parents, and realized we would save a lot of time by putting the information we had collected into an organized, easy-to-use, and fun-to-read book.

Our research and writing began—and so did our family crises—one right after another. Trips to the emergency room and the vet, car trouble, unexpected and extended business trips . . . well, let's just say that the month of chicken pox made the rest of it look easy. Our families had no idea how many museums and nature centers they'd get to explore, park playsets they'd get to test, meals they'd get to eat out, or new cultural events they'd get to enjoy. Nor did our husbands realize how many meals they were going to have to cook, or how much housework they would be faced with. In spite of the obstacles, things came together in extraordinary ways, with the help of many special people.

We believe this guidebook will be helpful to many of you "at-home" moms and dads, working parents, "weekend" parents, grandparents, and other relatives, as well as to teachers, homeschoolers, and babysitters. Whether you have just arrived for a short visit, have relocated to South Florida, or have lived here for years, this book will help you find some very special places to make memories with the children in your life.

And now for a word about the places listed in this book. We looked for those appropriate for children up to 12 years of age and tried to cover a broad range of interests. Most are free or cost no more than the price of a movie. Each chapter provides alphabetical listings for Dade, Broward, Palm Beach, and Monroe counties. We've included mailing addresses so you can write ahead for brochures, maps, schedules, or reservations. Note that the weeks from mid-December to after Easter are South Florida's coolest, driest, and busiest. This means that reservations are a must. You'll also find that during summer months some schedules change to accommodate children's vacations and to get the most out of those wonderful long summer evenings, while other places close until after Labor Day.

In a fast-growing area like South Florida, it's very important to call before you go anywhere to confirm the address, hours, cost, and other relevant information, such as wheelchair and stroller access. Most people are happy to give you directions, which is important because maps often do not reflect the area's rapid development. When getting directions for locations in the Florida Keys, be aware that addresses usually include "Mile Markers," which refer to the number of miles traveled from the beginning of U.S. Highway 1 in Key West. Be sure also to find out whether sites are on the ocean or bay side of the highway. For example, John Pennekamp Coral Reef State Park in Key Largo is at Mile Marker (M.M.) 102.5, ocean side. We have confirmed and reconfirmed the information in this book, but you should call ahead anyway. We do!

We have not received any compensation from the organizations or companies listed in this book, nor have we maliciously omitted anyone. As you explore on your own, if you find a favorite spot that we have not mentioned in this guide, please share it with us through Chronicle Books, 275 Fifth Street, San Francisco, California 94103. Our plans include a second edition to *Places to Go with Children in Miami and South Florida*; you may see your suggestions in print there! A Spanish edition of this book is also available; contact us through Chronicle Books if you can't find it in your local bookstores.

We've enjoyed working on this project, and hope it is helpful to all of you who realize that children need to be involved in our world if they are to make it theirs.

On Safari in South Florida

South Florida is a land full of adventures, with a wide variety of wonderful places to go for fun and excitement. You can visit a world-class zoo with elephants, giraffes, orangutans, koalas, and kangaroos; explore shipwrecks full of golden treasures; ride on an airboat through a "sea of grass" like no other on earth; inspect butterflies in a park of their own; and hold baby sea turtles. Each adventure we give our children is a gift that may inspire a new idea, discovery, or question about this world of ours.

Dade County

☐ **HMS *Bounty***
401 Biscayne Boulevard, Miami 33132. (Located at Bayside Marketplace.) (305) 375-0486. Sunday through Thursday, noon–8 P.M.; Saturday, 10 A.M.–10 P.M.; Friday, noon–10 P.M. Adults, $3.50; seniors over 50, $2; children ages 5 to 12, $1.50; children ages 4 and under, free. Group rates available.

Ahoy, mates! Climb on board the HMS *Bounty*, a magical ship enjoyed by young and old. The ship's claim to fame was its role in the filming of Metro-Goldwyn-Mayer's *Mutiny on the Bounty*, starring Marlon Brando and Trevor Howard in 1961. It was recently used in a film adaptation of Robert Louis Stevenson's novel *Treasure Island*. Built in Nova Scotia, the *Bounty* has sailed nearly 100,000 miles. The boat's hosts are dressed in 18th-century pirate garb and give a 30-minute tour that tells the historical background of the ship. **Tips:** Restrooms available at Bayside Marketplace. No stroller or wheelchair access on ship. For party information, see listing in "Celebrate in Style."

☐ **Miami Metrozoo**
12400 SW 152nd Street, Miami 33137. (Go ¼-mile west of Florida Turnpike; three miles west of U.S. 1.) Zoo information, (305) 251-0400;

educational programming, 255-5551. Daily, 9:30 A.M.–5:30 P.M.; ticket booth closes at 4 P.M. Residents of Florida (9:30–11 A.M., Monday through Saturday): adults, $5; children ages 3 to 12, $2.50; Nonresidents (and residents after 11 A.M. Monday through Saturday, and all day Sundays): adults, $8; children ages 3 to 12, $4. Monorail included with admission. Inquire at information booth about family memberships. No rainchecks.

One of the best entertainment investments for local families to make is a membership to this 285-acre cageless zoo, where you will see different animals and events each time you come. PAWS, the children's zoo completed in early 1989, provides you and your children with an opportunity to view animals up close. A petting yard, an amphitheater show, and elephant rides and performances are among the highlights. A small play area, a snack shop, and a gift store are also found in the PAWS vicinity.

A larger playground area is located in the center of the zoo. There you will also find restrooms, eating facilities, kiddie rides, and paddle boat rentals. Another playground can be found near the African elephants.

"Wings of Asia," a free-flight aviary, offers children a chance to see 150 kinds of tropical plants, and over 300 birds of 75 different species. Take a

Safari excitement awaits visitors at PAWS, Miami Metrozoo's children area.

walk through a rain forest, complete with darting birds, waterfalls, ponds, a swinging bridge, and a lookout tower. This sight and sound experience will make you and your children feel like you're on a jungle adventure!

The entire family can take part in the zoo's educational and recreational programs. There are camps for kids, family or group sleep-overs, early-morning breakfasts, after-school programs, and "behind-the-scene" tours. But don't let all of these events steal the show, because the animals themselves really make the zoo what it is—a fascinating and educational experience for everyone. Kangaroos and koalas, chimpanzees and chinchillas, flamingos and felines, gorillas and giraffes—these are the stars of Metrozoo. **Tips:** Best time to visit is in the morning (get to the aviary by 10:30 A.M. to get a close-up view of the birds as they are being fed) or late afternoon, when the weather is cool and the animals are ready to perform. Not a lot of shade, especially near play area. Pick up a complimentary map as you enter, and be prepared to do a lot of walking. A monorail tour is available for an additional fee. Rental strollers for children and adults are available. Diaper-changing table in PAWS' restroom. For party information, see listing in "Celebrate in Style."

□ **Miami Seaquarium**
4400 Rickenbacker Causeway, Key Biscayne 33149. (Ten minutes from downtown Miami.) (305) 361-5703. Daily, 9:30 A.M.–6:30 P.M. Tickets sold until 5 P.M. Shows begin at 10 A.M.; last show begins at 4 P.M. Adults, $13.95 plus tax; children ages 4 to 12, $9.95 plus tax; children under 4, free. Group rates for field trips. Stroller rental $3 per day. AE, MC, V accepted. Rainchecks available.

You definitely get a taste of Florida by visiting the Miami Seaquarium. Dolphins, sharks, sea lions, whales, and manatees are featured here in six different shows that run continuously.

A close-up view of a 10,000-pound killer whale doing tricks in the water is an awesome sight. Dolphins perform acrobatics and sea lions may even give you a kiss. Plus, you can feed the dolphins at their play pool. Perhaps your child's favorite part of the day will be peeking inside one of the 30 aquariums that line the walls of the main building, where tropical fish will keep them entertained for a long time.

To get a bird's-eye view of the attraction, take the monorail ride; for a dolphin's-eye view, try the Show Queen Island Cruise. **Tips:** Cafeteria and snack shops on grounds. Picnic areas outside of gate; playground directly inside gate. Film available in gift shop. Approximately four hours to tour—best time to visit is prior to 4 P.M. to see all shows. Not all shows have stroller access—you must either fold it and carry it with you, or park it outside the arenas. For party information, see listing in "Celebrate in Style."

☐ **Miccosukee Indian Village and Airboat Tours**
Twenty-five miles west of the Florida Turnpike on Tamiami Trail (U.S. 41). Mailing address is P.O. Box 440021, Miami 33144. (305) 223-8380 (weekdays); 223-8399 (weekends). Daily, 9 A.M.–5 P.M. Adults, $5; children ages 5 to 12, $3.50; children under 5, free. Airboat rides $6 per person for 20 minutes. Parking is free.

Tribal members live in traditional village fashion; their homes, called "chickees," are thatch-roofed, open-sided structures. Crafts such as basketry, beading, and patchwork are on display; watch men and women at work as they demonstrate their craft specialties. Older children will enjoy watching an alligator wrestling match. Annual events at the village include a music and crafts festival in July and an Indian arts festival in December. For event information, see listings in "Mark Your Calendar," and for tour information, see listing in "By Land, Sea, and Air."

☐ **Monkey Jungle**
14805 SW 216th Street, Miami 33170. (Four miles west of Florida Turnpike exit SW 216th Street, or about three miles west of U.S. 1.) (305) 235-1611. Daily, 9:30 A.M.–6 P.M. Adults, $8.25; children ages 4 to 12, $4.50; children under 4, free. Resident passes available. AE, MC, V accepted. Rainchecks available in gift shop in case of inclement weather.

Nearly 500 primates, most running free, live in this 20-acre reserve (plans are underway to expand the facility). Stroll the protected walkways while the monkeys roam around you. Some species are in cages. Children can feed many of the monkeys by placing raisins and peanuts (available at the concession area) in metal bowls that swing on a chain. The Java monkeys will anxiously watch and then pull the chain up to reach in for their snack. These monkeys are excellent skin divers in the wild; see a demonstration of their swimming skills during a show at the Monkey Swimming Pool.

Other shows focus on the natural world of chimpanzees and life in the Amazon Rain Forest. A show schedule is given to you when you enter the attraction. Other primates to watch for include the Sumatran orangutans, lowland gorillas, and squirrel monkeys. Field trips are available and special educational presentations can be made by appointment. **Tips:** Check out show schedules and plan your stay around these. Remember to keep an eye on younger children, and especially on little fingers—the monkeys may bite. Concession and picnic area on grounds. Stroller manuevering is difficult in some areas due to bark-chip paths.

☐ Orchid Jungle

26715 SW 157th Avenue, Homestead 33031. (One mile west of U.S. 1; 25 miles south of Miami.) (305) 247-4824; (800) 327-2832. Daily, 8:30 A.M.– 5:30 P.M.; closed Thanksgiving and Christmas. Adults, $5; teens ages 13 to 17, $4; children ages 6 to 12, $1.50; children under 6, free; seniors age 65 and over, $4. Group discounts available.

As the largest outdoor orchid garden in the U.S., this lush tropical jungle covers 20 acres and contains nearly 250,000 plants of 9,000 different varieties. There are display houses and conservatories that may interest older children; however, parents should be cautious with children who like hands-on activities. Remember that many of the tropical plants found here, including ferns, bromeliads, and staghorns, are delicate and easily bruised. Ladies who visit Orchid Jungle receive a free orchid. There are many gorgeous photo opportunities—this would be a lovely place to take a family photo, or to teach an older child about tropical plants and photography. **Tips:** Not recommended for toddlers. Plan to spend at least an hour to see the garden. Patio gift shop sells such collectibles as Hummels, Precious Moments, and Christmas plates. Gravel paths are not good for strollers or wheelchairs.

☐ Parrot Jungle and Gardens

11000 SW 57th Avenue (South Red Road), Miami 33156. (305) 666-7834. Daily, 9:30 A.M.–6 P.M. Tickets sold until 5 P.M. Adults, $9.75; children ages 3 to 12, $4; children under 3, free. Memberships available. AE, MC, V accepted.

This jungle will delight you and your children. As you wind your way through the lush tropical forest, have some fun identifying strange trees and unusual plants (there are signs to help!). The shady trail will take you near an alligator pool, a parrot island, a cactus garden, and the famous Flamingo Lake, where scenes from *Miami Vice, The Miss Universe Pageant,* and other television specials have been filmed.

The parrots here will amaze you and your youngsters with their acrobatic routines, bicycling tricks, high-wire acts, and roller-skating demonstrations. New shows and programs have been added since ownership changed in 1989, including festivals, a children's petting zoo and play area, and a tortoise exhibit. **Tips:** Plan to spend 2½ hours to tour. Stroller rentals available for $1; wheelchairs available free of charge. The Parrot Cafe opens daily at 8 A.M. for breakfast, lunch, and snacks. Snacks also available near Flamingo Lake and original entrance building within the gardens. Picnic tables located near parking lot outside entrance. For party information, see listing in "Celebrate in Style."

□ Spotted Acres Farm

13401 SW 224th Street, Goulds. Mailing address is P.O. Box 397, Goulds 33170. (305) 258-3186. Open exclusively for school field trips on weekdays, September through June, 9 A.M.–noon (one reservation per day for 1½-hour tour), minimum field trip cost $100. Open to families November through May, one Saturday morning per month, 10 A.M.–noon, $2 per person.

Take advantage of an opportunity to feed a baby pig, touch a rooster, and milk a goat. It's not often that city kids get the chance to see life on a working farm, but at Spotted Acres, they can get the flavor! Teachers can take their classes here on a field trip, or families can come on one of the Saturdays designated each month (call first for reservations).

In the spring children may see a baby animal come into the world—not something they see every day! They may also touch and caress the various animals and get a good idea of the way a farm is run. If time permits, kids will get to ride a horse. Make sure there are plenty of adults to help supervise children, especially in large groups. **Tips:** Recommended for children ages 3 and up. Plan to spend about 1½ hours to tour, and bring drinks with you. You must have a reservation—be sure to schedule far in advance. No restroom facilities on grounds. Tours arranged for special groups.

□ Weeks Air Museum, Inc.

14710 SW 128th Street, Miami 33186. (Located in a hangar at Tamiami Airport.) (305) 233-5197. Daily, 10 A.M.–5 P.M. Adults, $4; seniors age 65 and over, $3; children age 12 and under, $2. AE accepted. Annual memberships available.

Children and adults who have traveled with Snoopy on his Sopwith Camel will enjoy seeing a real one on display. This museum has an interesting collection of aircraft from the beginning of flight to the end of the World War II era. The museum was opened to the public in 1987 by champion acrobatic pilot Kermit Weeks.

Over 30 aircraft are on display, and some date back to 1916. Many of the aircraft have been rebuilt and restored, and are in flying condition. A wide variety of engines, propellers, and model planes can be examined. Video booths offer information on the museum's history and memorabilia, and on aircraft-related topics. **Tips:** There is a coffee shop at the airport and a gift shop at the museum. Plan to spend between 30 minutes and two hours to tour. Field trips available with advance reservations.

Broward County

□ Atlantis the Water Kingdom

2700 Stirling Road (just east of I-95), Hollywood 33020. (305) 926-1000. Seasonal hours in spring and summer, depending on school-year calendar; call for exact dates and times. Adults, $11.95 plus tax; children ages 3 to 11, $9.95 plus tax; children under 3, free. AE, MC, V accepted. Seasonal pass available; call for prices and group rates.

Over 65 acres of fun for everyone. The name says it all—water is the main attraction, with one mile of water slides, a wave pool, and Kiddie Cove play area. The All-Star Water Ski Show is a hit with everyone. And be sure to visit the only water maze in South Florida—there's one for every age group. In addition to the water wonders, there are 80 rides, specialty shows, and attractions. If you aren't tired yet, cool off inside the 5,000-square-foot room full of video games. **Tips:** Gift shop and concessions on grounds. Estimated time to tour is five hours; best time to visit is in the morning. This is an outside water attraction, so bring bathing suits, towels, and plenty of sunscreen and drinks.

□ Butterfly World

3600 West Sample Road, Coconut Creek 33073. (Located in Tradewinds Park, just west of the Florida Turnpike, or four miles west of I-95.) (305) 977-4400. Monday through Saturday, 9 A.M.–5 P.M.; Sunday, 1–5 P.M. Adults, $6; seniors, $5; children ages 3 to 12, $4; children under 3, free; tickets can be purchased until 4 P.M. AE, MC, V accepted. Resident passes, group rates, and tours available. Additional fee charged at Tradewinds Park entrance on weekends.

Butterfly World, a three-acre attraction located within Tradewinds Park, is home to thousands of butterflies representing over 150 species from around the world. The first of its kind in the U.S. and the largest in the world, this facility allows these graceful insects to fly freely in a screened-in garden. Select vegetation has been planted to attract the butterflies. You can observe their entire life cycle in a breeding laboratory. There is also a museum that houses a collection of unusual butterflies and other interesting insects, such as giant beetles and exotic walking sticks. **Tips:** Snack bar and picnic facilities on grounds. Plan to spend one hour to tour. Gift shop has souvenirs and film. Field trips are available by reservation. Staff requests that children be accompanied by adults while touring the facility. Best time to visit is between 10 A.M. and 3 P.M. on sunny days. For information on Tradewinds Park, see listing in "Under the Sun."

□ **Flamingo Gardens**
3750 Flamingo Road, Fort Lauderdale 33330. (Take I-95 to State Route 84; take 84 west to Flamingo Road, turn south, and go three miles to entrance.) (305) 473-2955. Daily, 9 A.M.–5 P.M. Adults, $6.50 (20% discount with Medicare card); children ages 4 to 14, $3.25. Memberships available. AE accepted. Rainchecks are available.

This 60-acre botanical garden has a little bit of everything, yet doesn't overwhelm the little ones. They get to see crocodiles, alligators, monkeys, flamingos, and exotic birds. There's a petting zoo where they can hand-feed baby animals. Walk among the acres of orange groves and visit the Antique Car and Florida Everglades Museums. There's a mile-long tram ride, too. And here's a quest for your children—send them in search of Florida's largest tree, located within the park. **Tips:** Gift shop, film, and snacks available on grounds. Plan to spend about three hours to tour. Picnic areas are located within the park.

□ **Goodyear Blimp** *Enterprise*
1500 NE Fifth Avenue, Pompano Beach 33060. (305) 946-4629 or 946-8300. Daily, 9 A.M.–5 P.M. Free admission.

The *Enterprise* is one of only three touring Goodyear blimps in the world, traveling as far west as Dallas, Texas, and as far north as Montreal, Canada. Take a look at the airship and operating hangar at Pompano Beach Air Park (November through May—the *Enterprise* tours during the other months). Your self-guided tour will take about 20 to 30 minutes.

□ **International Swimming Hall of Fame Museum**
Museum: 1 Hall of Fame Drive, Fort Lauderdale 33316. (One block west of A1A.) (305) 462-6536. Monday through Saturday, 10 A.M.–5 P.M.; Sunday, 11 A.M.–4 P.M. Adults, $4; students, seniors, and military personnel, $2; family rate, $10. Pool: 501 Seabreeze Boulevard (next to museum). Daily, 10 A.M.–4 P.M. Adult resident, $2; adult nonresident, $3; students, seniors,

and military personnel residents, $1.50; students, seniors, and military personnel nonresidents, $2.

Older children will enjoy seeing the 50-meter, 10-lane Olympic-sized swimming pool, as well as Olympic gold medals belonging to Mark Spitz and Johnny Weissmuller. These and other memorabilia from swimming events in 107 nations—like trophies and medals of diving, water polo, and synchronized swimming events—are on display. **Tips:** No access for strollers or wheelchairs. Plan to spend one hour to tour. Gift shop on grounds. For swimming information, see listing in "On Your Mark, Get Set, Go!"

☐ **Native Village**
3551 North State Road 7 (between Stirling and Sheridan roads), Hollywood 33314. (305) 961-4519. Monday through Saturday, 10 A.M.–4 P.M. Guided tour (includes alligator wrestling, snakes, and turtles): adults, $8; children under 12, $5; self-guided tour: adults, $3, children under 12, $2.

Displays of wild animals, venomous and nonvenomous snakes, and an alligator wrestling show make for an exciting learning experience for children. This one-acre village also features Seminole and other Indian tribal crafts (you can watch an Indian woman creating beaded artwork). The craft shop is usually open one hour after the ticket booth closes. Children will enjoy examining the artifacts on the touch tables and seeing the thatch-roofed chickee huts. **Tips:** Plan on spending an hour for the guided tour, less for the self-guided tour. Alligator wrestling is only performed Tuesdays through Thursdays and on some Saturdays.

☐ **Ocean World**
1701 SE 17th Street Causeway, Fort Lauderdale 33316. (305) 525-6611. Daily, 10 A.M.–6 P.M. (gates close at 4:30 P.M.). Adults, $8.95; children ages 4 to 12, $6.95; children under 3, free with paying adult. MC, V accepted. Group rates and resident passes available.

Ocean World, Fort Lauderdale's famed aquatic park, has seven shows you won't want to miss. The stars include dolphins, sharks, alligators, sea lions, and turtles. The aviary, complete with parrots and toucans, adds a twist to this marine-life park. Ocean World's own cruise boat, *Miss Ocean World*, jaunts along the Intracoastal Waterway for a fun 45-minute sightseeing adventure. **Tips:** Eating facilities, gift shop, and film on grounds. Plan to arrive prior to 4:30 P.M. to see all seven shows. For party information, see listing in "Celebrate in Style."

□ **Publix Refrigerated Distribution Center**

777 SW 12th Avenue, Deerfield Beach 33442. (305) 429-0122. Tours given Tuesday through Friday, at 9 and 11 A.M., and 1 and 3 P.M. Free admission.

School groups will be especially interested in a trip to one of the largest grocers in the state. While visiting this refrigeration facility, children are treated to orange juice and ice cream while learning about the bakery, dairy warehouse, and bottling areas. **Tips:** Recommended for children ages 5 and up. Tours must be scheduled two weeks in advance.

Palm Beach County

□ **Burt Reynolds Ranch**

16133 Jupiter Farms Road, Jupiter 33478. (407) 747-5390. Daily, 10 A.M.– 4:30 P.M. Free admission.

There's an especially nice petting zoo for children at the B.R. Ranch. Follow a boardwalk path and view the llamas, ponies, turkeys, sheep, goats, and other animals. Stop in the Western Wear Store for a look at a large preserved bear named Ted. There are a few children's items for sale in the

Primate families always entertain children and mimic their audience.

store, but the tots would probably prefer to sit in the old-fashioned barbershop chairs or glance at the photos of Burt around the store. There's also a feed store that's open to the public, packed with pet items and people items, too! The back of the ranch is private property, so remember to stay in the petting zoo and store area.

□ Dreher Park and Zoo

1301 Summit Boulevard, West Palm Beach 33405. (Just east of I-95; from the Florida Turnpike take the Okeechobee Boulevard exit east to I-95 south.) (407) 585-2197. Daily, 9 A.M.–5 P.M.; tickets sold until 4:15 P.M. Closed on Thanksgiving and Christmas. Adults, $5; seniors over 60, $4; children ages 3 to 12, $3; children under 3, free. Groups of 15 or more receive a 50% discount. MC, V accepted. Annual memberships available.

This 32-acre zoo and park is home to nearly 100 species of domestic and exotic animals, which you can see in natural settings of trees, ponds, and grassy areas. There are even some endangered animals here, including giant Aldabra tortoises, woolley monkeys, Brazilian tapirs, and Florida panthers. The petting zoo is always a hit with little ones.

You might also enjoy the reptile exhibit featuring both venomous and nonvenomous snakes. There's always a special event at the zoo during weekends and holidays, so you might want to call for a schedule before planning your trip. **Tips:** Plan to spend two hours to tour. Gift shop with film and souvenirs on grounds. No feeding of the animals permitted.

□ Lion Country Safari

Southern Boulevard (State Road 80), West Palm Beach. (Ninety minutes from downtown Miami; 15 miles west of Florida Turnpike exits 93 or 99. From I-95 take exit 50; from the coastal areas, go west on Southern Boulevard.) Mailing address is P.O. Box 16066, West Palm Beach 33416-6066. (407) 793-1084; campground, 793-9797. Daily, 9:30 A.M.–5:30 P.M. Tickets sold up to 4:30 P.M., when wildlife preserve closes. Adults, $11.25; children ages 3 to 16, $9.95; children under 3, free. Group rates available.

Open since 1967, Lion Country Safari was North America's first cageless zoo. As interesting for adults as it is for kids, you'll drive through several hundred acres of a natural wildlife preserve. Watch from your car as over 1,000 wild beasts, including lions, giraffes, elephants, zebras, chimpanzees, antelopes, ostriches, and rhinos roam freely in a natural setting. Stretch your legs during a visit to Safari World, where you'll find boat rides, jeep tours, a free-flight aviary, reptile displays, a dinosaur replica park, miniature golf, and an "old-tyme" carousel. Don't miss the wonderful Great American Farm Yard that has a variety of domestic and exotic animals, often including zebras, llamas, miniature horses, and baby ostriches. You can purchase bottles of milk at the barn to feed the animals. An unusual collection of chickens gathers here as well, including some that have feathered feet, lay different-colored eggs, or whose wild plumage gives them a "punk" look!

Adventurers can cruise on the Safari Queen that will take them past Gibbon apes, flamingos, and spider monkeys. The complete campground facilities include a swimming pool, child's playground, and general store. **Tips:** Gift shop, snacks, and refreshments on grounds. Watch in newspapers for special discount price coupons; souvenir program is a nice keepsake. Changing table available in women's restroom behind film/gift area. Picnic area with lots of trees just past entrance on right.

□ **Rapids Waterslide and Miniature Golf**
6566 North Military Trail (between 45th Street and Blue Heron Boulevard), West Palm Beach 33407. (407) 842-8756. Golf: daily, noon–10 P.M.; $3.50 per person. Waterslide: daily, noon–5 P.M.; $7 per person. Combination ticket, $10. Ask about the Fun Day Pass. Personal checks accepted.

This nicely landscaped and shady amusement center has 19 holes of miniature golf, plus a huge waterslide with four flumes for you to enjoy all day. There is a convenient refreshment stand, dressing facilities, and sundeck. Don't forget the sunscreen!

Monroe County
Don't miss a stop at the information and visitors' centers on your way down the Keys! They often have maps, discount tickets, and menus for you, free of charge.

□ **African Queen**
Mile Marker 100, Key Largo 33037. (In front of the Holiday Inn.) (305) 451-4655. Free admission.

The legendary ship, *The African Queen,* from the 1951 movie by the same name (starring Humphrey Bogart and Katherine Hepburn), is now a tourist attraction docked outside the Key Largo Holiday Inn. Plans are being made for the boat to take passengers on a short trip to the Atlantic Ocean and back.

After starring in the movie, the 30-foot boat was used in Africa as a government supply vessel. In 1968 she was brought to the U.S. and used as a fund-raiser for cancer research. In the early 1980s the boat was refurbished and has appeared in parades and races.

□ **Mallory Square Sunset**
Mallory Square, Key West.

The sunset is breathtaking, the entertainment is unusual, and both are free (although a hat may be passed). The street theater performed here changes daily, but expect to see fire-eaters, trained cats, contortionists, tight-rope walkers, comedians, magicians, mimes, and jugglers. Locally produced art is also on display and for sale. Most hotels and shops in Key West post daily sunrise and sunset times, so there's no excuse to miss this free show.

Other fun things to do in the area (for free!) include going to South Beach to find baby crabs to watch or chase near the pier, or watching the fishing boats unload their catch of the day around 6 P.M. at Land's End Village.

□ **Mel Fisher's Treasure Exhibit**
200 Greene Street, Key West 33040. (305) 294-5413. Daily, 10 A.M.–5:15 P.M. Adults, $5; children ages 7 to 12, $1; children under 6, free.

See gold, silver, jewelry, coins, and gems that world-renowned Mel Fisher found during his quests under the sea. Some date back to shipwrecks from the early 1600s.

□ **Southernmost Point**
Corner of Whitehead and South streets.

The southernmost point in the United States can't help but be thrilling, even if only to say "I was there!" It's free and a good place to meet people from around the world.

□ **Theater of the Sea**
Mile Marker 84.5, Islamorada. Mailing address is P.O. Box 407, Islamorada 33036. (305) 664-2431. Daily, 9:30 A.M.–4 P.M. Adults, $9.50, children ages 4 to 12, $5.50; children 3 and under, free. AE, MC, V accepted. Annual membership for local residents available. Rainchecks available if needed.

Open since 1946, Theater of the Sea is known for its famous dolphins, sea lions, and marine exhibits. Both entertaining and educational, you can watch one of the shows that run continuously, or take a guided tour of the tidal pools carved from native coral rock and filled with sea life. You can get some great photos here.

Here in this second-oldest marine-life park in the world, you and your family can participate in the shows and often meet the "stars" face to face. Be prepared with the video camera as volunteers get kissed by sea lions, touch dolphins, turtles, and sharks, or feed stingrays. Kids can also experience marine life firsthand when they hold a sea urchin or examine crabs and sharks. The bottomless boat rides also give insight into the life below.

Tips: Snack bar on grounds. Gift shop sells film. Guided tours and group rates available. Plan on 90 minutes to tour. For party information, see listing in "Celebrate in Style."

□ Turtle Kraals

Land's End Village (where Margaret Street meets the Gulf), Key West 33040. (305) 294-2640. Monday through Saturday, 11 A.M.–11 P.M.; Sunday, noon–11 P.M. Free admission.

Turtle Kraals is home of the huge loggerhead turtles that weigh up to 400 pounds. Kids will enjoy the touch-tank filled with marine life. There's an aviary here as well, and if you're hungry, try the full-service waterfront restaurant. For more information, see listing in "Come and Get It!"

Tracing the Past

Indians, pirates, Spanish explorers, wreckers, slaves, pioneers, English soldiers, railroad workers, and immigrants from all over the world play important roles in South Florida's past, present, and future. Fortunately, South Florida has many hands-on ways for children to touch the past and wonder about the future—the best ways are listed here.

The first known human presence in South Florida can be traced to about 8000 B.C., when Paleo-Indians inhabited the area. Then came the Hobe, Tequesta, Creek, Miccosukee, and Seminole Indians. Spanish explorer Ponce de León, in search of the Fountain of Youth, saw Biscayne Bay in 1513; he brought "gifts" of smallpox and other diseases to the Tequesta Indians who had inhabited the area since 2000 B.C. By 1763, the few surviving families (less than 100) departed for Cuba.

England gained control of Florida in 1763; Florida became a United States territory in 1821, gained statehood in 1845, seceded from the Union in 1861, and reunited with the United States in 1868. A long and bloody war with the Seminole Indians broke out in 1835; the Third Seminole War ended in 1858. A peace treaty between the Seminoles and the U.S. has yet to be signed.

Fitzgerald, Flagler, Tuttle, Brickell, and Merrick are a few names you will encounter as you explore South Florida's more recent past. The actions of these pioneer men and women during the late 19th and early 20th centuries shaped the past and influence the present. A trip to Miami Beach on the Tuttle Causeway, a drive down Flagler Street or a visit to Tequesta will be more interesting when children know something about Julia Tuttle, Henry Flagler, and the Tequesta Indians.

Many South Floridians have ethnic roots in countries throughout the Caribbean and Latin America, Africa, Europe, and Asia. South Florida's immigrants have had many motives for developing communities here; Bahamians, African Americans, Conchs, wreckers, Cubans, Haitians, Nicaraguans, Norwegians, Finns, Japanese, Mexicans, and more have influenced the area's historical and geographical maps.

The *Dade County Environmental Story*, edited by Sandra Ross, Dennis M. Ross, and Joseph E. Podgor Jr., is an excellent resource for parents and older children. Written as a social studies teachers' guide, it describes the county's natural and cultural history, as well as the impact humans have had on the environment. A reader companion, written in a narrative style at the 4th grade level, is also available. Contact Friends of the Everglades Environmental Information Services at (305) 888-1230. The Monroe County Public Schools have also developed an edition of this book. Call (305) 296-6523.

Dade County

□ The Ancient Spanish Monastery
16711 West Dixie Highway, North Miami Beach 33160. (305) 945-1462. Monday through Saturday, 10 A.M.–5 P.M.; Sunday, noon–5 P.M. Adults, $3; children ages 13 to 18, $1.50; children ages 7 to 12, 75¢. AE accepted.

Built in 1141, The Ancient Spanish Monastery is the oldest building in the Western Hemisphere. It was built in Spain and relocated to Miami in the 20th century, after William Randolph Hearst saw it in 1925 while visiting Spain. He had it dismantled and shipped to the United States, where the boxes were quarantined due to an outbreak of hoof-and-mouth disease. The carefully numbered and boxed stones were jumbled together and kept in a warehouse for 26 years. In 1952 they were bought and shipped to Miami; 19 months and $1.5 million later they were reassembled. **Tips:** Plan on spending about 40 minutes to tour the monastery. Group tours can be arranged. Picnic facilities are available. For party ideas, see listing in "Celebrate in Style."

□ Art Deco District
From Sixth to 23rd streets on Miami Beach, between Lennox Avenue and Ocean Drive. Tours (minimum of 10 people per group) can be arranged by contacting the Dade Heritage Trust at (305) 638-6064.

The Art Deco District is a one-mile-square area with more than 800 buildings representing the famous architecture styles of the 1920s, '30s, and '40s. Come see the world-renowned pastel buildings along the streets of this designated historic district, which demonstrates the distinctive architectural style of the period between the two world wars. **Tips:** Note that the ninety-minute tours on Saturday mornings, sponsored by the Miami Design Preservation League, are not appropriate for children. Call (305) 672-2014 for more information. Some areas are not safe to visit in the evenings. For information about Art Deco Weekend Festival, which is held annually in January to show off the area, see listing in "Mark Your Calendar."

☐ Barnacle State Historic Site

3485 Main Highway, Coconut Grove 33133. (305) 448-9445. Tours: Thursday through Monday, 9 and 10:30 A.M., 1 and 2:30 P.M. Adults, $1; children under 12, 50¢.

In 1886 Commodore Ralph Middleton Munroe, naval architect and photographer, early pioneer and community leader, moved to what he named "Cocoanut Grove" and built his beautiful and ingenious frame home. He was the head, or commodore, of the Biscayne Yacht Club for 22 years, from whence came his nickname "Commodore" (Commodore Plaza was named after him). The home, boathouse, and grounds have been restored and are maintained by the park service, and provide a great way to experience life in Miami at the turn of the century. **Tips:** Tours start promptly, so get to the entrance several minutes early; the guide will unlock the door to take anyone waiting, and lock the door once they are in. Tours last at least an hour, commencing with a tour of the grounds before entering the house. Toddlers and small children will be tempted to play with the antiques that are displayed in the house, so be prepared to carry your children or hold their hands. No stroller access in the house.

☐ Black Archives History and Research Foundation of South Florida, Inc.

Caleb Center, Seventh Floor, 5400 NW 22nd Avenue, Miami 33142. (305) 638-6064. Monday through Friday, 9 A.M.–5 P.M.

This nonprofit organization was incorporated in 1977 to spearhead African-American heritage observances throughout Dade County. These include programs in the humanities and in literary, visual, and performing arts. The research center is a treasure chest of original historical materials such as letters, photographs, noncurrent records, clippings, manuscripts, and oral history tape recordings that document the history of the various black communities in Dade County from 1845 to the present.

The Black Archives sponsors the ongoing development of the Historic Overtown Folklife Village, which will encompass eight blocks from NW Eighth Street north to NW 10th Street, with NW Second Avenue on the east and NW Third Avenue on the west. They also hold an annual Black Heritage Fair, an Adopt-a-Pioneer History program, and many other activities. **Tips:** Tours can be arranged for a minimum of 10 people. Call for individual appointments.

☐ Cape Florida Lighthouse

1200 South Crandon Boulevard, Key Biscayne 33149. (Located in Bill Baggs/

Cape Florida State Recreation Area.) (305) 361-5811. Tours: Wednesday through Monday, 10:30 A.M. and 1, 2:30, and 3:30 P.M. Adults, $1; children under 6, free. Park admission for Florida residents: driver, $1; passengers, 50¢; children under 6, free. Nonresidents: driver, $2; passengers, $1; children under 6, free.

Built in 1825, the lighthouse is the oldest structure built in South Florida. Climb the 122 steps up the 95-foot-tall building and your reward is an amazing view (look out into the sea to find the community of houses built on stilts, known as Stiltsville). When you're back on the ground, you can find out how a lighthouse keeper in the early 1900s might have lived. While you're in the past, imagine the battle between the Seminole Indians and the settlers in 1836, when the Seminoles killed the lighthouse keeper's aide and tried to burn down the structure. For more information, see Bill Baggs/Cape Florida State Recreation Area listing in "Under the Sun."

□ **Cauley Square**
22400 Old Dixie Highway (one block west of South Dixie Highway, across the railroad tracks), Goulds 33170. (305) 258-3543. Monday through Saturday, 10 A.M.–4:30 P.M.

When William H. Cauley built this complex in 1919, it included a commissary, offices, luxury apartments, restaurants, and warehouses. The area has been converted to a unique shopping area. Many of the shops are strictly for older children and adults because of the variety of small and fragile items; however, for older kids it's like taking a tour of great-grandma's attic! There are plenty of unusual treasures here—this could almost be classified as a museum area! **Tips:** There are narrow stairs to get to the second floor shops. Much of the area outside is covered with pine bark chips, so stroller access is difficult. For event information, see listing in "Mark Your Calendar."

□ **Chapman House/Ethnic Heritage Children's Folklife Museum**
1200 NW Sixth Avenue, Miami 33136. Call the Black Archives for information: (305) 638-6064. Monday through Friday, 9 A.M.–3 P.M. Field trips can be arranged. Free admission.

Dr. W. A. Chapman, a black physician, was called to serve as the first "colored consultant" for the State Board of Health in Jacksonville in 1939. He was also a church and civic leader in the area known as Colored Town (renamed Overtown in the 1940s), and built his 17-room home near Booker T. Washington High School, where it stands today. The Chapman

House was declared a historic site by the City of Miami Commission, and is listed in the National Register of Historic Places.

The Ethnic Heritage Children's Museum focuses on the folk arts and lives of children who have come to South Florida in migrant and immigrant groups. Exhibits change annually.

Field trips can be arranged to include the Chapman House, a tour of the Historic Overtown Folklife Village area (see listing under "Black Archives" in this section), and a visit to the planetarium at Booker T. Washington Junior High School at 1200 NW Sixth Avenue. **Tip:** These trips are best for children in 4th to 12th grades.

□ **Charles Deering Estate**
16701 SW 72nd Avenue, Miami 33157. (305) 235-1668. Weekends only, 9 A.M.–5 P.M. Adults, $4; children ages 6 to 12, $2; children under 6, free.

A visit to this 350-acre bay-front estate will take you on a journey that spans 10,000 years, beginning with the Paleo-Indians who hunted and gathered food in this area. Tequesta Indian archaeological sites located on the grounds date back to around 500 A.D. Remains of Cutler, a late 19th-century town, can be seen, as can the Richmond Cottage, built in 1896. In 1916, Charles Deering (brother of James Deering of Vizcaya) bought the entire property and built his Mediterranean Revival-style mansion. In 1985 the State of Florida and Metropolitan Dade County bought the property and opened it to the public. Available tours include a 90-minute visit to the houses and grounds. This is an excellent place for school field trips. For more information, see listing in "Under the Sun."

□ **Coral Castle**
28655 South Dixie Highway, Homestead 33030. (305) 248-6344. Daily, 9 A.M.–9 P.M. Adults, $6.75; children ages 7 to 15, $4.50; children under 7, free.

Mystery surrounds this stone castle, built by Latvian immigrant Edward Leedskalnin. He single-handedly dug the 1,000 tons of coral used for the huge sculptures to impress the woman who left him the night before their wedding. The castle was built over a 20-year period, from 1920 to 1939. **Tip:** Allow about 45 minutes to tour.

□ **Dade Heritage Trust**
Historic Preservation Center, 190 SE 12th Terrace, Miami 33131. (305) 358-9572.

Call the office or stop by to pick up their excellent materials designed to help children and adults get to know Dade County as it once was. The friendly staff is willing to help you provide age-appropriate outings that introduce children to the history around them. If you are interested in exploring old Dade County sites (rather than just driving past them), the staff can arrange tours for children ages one and older. They request that groups have at least 10 people. A coloring book for younger children, a "Preservation Activity Book" for older children, and other materials describing Dade County's historic sights are available at the office.

☐ First Coconut Grove Schoolhouse

3429 Devon Road (on grounds of Plymouth Congregational Church), Coconut Grove 33133.

School-age children will enjoy visiting the first public school in what is now Dade County. Built in 1889 to serve as a Sunday School across from the Peacock Inn, the school was constructed of lumber that Coconut Grove pioneers salvaged from wrecked ships. It was sold in 1902 to serve as a home; the Ryder Corporation bought it in 1969, donated it to Plymouth Congregational Church, moved it to church property, and restored its original appearance. **Tip:** Tours can be arranged for groups of at least 10 people. Call the Dade Heritage Trust at (305) 638-6064.

☐ Florida Gold Coast Railroad Museum

12400 SW 152nd Street, Miami 33177. (Follow signs to Miami Metrozoo; the museum is on the right as you approach the Metrozoo's west parking lot.) (305) 253-0063. Monday through Friday, 10 A.M.–3 P.M.; Saturday and Sunday, 10 A.M.–5 P.M. Weekdays: adults, $2.50; children ages 3 to 11, $1.50. Weekends: adults, $4.25; children ages 3 to 11, $2.25.

A popular school field trip destination, children have a chance to see a whole room full of miniature trains, explore several old railroad cars, and take a trip on a real train. Hold on to small children's hands in the "Ferdinand Magellan" (U.S. Presidential Car #1); it's not a hands-on display. **Tip:** Strollers do not fit on the trains, so bring an alternative or be prepared to leave it outside while you're inside. For party information, see listing in "Celebrate in Style."

☐ Florida Pioneer Museum

826 North Krome Avenue (east side, north of Silver Palm; just look for the

The Gold Coast Railroad Museum,
equipped with antique and model trains,
is a favorite touring spot in South Florida.

yellow and white buildings), Florida City 33034. (305) 246-9531. Daily,
except Christmas and New Year's, 1–5 P.M. Adults, $1.50; children, 75¢.

A railroad agent's 10-room home, an old Homestead depot, and a caboose can all be explored at this small museum. The buildings were constructed around 1904 from durable Dade County pine, and are painted "Flagler yellow" as prescribed by Henry Flagler for his Florida East Coast Railway Company buildings and hotels.

☐ **Hialeah Park**
Corner of East Fourth Avenue and 79th Street, Hialeah 33010. Mailing address is P.O. Box 158, Hialeah 33011. (305) 885-8000; (800) 423-3504, in Florida. Daily, 9:30 A.M.–4:30 P.M. except during racing dates. Free admission during off-season. Cost varies according to seating location; children ages 17 and under admitted to races free with adult.

Whether you prefer watching the horses run for fun or for money, you and the little ones will enjoy a few hours at this National Historic Site. The clubhouse opened in 1925—look for displays of historic carriages and thoroughbred racing silks. Gates open early on designated Saturday and Sunday mornings to let you eat breakfast (7:30–9:30 A.M.), watch the horses work out, and count the several hundred Cuban flamingos. **Tips:** If you take the Metrorail to the Hialeah station, located in the park, the information booths and gift shops will give you a free return Metrorail pass. For more information, see listing in "On Your Mark, Get Set, Go!"

☐ **Historic Coral Gables House**
907 Coral Way, Coral Gables 33134. (305) 442-6593. Sunday, 1–4 P.M.; Wednesday, 10 A.M.–4 P.M. Group tours may be arranged on other days. Adults, $1; children, 50¢.

Get an idea of life in Coral Gables during the 1920s by touring the boyhood home of the city's founder, George Merrick. The city acquired the home in 1976, restored it, and opened it to the public. Keep an eye on toddlers and small children, as there are many things that they will want to touch, but shouldn't. The annual Christmas party is great for children; call for information.

☐ **Historical Museum of Southern Florida**
101 West Flagler Street, Miami 33130. (305) 375-1492. Monday through Wednesday, Friday and Saturday, 10 A.M.–5 P.M.; Thursday, 10 A.M.– 9 P.M.; Sunday, noon–5 P.M. Adults, $3; children ages 6 to 12, $2; contributions on Monday only. Yearly memberships available for individuals, couples, and families.

A great place for children and adults to get a better idea of 10,000 years of South Florida's history. They will enjoy the life-size displays of Indian families, Florida animals, and marine life. Several exhibits are set up to teach children about various aspects of Florida life.

The museum sponsors outings that include canoe trips and nature hikes. During Christmas vacation, special classes for children teach holiday arts and crafts. They learn to make holiday kites, piñatas, and Christmas ornaments from around the world.

"The Museum's Traditions: The South Florida Folklife Festival" and the ongoing folklife program explores the beliefs, customs, art, crafts, music, food, dance, drama, play, occupational/technical skills, architecture, and oral literature of the area's distinct cultural groups. Workshops, lectures, concerts, and other activities are offered. Call or write for their free brochure, available in Spanish and English.

☐ Ichimura Miami-Japan Garden

Located on Watson Island, just opposite downtown Miami on the north side of MacArthur Causeway, just east of the bridge. (305) 579-6944. Open daily from 9 A.M.–5 P.M. Call the City of Miami Parks, Recreation and Public Facilities Operations Division, (305) 575-5256, to arrange for tours, field trips, and rentals. Free admission.

A one-acre garden built and donated to the city of Miami by Kyoshi Ichimura, a Japanese industrialist and founder of the Ricoh Corporation's copy machine company. Completely restored in 1988, a new *hakkaku-do* (the octagonal pavillion) as well as the original pagoda, lanterns, and stone *Hotei* figures can be seen as you wander down winding paths.

☐ Little Havana/Calle Ocho

Area from State Road 836 (Dolphin Expressway) and Miami River south to Dixie Highway, I-95 on the east and SW 27th Avenue on the west. The main street is Calle Ocho (SW Eighth Street/Tamiami Trail). (From 27th Avenue east, Calle Ocho is one-way, so you need to take SW Seventh Street to travel west.) Call Little Havana Development Authority, (305) 324-8127, for information on group tours. Free tours are given Monday through Friday, 9 A.M.–4 P.M.

If you live in Miami, or are just here for a visit, plan to spend a couple of hours getting to know this part of town. And don't worry if you don't speak Spanish—shop and restaurant owners, and even people on the street, will be happy to find someone who can help you find what you need. There are several historic sites in this area, and the Little Havana Development Authority can provide you with a written self-guided tour on request, or will provide groups with a free guide. Be sure to visit:

☐ **El Crédito Cigars**, 1106 SW Eighth Street, (305) 858-4162. This cigar manufacturer has been operating since 1907, and you can watch them make cigars by hand.

☐ **Cuban Memorial Plaza**, Memorial Boulevard and Eighth Street, dedicated to the "Martyrs of the Assault April 17, 1961."

☐ **Máximo Gómez Park**, popularly known as "Domino Park." The game is taken very seriously, and dominoes is the only thing people play here.

☐ Open fruit and vegetable **market** on Calle Ocho.

☐ **Casa de los Trucos and La Casa de las Piñatas.** (For information, see listings in "Bytes, Kites, and Toy Delights.")

☐ **Miami Biltmore Hotel**
1212 Anastasia Avenue, Coral Gables 33134. (305) 445-1926. Free 30-minute historic tours depart from the hotel lobby every half hour from 3:30–5 P.M. on Sundays. High tea is available from 3–5 P.M. for $5.50 per person.

This National Historic Landmark was a hotspot for the wealthy of the 1920s and '30s. The 26-story tower is a replica of the Giralda Tower in Sevilla, Spain. After World War II, the hotel was used as a veteran's hospital, and was vacant from 1968 until it was completely restored in 1986. It now houses two restaurants, a spa, and North America's largest hotel pool. **Tips:** The tour is interesting for older children accompanied by an adult. Customized tours are available if you have younger children; call for reservations. Also, ask for information about special activities for children

Miami's famous Biltmore Hotel offers children a hands-on experience with history.

in the pool area, usually scheduled from 10 A.M.-6 P.M. on Sundays. For information on Christmas at the Biltmore, see listing in "Mark Your Calendar."

☐ **Vizcaya Museum and Gardens**
3251 South Miami Avenue, Miami 33129. (Take the Metrorail to the Vizcaya exit.) (305) 579-2813. Daily, 9:30 A.M.–5 P.M. Closed Christmas. Adults, $6.50; persons in wheelchairs, $4.50; children ages 7 to 18, $4. Memberships are available. AE accepted.

Built by James Deering, cofounder of International Harvestor, Vizcaya (a Basque word meaning "elevated place") was completed in 1916, and is now operated by the Metro Dade County Department of Parks and Recreation. Ten acres of formal gardens overlooking Biscayne Bay surround this 70-room Italian palace, which houses a collection of European art from the 15th through 19th centuries. Sound and light shows are held here, as well as the annual Shakespeare Festival, Italian Renaissance Faire, and a beautiful Christmas tree display. Learning packets are available for children who visit with school groups; coloring books are available in the gift shop.
  In 1984, the Ellis A. Gimbel Garden for the Blind, located at the south end of the Formal Gardens, was dedicated at the Vizcaya. Many of the plants here have unique textures, are especially aromatic, and need no identifying labels. They include blue sage, rosemary, lavender, mint, white butterfly ginger, lemon grass, and society garlic, as well as bay, allspice, eucalyptus, and camphor trees. On the west side of the Formal Gardens you can get a good idea of different architectural features by feeling the marble, terra-cotta, limestone, and wrought-iron textures. A narrative tape is available by contacting Vizcaya personnel at 579-2808. **Tips:** Strollers are not allowed inside the mansion, and are somewhat difficult to manuever on the grounds and in the gift shop. On the bay side of the grounds there is no barrier, so hold on to young explorers. No food or refreshments may be brought on the premises. For special event information, see listings in "Mark Your Calendar."

Broward County

☐ **Bonnet House**
900 North Birch Road, Fort Lauderdale 33301. (305) 563-5393. Tours available Tuesday through Thursday, 10:30 A.M. and 1:30 P.M.; Sundays in the summer, 1:30 P.M. Reservations required. Adults, $7.50; students and adults ages 60 and older, $5; children ages 6 and under, free.

Built in the 1920s by Frederic and Evelyn Bartlett, the Bonnet House (also known as the Bartlett House) is part of a $36-million, 35-acre estate on Fort Lauderdale Beach. It has been restored to its original elegance, and now offers tours, seminars, and workshops. **Tips:** This is best for older children who have had previous experiences in this type of museum; call for information about programs in progress for children.

□ **Fort Lauderdale Historical Society**
219 SE Second Avenue, Fort Lauderdale 33301. (305) 463-4431. Tuesday through Saturday, 10 A.M.–4 P.M.; Sunday, 1–4 P.M. Donations accepted. Memberships available.

Explore Fort Lauderdale and Broward County's history through permanent exhibits that date from the Seminole Indian era through World War II. Temporary and/or traveling exhibits are also featured occasionally. Field trips or group tours may be arranged for a small fee. An annual Seafood Festival is held the second Saturday in April. **Tips:** Plan to spend 30 to 40 minutes to tour. There are no picnic facilities.

□ **Hillsboro Lighthouse**
Go east on Hillsboro Boulevard to Route A1A; go south to Hillsboro Beach.

Designated a major historic landmark in 1907, this is one of the most powerful lighthouses in the United States.

□ **Himmarshee Village**
Composed of an eight-block historical area in downtown Fort Lauderdale. Go north on First Avenue, turn left on SW Second Street, cross the railroad tracks, and turn left onto SW Second Avenue.

The Discovery Center, the New River Inn (Fort Lauderdale's first hotel), the King-Cromartie House (which now houses a pioneer residence museum, and is included in the Discovery Center tour), the Fort Lauderdale Historical Society Museum (see listing in this section), the Bryan House (now a restaurant—they serve marinated and fried alligator bites), and several antique shops and restaurants can be found in this historical area. For more information on the Discovery Center, see listing in "On Safari in South Florida."

□ **Museum of Archaelogy**
203 SW First Avenue, Fort Lauderdale 33301. (305) 525-8778. Tuesday

Historic lighthouses scattered along the Florida coast offer a hint of the past to viewers.

through Saturday, 10 A.M.–4 P.M.; Sunday, 1–4 P.M. Adults, $1; senior citizens and children, 50¢. Annual memberships available.

Discover life among the Tequestas 2,000 years ago, or imagine seeing the Ice-Age mammals whose bones are on display. The museum also exhibits pre-Colombian, African, and other cultural artifacts. A marine archaeological exhibit depicts shipwrecks. The "Sense of Egypt" room, a favorite with children, is set up to look like an Egyptian tomb.

Classes for children are offered, as are monthly special exhibits and annual events. **Tips:** It's best to visit this museum in the afternoon, with children ages 5 to 12. Plan to spend about an hour to tour. The museum closes for a period during the summer, so call before you go to be sure it's open.

□ **Plantation Historical Museum**
511 North Figtree Lane, Plantation 33322. (305) 581-3203. Tuesday through Thursday, 1–4 P.M. Free admission.

Look at antiques that you might find in "Granny's Attic," artifacts from various Florida Indian tribes, and other relics from the history of the town of Plantation.

□ **Stranahan Historical House Museum**
One Stranahan Place, 335 SE Sixth Avenue (take Las Olas Boulevard to the New River Tunnel), Fort Lauderdale 33301. (305) 463-4374 or 524-4736. Wednesday, Friday, and Saturday, 10 A.M.–4 P.M.; Sunday, 1–4 P.M. Adults, $3; students, $1.

Built in 1901 by Florida pioneers Frank Stranahan and Ivy Stranahan, this is the oldest building in Broward County. Mr. Stranahan was a businessman who began trading with the Seminoles in 1892. His store served as an outpost on the road south to Lemon City (what is now North Miami), then became their home. It is now a museum.

Palm Beach County

□ **The Cason Cottage and Museum**
5 NE First Street, Delray Beach 33483-0042. (305) 243-0223. Tuesday through Saturday, 10 A.M.–3 P.M. Free admission.

Cason Cottage houses a museum with art, artifacts, and records of Delray Beach, and is also home to the Delray Beach Historical Society. The house was built between 1915 and 1920 by Dr. and Mrs. John R. Cason, Sr., and the family played a major leadership role in the development of the area. A visit to the Cottage will give children an idea of what South Florida was once like. Older childen may enjoy listening to pioneer citizens' tape-recordings of oral histories available at the Cottage. Special events and exhibits for children are also scheduled throughout the year.

□ **Henry Morrison Flagler Museum/Whitehall**
Whitehall Way, Palm Beach. (Take the Okeechobee Road East exit off I-95 or the Florida Turnpike, continue east into Palm Beach to the first traffic light. Turn left on Cocoanut Row, continue until the fourth light [Whitehall Way]. The museum is on the left.) Mailing address is P.O. Box 969, Palm Beach 33480. (407) 655-2833. Tuesday through Saturday, 10 A.M.–5 P.M.; Sunday, noon–5 P.M. Adults, $3.50; children ages 6 to 12, $1.25.

The arrival of Henry Flagler's railroad in 1894 provided the catalyst for much growth in the Palm Beach area. He built beautiful hotels for wealthy visitors, and in 1901 spent $2.5 million to create Whitehall, a personal palace to enjoy with his bride. His home has been restored and preserved as a museum that displays his collection of treasures from around the world. Children will especially enjoy the playroom and dollhouses on the second floor, as well as a trip outside to board "Rambler," Flagler's private railroad car.
    A very popular annual open house is held in February, with clowns, magic shows, special exhibits, fireworks, and other family activities. For more event information, see listing in "Mark Your Calendar." **Tips:** Regular tours of the museum last about 45 minutes, and are too long for children under age 5. Special tours for children may be arranged by calling in advance. The staff welcomes school groups and clubs throughout the year. Only a few of the upper rooms are air conditioned, so plan your visit accordingly.

□ **Loxahatchee Historical Museum**
805 North U.S. 1 (in Burt Reynolds Park), Jupiter 33477. (407) 747-6639. Tuesday through Friday, 10 A.M.–3 P.M.; Saturday and Sunday, noon–3 P.M. Free admission; donations accepted. Call for information on memberships.

Open since 1988, this museum offers a permanent exhibit and library. Explore what was going on in Jupiter in 500 B.C., or see how the arrival of

Henry Flagler's railroad changed the area. Reenactments of the Seminole Indian Wars are performed periodically; call for information.

Another attraction here is the Dubois House, built on an ancient Indian mound in 1898. Inside you'll find displays of antique furntiture and clothing that give children an idea of how early South Floridian pioneers lived. The house is open to the public on Sundays, from 1 to 3 P.M., weather permitting; tours can be arranged during the week by calling the museum staff. You can also arrange to participate in archaeological digs in the area around the museum.

When you're in Jupiter, don't miss a tour of the Jupiter Lighthouse, located just north of the museum, built in 1860 and still in use today. The lighthouse and the small museum located at its base are open to the public on Sunday from noon to 2:30 P.M., weather permitting; the Historical Society staff can arrange for special tours at other times. For more information, see listing for Dubois Park in "Under the Sun."

☐ **The Morikami Museum and Japanese Gardens**
4000 Morikami Park Road, Delray Beach 33446. (Take Linton Road exit off I-95 and head west about 4 miles. Go south on Carter Road, and then west on Morikami Park Road.) (407) 499-0631 (recording) or 495-0233. Tuesday through Sunday, 10 A.M.–5 P.M. Closed Easter, Thanksgiving, Christmas, and New Year's. Free admission; donations accepted. Memberships available.

George Morikami, a pineapple and winter vegetable farmer, donated what is now one of the most popular parks in Palm Beach County's Department of Parks and Recreation. Within the 150-acre park you will find a museum, housed in an imperial Japanese home on a man-made island, and a two-acre traditional Japanese garden. You'll have to take off your shoes outside and put on paper ones before you tour the museum.

A *chanoyu*, or traditional Japanese tea ceremony, is held in the museum's Tea Ceremony Room on the third Saturday of each month, from October through April. The ceremony is held hourly from 1 to 4 P.M. for $2 per person, free for members (reservations not required). Japanese culture films for children are shown at 3 P.M. on Wednesdays and Fridays.

Wander down the one-mile nature trail through a wild area; explore the gardens and climb to the observation deck (but please don't play in the waterfalls!). Free garden tours are given at 2 P.M. on Wednesdays and Fridays. Picnic facilities with covered pavillions and open tables are available, and there are large grassy areas around the lake where you can spread out blankets.

Four traditional festivals are celebrated annually: *Bon* Festival (mid-August); *Oshogatsu* (New Year's in December and January); *Hatsume* ("First Bud," in February); and *Bunka-No-Hi* (Japanese Culture Days, in November). Check local newspapers or call for information. An entrance fee is charged at these festivals. **Tips:** Don't miss feeding the *koi* (large fish in the pond); fish food is available on the boardwalk. For more information about the festivals, see listings in "Mark Your Calendar."

Monroe County

☐ Audubon House and Gardens
205 Whitehead Street, Key West 33040. (305) 294-2116. Daily, 9:30 A.M.–5 P.M. Adults, $4.50; children ages 6 to 12, $1; children under 6, free. Cash payment only. Group rates available (15 people minimum, reservations required).

Completely restored, with the original furnishings intact, this house provides a glimpse of where John James Audubon found inspiration for his sketches of the Keys' native birds. Walk through the tropical gardens and enjoy the gallery of Audubon's prints and sculptures. The home actually belonged to a Mr. Geiger; Audubon was only an occasional visitor here. **Tips:** Staff suggests that this is appropriate for children ages 8 and up. Guided walking tours and video show available. No wheelchair or stroller access inside house. No drinking fountains or eating facilities. Plan to spend about 30 minutes to tour.

☐ East Martello Museum and Art Gallery
3501 South Roosevelt Boulevard (adjacent to the airport), Key West 33040. (305) 296-3913. Daily, 9:30 A.M.–5 P.M.; closed Christmas. Adults, $2.50; children ages 7 to 12, $1; children under 7, free. Tours available.

This museum was once a Civil War fortress. Today it houses many artifacts from Old Key West. For more information, see listing in "Adventures in the Arts."

☐ Fort Jefferson National Monument
U.S. Coast Guard Base, Key West 33040. (305) 247-6211.

This national park lies 68 miles west of Key West in the Dry Tortugas, and is accessible only by boat or seaplane. Built as a garrison for Federal troops during the Civil War, it later became a prison. Its most notable prisoner was

Dr. Samuel Mudd, who set John Wilkes Booth's leg, without realizing who he was treating, after Booth assassinated President Abraham Lincoln. In 1874 the fort was abandoned; it is now open for snorkeling, camping, swimming, and hiking. If you camp, make reservations; you'll need to bring everything, including water, with you. For transportation call one of the Key West outfitters, such as the Key West Seaplane Service, (305) 294-6978. For more information, see, "By Land, Sea, and Air."

□ Fort Zachary Taylor State Historic Site

West end of Southard Street, Key West. Mailing address is P.O. Box 289, Key West 33041. (305) 292-6713. Daily, 8 A.M.–sunset; fort area closes at 5 P.M. Florida residents: driver, $1.50; passengers, $1; non-residents: driver, $2.50; passengers, $2; children under age 6, free. Yearly passes are available at entrance. Cash payment only.

This National Historic Landmark was a stronghold for the Union during the Civil War. The largest collection of Civil War cannons in the U.S. was found here in recent excavations. A 40-minute guided tour begins at 2 P.M. daily, but you can explore on your own anytime. You'll also find one of the island's best public beaches located here, as well as a picnic area with barbecue grills, shaded by Australian pines. Birthday parties can be held in this area, and Civil War Days events take place here each winter.

□ Hemingway House

907 Whitehead Street, Key West 33040. (305) 294-1575. Daily, 9 A.M.– 5 P.M. Adults, $4; children ages 6 to 12, $1; children under 6, free.

The home of famed author Ernest Hemingway is now a National Historic Landmark. The furnishings are authentic and the house, which is 140 years old, abounds with many decendants of Hemingway's famed six-toed cats. (Most children think the cats are the best part of this museum.)

□ Key West Lighthouse and Military Museum

938 Whitehead Street, Key West 33040. (305) 294-0012. Daily, 9:30 A.M.– 5 P.M. Adults, $2.50; children ages 7 to 15, 50¢; children under 7, free.

Climb the 88 steps and get a sweeping view of Key West. Built in 1846, this lighthouse guided sailors until 1969. Recently renovated, there are handrails all the way up the winding staircase, and safety bars enclose the lookout area. The museum contains military artifacts.

☐ **Perky Bat Tower**
Near Mile Marker 17 on the Gulf side of U.S. 1, Sugarloaf Key.

Inspire your child's imagination with a visit to this tower, listed in the National Register of Historic Places. Clyde Perky built it in 1929 to attract the bats that would eat the mosquitoes that were attacking the guests who were visiting his Sugarloaf Lodge. The bats never showed up, but the tower has outlasted several hurricanes, and young inventors or storytellers might like to stop and take a look at one man's attempt to solve a problem.

☐ **Wrecker's Museum and Oldest House**
322 Duval Street, Key West 33040. (305) 294-9502. Daily, 10 A.M.–4 P.M. Adults, $2; children ages 2 to 12, 50¢.

This museum is located in the oldest house in Key West, originally built in 1829 on Duval Street. Some contend that the house on the corner of Angela and Margaret streets is the oldest, but whichever camp you side with, you'll find that the museum is filled with maritime history. It was the home of Captain Francis B. Watlington, a merchant seaman and "wrecker" (ask the staff to explain how wreckers got their name). The museum has a display of seagoing artifacts, model ships, documents, a small toy collection (including an elegant doll house), and many antiques. Group tours may be arranged in advance. Thank the staff as you leave—they are all volunteers! **Tips:** Tuesday is the best day for families to visit. Plan to spend about 30 minutes to tour. Strollers are fine, but no wheelchair access on grounds.

Adventures in the Arts

South Florida is a wonderful place for children to learn about the arts. On almost any weekend of the year, there is an art, dance, music, or theater event for children happening somewhere. This section describes the area's professional and nonprofit arts organizations.

Universities, community colleges, and high schools often host low-cost or free exhibits and performances that are usually close to home. These opportunities give children the chance to learn about and experience the arts in an informal environment. Commercial art galleries and those located on college campuses can provide a free education in the visual arts if you take the time to browse. Most welcome well-behaved children to exhibition openings, and children enjoy meeting the artists who created the works.

Don't overlook valuable and free community resources. Local and regional libraries host a variety of dance and musical performances, puppet shows, ethnic art exhibitions, dramatic storytelling events, and film presentations. Ask your local librarian about the bedtime storytelling hour, toy lending, "tell and touch," foreign language collections, Talking Books, Books-by-Mail, and "share box" (donate one of your books and pick another to take home). Broward County residents can call (305) 357-7777 to hear a four-minute story or fable.

Broward, Dade, Monroe, and Palm Beach counties have arts councils that can provide you with this year's information about cultural events. You can call or write to the following:

☐ **Broward Arts Council,** 100 South Andrews Avenue, Fort Lauderdale 33301. (305) 357-7457.
☐ **Metropolitan Dade County Cultural Affairs Council,** 111 NW First Street, Suite 625, Miami 33128-1964. (305) 375-4634.
☐ **Monroe County Fine Arts Council,** 1435 Simonton Street, Key West 33040. (305) 296-5000.
☐ **Palm Beach County Council of the Arts,** 1555 Palm Beach Lakes Boulevard, Suite 206, West Palm Beach 33401-2371.

The Children's Cultural Coalition of the Metropolitan Dade Cultural Affairs Council provides up-to-date information about children's programs through their publication *Classroom Cultural Catalogue: A Resource Directory for Teachers: Cultural and Scientific In-School and Field-Trip Programs.* Call (305) 375-5024. The Broward Arts Council also publishes a directory of professional artists and cultural organizations available for performances in the Broward County School District. Call (305) 357-7457.

Your children will enjoy whatever cultural events you choose if you take time to explain what to expect in the program, and tell them what kind of behavior is appropriate for the event. The following poem, written by Peggy Simon Tractman of Maximillion Productions in New York, gives children a good picture of what they they can see and do at the theater.

Matinee Manners

1. The theatre is no place for lunch.
   Who can hear when you go "crunch?"
2. We must wear our nicest clothes
   When we go to theatre shows.
3. Do not talk to one another
   (that means friends or even mother)
   When you go to see a show.
   Otherwise you'll never know
   What the play is all about
   And you'll make the actors shout
   Just to make themselves be heard.
   So, be still—don't say a word
   Unless an actor asks you to . . .
   A thing they rarely ever do.
4. A program has a special use
   So do not treat it with abuse!
   It's purpose is to let us know
   Exactly who is in the show—
   It also tells us other facts
   Of coming shows and future acts.
   Programs make great souvenirs
   Of fun we've had in bygone years.
5. Keep your hands upon your lap
   But if you like something, you clap.
   Actors like to hear applause
   If there is cause for this applause.
6. If a scene is bright and sunny
   And you think something is funny,
   Laugh—performers love the laughter
   But be quiet from thereafter.
7. Don't kick chairs or pound your feet
   And do not stand up in your seat.

Never wander to and fro—
Just sit back and watch the show.

8. And when the final curtain falls
   The actors take their "curtain calls."
   That means they curtsy or they bow
   And you applaud, which tells them how
   You liked their work and liked the show.
   Then, when the lights come on, you go
   Back up the aisle and walk—don't run
   Out to the lobby, everyone.

9. The theatre is a special treat
   and not a place to talk or eat.
   If you behave the proper way
   You really will enjoy the play!

Art

Art museums are wonderful community resources, but don't forget the possibilities for learning about art to be found at festivals, galleries, neighborhoods (for works of architecture, exterior art, and decoration), corporate offices, and public places.

Dade County

☐ **Artmobile**
101 West Flagler Street, Miami 33130. (This is the mailing and parking address; you won't find it parked here very often, though!) (305) 375-5048.

What's black and white and flowery all over? If you've spotted this 30-foot traveling museum, you know the answer is the Artmobile. Southeast Bank donated the vehicle to the Metro-Dade County Library in 1976; artist Lowell Nesbitt painted the exterior. Exhibitions of original works of art are displayed in the gallery-like setting; special exhibitions are presented during Black Heritage and Hispanic Heritage months (February and October, respectively).

*Art can be found in unexpected places—
even on the walls of neighborhood
restaurants.*

Public and private schools, festivals, and public events in most areas of Dade County may request sessions with the Artmobile, free of charge. Prior to its arrival date at a school, information about exhibit artists and works, as well as a glossary, are sent to the teacher in order to familiarize the children with what they will see. The Artmobile has served approximately 50,000 children per year. Ask your child's school or PTA to request the Artmobile if it hasn't been scheduled yet—the children really enjoy it.

□ **Bacardi Art Gallery**
2100 Biscayne Boulevard, Miami 33137. (305) 573-8511. Monday through Friday, 9 A.M.–5 P.M. Free admission.

In 1963 Bacardi Imports, Inc., established the gallery as a nonprofit community service in the visual arts. Exhibitions have included "Selections of Cuban Art," "American Prints from Colonial Times to 1950," "Urban Sculpture," "20th Century Mexican Masters," and "German Neo-Expressionists."

Group tours can be arranged by calling in advance. The gallery also works with the Dade County Public Schools to present an Art Education Workshop that provides children with the opportunity to develop their creative skills through hands-on activities.

□ Bass Museum of Art
2121 Park Avenue, Miami Beach 33139. (305) 673-7530. Tuesday through Saturday, 10 A.M.–5 P.M.; Sunday, 1–5 P.M. Adults, $2; students with I.D., $1; children under age 16, free. MC, V accepted.

Browse through this wonderful collection of paintings, sculptures, graphics, and textiles from the 14th through the 20th centuries. Special events and classes for children are offered throughout the year; call for information. **Tip:** Adult supervision is required.

□ Black Heritage Museum
Mailing address is P.O. Box 50327, Miami 33255. (305) 252-3535. Free admission; memberships available.

Begun in 1987 to showcase positive aspects of black heritage around the world, the exhibitions are presented in various locations in Dade County. A permanent display of paintings and traditional African art from seven countries can be seen at the Minority Student Support Services facilities at the University of Miami, on Dickenson Drive, Buildings 37B-C. Collections of dolls, art from Africa and Papua New Guinea, and other works have been displayed at the Bacardi Art Gallery, the Model City Cultural Arts Gallery, and at public libraries. Call for information concerning current exhibitions.

□ Center for the Fine Arts
101 West Flagler Street (Metro Dade Cultural Center), Miami 33130. (Take the Metrorail to Government Center, walk one block south, and go up the stairs.) (305) 375-1700. Tuesday, Wednesday, Friday, and Saturday, 10 A.M.–5 P.M.; Thursday, 10 A.M.–9 P.M.; Sunday, noon–5 P.M. Adults, $3; adult groups, $2.50 per person; children ages 6 to 12, $2; student groups (more than 10), $1 per person. Annual memberships: $35 (individual) and $50 (family). MC, V accepted.

At least 12 to 15 new exhibitions each year keep this museum interesting for everyone, children included. You can call or send for information (a study guide) that will acquaint children with an exhibition before they actually see it. Children of members are welcome to attend openings; they usually take place on Fridays from 5 to 6 P.M.

The Curator for a Day program (for children ages 9 and up) and Behind the Scenes tours (for ages 7 and up) give children hands-on experience with art exhibitions. Storytelling is offered on Tuesdays from June to August. Call for more information on these and other special events for children. **Tips:** Plan on spending about an hour to tour. The staff recommends weekday afternoons as the best time to visit. If you drive, there is a parking garage west of the Metro Dade Cultural Center; get your parking ticket validated in the museum and receive a parking discount. Joint tickets are available if you plan to visit the South Florida Historical Museum on the same day: adults, $5; children, $3. Strollers are not allowed during special ticketed exhibitions. Picnic tables are located on the plaza in front of the museum.

☐ **Cuban Museum of Arts and Culture**
1300 SW 12th Avenue, Miami 33145. (305) 858-8006. Monday through Friday, 10 A.M.–5 P.M.; Saturday and Sunday, 1–5 P.M. Free admission.

Appropriate for older children, the exhibitions introduce viewers to Cuban and other Latin American artists.

☐ **Gallery Antigua, Inc.**
5138 Biscayne Boulevard, Miami 33137. (305) 759-5355. Monday through Friday, 9 A.M.–5:30 P.M.; Saturday, 10 A.M.–6 P.M. Free admission. Major credit cards and personal checks accepted for art purchases.

A trip to this gallery will provide children with an opportunity to learn about African, African-American, and Caribbean art. Quarterly exhibitions may feature a single artist, groups of artists, or art representing a geographic area. The gallery is unique in Florida in its commitment to exhibit fine art produced by artists of the African Diaspora. Ask for a copy of their quarterly newsletter, *The Scene,* which includes art reviews, exhibition information, poetry, and suggested readings for children and adults.

☐ **The Lawrence Museum of Judaica**
Beth David Congregation, 2625 SW Third Avenue, Miami 33129. (305) 854-3911.

In 1989, Miami's oldest synagogue opened this museum to display approximately 150 artifacts and artworks, including items rescued from Czechoslovakian and other European synagogues destroyed by the Nazis. Two large carvings made from Honduran mahogany depict the Holocaust's suffering and death on one side, and Israel's hope and life on the other.

Tip: The museum welcomes older supervised children. Call for a tour appointment.

□ **Lowe Art Museum**
University of Miami, 1301 Stanford Drive, Coral Gables 33146. (305) 284-3536. Tuesday through Friday, noon–5 P.M.; Saturday, 10 A.M.–5 P.M.; Sunday, noon–5 P.M. Adults, $2; senior citizens and non-UM students, $1; members, children ages 16 and under and UM students, free. Memberships available. AE, V accepted in gift shop.

Permanent displays are augmented by new exhibitions every eight weeks. Call or send for a calendar to decide in advance if the current exhibition is appropriate for your child. Art classes and camps for children ages 3 and up are offered during the summer and holidays. Call for information about special events, including children's activities at the Beaux Arts Festival. **Tips:** Plan to spend about 45 minutes to visit, and come early in the day. You can schedule group tours in the morning before the museum opens. There are lots of grassy areas for picnics on campus, or try out the cafeteria and other eateries on campus. For more information about the Beaux Arts Festival, see listing in "Mark Your Calendar."

□ **Miami Youth Museum**
5701 Sunset Drive, South Miami 33143. (Located in the Bakery Center, third level.) (305) 661-ARTS. Monday through Friday, 10 A.M.–5 P.M.; Saturday and Sunday, noon–5 P.M. Adults and children, $3. Memberships available. Cash payment only.

This is an excellent place to enjoy, experience, and learn about art with your youngsters. The museum provides rotating and permanent exhibitions designed especially for children, as well as related hands-on activities that allow them to explore many different artistic expressions. Toddlers may enjoy these activities, but they really appeal more to preschoolers and older children.

A gift shop is located at the museum, where children can buy small bags of recycled materials that can be used for arts and crafts projects. "Ed-U-Kits," offered for rent at the museum's resource center, will interest elementary school age children. Each kit includes hands-on materials that teach them about art, Florida's environment, patchwork quilting, Miami's history, and more. **Tips:** You'll need to spend about 90 minutes with your children to tour; please stay with them in the museum!

☐ Metropolitan Dade County Art in Public Places

111 NW First Street, Sixth Floor, Miami 33128. (The art can be seen throughout Dade County; many pieces are sited in or near Metrorail stations.) (305) 375-5362.

Over 350 works of art (mostly contemporary art) can be seen in parks, plazas, public libraries, hospitals, and transit facilities (including Miami International Airport) throughout Dade County. All kinds of art, including sculptures, paintings, photographs, mixed media, prints, ceramics, weavings, and fountains have been commissioned, sited, and maintained through this program. A self-guided Metrorail Art Tour booklet will lead you to many of the works. The information office can tell you about field trips and community programs related to the Art in Public Places program. **Tips:** You may touch the artworks that are within reach. Don't tour more than three or four sites (five or six for older children) and take drinks or a picnic with you. There are several places near the Metrorail stations suitable for picnics, such as Bayfront Park (accessible from the Metromover). Call for information about special Metrorail passes.

☐ Mitchell Wolfson, Jr., Collection of Decorative and Propaganda Arts

Miami-Dade Community College, Wolfson Campus, 300 NE Second Avenue, Building 1, Room 1365, Miami 33132. (305) 347-3429. Monday through Thursday, 10 A.M.–5:30 P.M. Free admission.

Children at least 5 years old will enjoy this collection of art objects that includes toys, sculptures, and posters from the 1888-1945 period.

☐ Model City Branch Library

2211 NW 54th Street (in Caleb Center), Miami 33142. (305) 638-6978. Monday through Friday, 9 A.M.–5 P.M. Free admission.

Forty-five hand-woven cloths, quilts, and tapestries from many African countries are on display in this library. Ask the librarian for a guidebook that describes the origin and meaning of each one.

☐ North Miami Museum and Center of Contemporary Art

12340 NE Eighth Avenue, North Miami 33161. (305) 893-6211. Monday through Friday, 10 A.M.–4 P.M.; Saturday, 1–4 P.M. Free admission; memberships available.

This nonprofit fine arts center offers a visual arts experience that showcases Florida artists. New exhibits are displayed every five weeks. Classes for children are available on Saturdays; group tours or field trips for children can be arranged. Call for information. **Tip:** Plan to spend up to an hour to tour.

Broward County

☐ Art and Cultural Center of Hollywood
1301 South Ocean Drive, Hollywood 33019. (305) 921-3275. Tuesday through Saturday, 10 A.M.–4 P.M., Sunday, 1–4 P.M. Adults, $2; children, $1; children under age 12, free. Donations accepted on Tuesdays. Memberships available. Cash payment only.

This museum of contemporary paintings and sculptures also sponsors several annual special events for children, including concerts and workshops, and a summer program on Saturdays for children ages 4 to 12. Concerts are presented on Sundays at 2:30 P.M. Birthday parties and field trips are available by special arrangement. **Tips:** The museum staff suggests that children visit from 10 A.M. to 1 P.M., and that you collect all the brochures containing exhibit information when you arrive.

☐ Broward Art Guild
207 South Andrews Avenue, Fort Lauderdale 33301. (305) 764-2005. Monday through Saturday, 10 A.M.–4 P.M.; Sunday, noon–4 P.M. Free admission; memberships available.

This nonprofit art guild brings in a new exhibition about every six weeks. Eight days following each opening (the following Saturday) children are invited to attend "Children's Opening-Night Day," a free event designed just for them, from noon to 2 P.M. The program includes a hands-on art activity, a gallery/exhibition tour, entertainment, refreshments, and balloons.

Art classes are available on Saturdays and after school for children ages 6 to 15 (younger children admitted according to their ability). A summer art camp is also offered. Call for information. **Tip:** Wear clothes you won't mind getting dirty (or bring a paint smock) to the activities.

☐ Museum of Art
One East Las Olas Boulevard, Fort Lauderdale 33301. (305) 525-5500. Tuesday, 11 A.M.–9 P.M.; Wednesday through Saturday, 10 A.M.–5 P.M.;

Sunday, noon–5 P.M.; closed on all national holidays. Adults, $3.25; senior citizens, $2.75; students, $1.25; children under age 12 admitted free with adult. AE, MC, V, personal checks accepted.

The museum displays a fascinating collection of 20th-century contemporary American art. It also houses the largest collection of ethnographic art in South Florida, including pre-Colombian, Oceanic, American Indian, and West African material, in addition to a collection of the world's foremost CoBrA (the Copenhagen, Brussels, and Amsterdam movement) paintings. In 1986 the museum moved to its new home, which has a 262-seat auditorium, sculpture terrace, art library, and bookstore.

Delightful "Children's Openings" happen one Saturday morning each month, from 10 A.M. to noon. Free to the public, the openings use hands-on, mixed-media art activities, as well as an exhibition tour conducted by trained docents, to acquaint children ages 3 to 10 with current exhibitions. Performances by dancers, musicians, and other entertainers, as well as refreshments and balloons, are provided.

"Kids' Eye View" is a program designed for children from preschool age to 8th grade who are enrolled in day-care and after-school-care centers. Groups may arrange to come to the museum for improvisational tours of exhibitions conducted by trained guides. Participatory activities are also included. Tours take place Tuesday through Thursday, from 3 to 5 P.M., and last about one hour. Arrangements may be made for museum staff to visit the children's center. Call the tour coordinator for more information. **Tip:** You can park in the Municipal Parking facility located on SE First Avenue, east of the museum.

□ **Young at Art Children's Museum**
801 South University Drive (just south of Broward Boulevard), Building C, Suite 136 (in The Fountains, near Lionel Playworld on south end of mall), Plantation 33024. (305) 922-3484. Tuesday through Sunday, 11 A.M.– 5 P.M. Adults and children, $2.50. Family memberships available. Cash payment only.

Hands-on, interactive exhibitions make this new museum (opened in July 1989) an exciting learning experience. Their goal is "to help children from infancy through adolescence understand and enjoy the complex world in which they live through the arts." One room displays exhibits that teach about line, color, shape, and texture. Another room features rotating exhibitions, such as "The Nature of Art." Two rooms are available for art classes and birthday parties; if you are a museum member you can host a special party there. A small gift shop and Recycle Arts Center are located near the front of the museum. Group tours and field trips may be arranged in advance; call for more information. **Tips:** Visit during the week if possible, and plan to spend about two hours to tour. Stroller access, wheelchair access, and changing area for babies provided. No picnic facilities.

Palm Beach County

□ The Boca Raton Museum of Art

801 West Palmetto Park Road, Boca Raton 33432. (407) 392-2500. Monday through Friday, 10 A.M.–4 P.M.; Saturday and Sunday, noon–4 P.M. Free admission.

This nonprofit cultural organization has served the community for over 40 years. In addition to the collections and international exhibitions found here, the museum sponsors classes for children in their Museum Art School, and hosts art tours, workshops, and other community events, such as art fairs in shopping malls. Call for information about current classes and activities for children.

□ Children's Museum of Boca Raton

498 Crawford Boulevard, Boca Raton 33432. (407) 368-6875. Tuesday through Sunday, noon–5 P.M.; school tours may be scheduled from 9 A.M. to noon. Adults and children, $1; children under age 2, free. Annual memberships available. Cash payment only for admission.

One of Boca Raton's oldest houses provides a home for this museum designed just for children. Special events include "Kidsfest," "Breakfast with Santa," and drawing and painting workshops. Birthday parties may be held at the museum. **Tips:** Picnic tables and soda machines are available; parking lot is behind the museum. Tours are available in Spanish. Formerly called the Singing Pines Museum for Children.

□ Norton Gallery of Art

1451 South Olive Avenue (south of Okeechobee Road), West Palm Beach 33401. (407) 832-5194. Tuesday through Saturday, 10 A.M.–5 P.M.; Sunday, 1–5 P.M. Memberships available. Free admission; donations requested. AE, MC, V accepted.

Steel magnate Ralph H. Norton founded this museum in 1941. Its permanent collection includes paintings by French impressionist and 20th-century artists (including Gauguin, Renoir, and Monet). An excellent library houses over 3,000 art books and periodicals.

Classes for children are offered on occasion throughout the year, and field trips or group tours may be arranged. Call for more information.
Tips: The staff recommends spending an hour in the late morning or early afternoon to tour the museum.

☐ The Society of the Four Arts

Four Arts Plaza, Palm Beach 33480. (407) 655-7226 for the galleries and offices; (407) 655-2766 for the library. Galleries open December 3 to April 16: Monday through Saturday, 10 A.M.–5 P.M.; Sundays, 2–5 P.M. Library open November 1 to April 30: Monday through Saturday, 10 A.M.–5 P.M. May 1 to October 31: Monday through Friday, 10 A.M.–5 P.M.

Incorporated in 1936 as a nonprofit organization, the Society of the Four Arts provides programs for adults and children in art, music, drama, and literature. The library here is the only public library on the island of Palm Beach. Students from the Palm Beach County Schools provide artwork for an annual children's art show presented in the gallery. The library's Children's Room has over 7,000 books and is staffed by a full-time children's librarian. During the summer. films for youngsters are presented in conjunction with the Parks and Recreation Department. There is a special collection of sea shells in the library and in the gallery lobby.
Tips: Picnics are not permitted in the botanical gardens, but this is a beautiful place for a supervised walk. Stay on the paths, and please don't touch the flowers or anything in the sculpture garden.

Monroe County

In addition to the museums, there are several art galleries in Key West that children may enjoy. Just remember that they are not places where children are free to run around and pick things up!

☐ East Martello Museum and Art Gallery

3501 South Roosevelt, Key West 33040. (Go north on A1A, the Atlantic side of the island past the airport.) (305) 296-6206. Daily, 9:30 A.M.–5 P.M. $2.50.

A Canadian welder named Stanley Papio moved to Key Largo in 1949 and started turning junk into sculptures in his yard. His neighbors called the police several times to have the "eyesores" removed. Now his works are collected here, and some people call him a genius along the lines of Picasso, Dalí, and Warhol. Other collections include painted wood carvings of Key West street scenes by Mario Sánchez, a local Cuban artist. For more information, see listing in "Tracing the Past."

□ **Haitian Art Co.**
600 Frances Street (corner of Southard Street), Key West 33040. (305) 296-8932. Daily, 10 A.M.–6 P.M. Major credit cards accepted.

A collection from over 200 artists working in Haiti is displayed in this gallery. Oils and acrylics on canvas, wood sculptures, oil drum cutouts, and painted cedar box cubes can be seen and purchased. Group tours and field trips can be arranged for children ages 3 and up.

Dance

Dade County

□ **Ballet Concerto**
3410 Coral Way, Miami 33145. (305) 446-7922.

In-school performances, including classical ballets and informal concerts, are available for children in grades K through 12 in Dade County schools. Call for information about children's ballet performances open to the public.

□ **Ballet Flamenco La Rosa**
4545 NW Seventh Street, Suite 13, Miami 33126. (305) 444-8228.

Children ages 3 and up will enjoy performances of this lively Spanish dance form. The origins of flamenco and other forms of Spanish dance are discussed and demonstrated to students in grades K through 12 throughout Dade County. Call for performance dates.

□ **Ballet Theatre of Miami**
1809 Ponce de Leon, Coral Gables 33134. (305) 442-4840.

The Ballet Theatre of Miami is a a nonprofit, professional ballet company that performs traditional classical and modern ballet. Performances of "The Nutcracker" are held every December at the Gusman Center for the Performing Arts. The company also performs special programs in elementary through high school classes within Dade County. **Tip:** All public performances except "The Nutcracker" are appropriate only for older children (ages 10 to 12) who have a basic understanding of ballet.

☐ Chiumba Imani Dance Theatre
% Model City Cultural Arts Center, 6161 NW 22nd Avenue, Miami 33142. (305) 638-6770. Cost and times vary according to performance; call for information.

Since 1978, director Chiku Ngozi and her dancers and drummers have presented East and West African dance, traditions, and culture through performances in various Dade County locations. They perform in the Model City Cultural Arts Center, Caleb Auditorium, in festivals, and in Dade County classrooms.

☐ InnerCity Children's Touring Dance Company
4256 NW Seventh Avenue, Miami 33127. (305) 756-5595.

About 250 children ages 2½ to 17 are trained in dance in late afternoon and evening classes. The performing group incorporates students ages 8 to 16. They perform throughout Florida for social groups and community activities, such as the Miami Book Fair International.

Each summer a group of students travels to Dakar, Senegal, in West Africa to learn dance, percussion, history, traditional medicine, hospitality, and cuisine, sponsored by the State of Florida Division of Cultural Exchange. A summer performing camp in Miami is also offered. Call for information.

☐ Junior Ballet Company of the Cultural Arts Society of South Florida
8027 Biscayne Boulevard, Miami 33138. (305) 757-4843.

Founded in 1971 and dedicated to bringing free cultural programs to the community, the Cultural Arts Society of South Florida sponsors several free ballet performances throughout Dade County. Check for newspaper announcements about performances at the Dade County Youth Fair, Vizcaya, and the Jackie Gleason Theatre of the Performing Arts. The Cultural Arts Society also sponsors a full two-hour program for families

Students in the InnerCity Children's Touring Dance Company provide lively performances at community events.

with older children at the North Miami Beach City Hall Auditorium. Laura Rose May serves as the artistic director. Call for performance information.

☐ Miami City Ballet
905 Lincoln Road, Miami Beach 33139. (305) 532-4880.

"Ballets for Young People," presented by the Miami City Ballet, provide an outstanding opportunity for children to learn about and enjoy child-size bites of ballet. Artistic director Edward Villela introduces and explains each segment of the performance. The ballet is followed by an activity designed to make the afternoon even more fun for the children; past activities have included a behind-the-scenes look at ballet and a fashion show featuring children's bathing suits and dance clothes. Coloring/activity books that explain various aspects of ballet are available. Call for performance information in Dade, Broward, and Palm Beach counties.

☐ Miami Repertoire Ballet Company
8781 SW 134th Street, Miami 33176. (West side of South Dixie Highway, just north of The Falls shopping area.) (305) 251-5822.

Watch for special performances for children, such as "Snow White" and "Cinderella" in the spring and "The Nutcracker" in December. The Company performs in public and private schools (contact your PTA to request a performance), at the annual Arti Gras in North Miami in March, in local shopping malls, and at festivals throughout the area. Ticket prices are very reasonable. Note that when you call the number given in this listing for Miami Repertoire Ballet performance information, you will reach the Ravich Ballet. This is the dance-school side of the organization.

Broward County

☐ Fort Lauderdale Children's Ballet Theatre
934 NE 62nd Street (Cypress Creek Road), Fort Lauderdale 33334. (305) 491-4668.

Each year two full-length ballets, such as "Sleeping Beauty" and "Coppelia," are presented for children ages 3 and up. A special feature is that some performances incorporate children ages 5 and older chosen from auditions in Dade, Broward, and Palm Beach counties. The ballets can be seen at festivals, the Main Library, and other sites throughout Broward. Lecture demonstrations are presented in the schools. This theater also houses a performing arts school that offers dance, drama, and voice classes. Call for performance and school information. **Tip:** Performances last about 90 minutes, so plan ahead.

☐ Miami City Ballet
(305) 463-0109.

See listing under Dade County.

Palm Beach County

☐ Ballet Florida
4704 Broadway, West Palm Beach 33407. (407) 844-2900 or 842-7631. Hours and cost vary according to performance.

A professional dance company and school, Ballet Florida presents ballet for children ages 3 and up. Performances have included "Sleeping Beauty" and "Coppelia," and have taken place at various sites, such as at the Royal Poinciana Playhouse, at libraries, and at the Dreher Park Zoo.

□ **The Florida Youth Ballet**
337 First Street (in The Children's Gym), Jupiter 33458. (407) 626-9631 or (407) 747-3646.

Young dancers (ages 11 to 14) from the Fiona Fairrie School of Ballet perform at festivals and other events throughout Palm Beach County. Call for information about upcoming performances or about the school.

□ **Miami City Ballet**
(407) 659-1328.

See listing under Dade County.

Music

Dade County

□ **An Afternoon of Music for Children**
Temple Beth Am Concert Series, Temple Beth Am, 5950 North Kendall Drive, Miami 33156. (305) 667-6667.

This concert series provides an excellent opportunity for children and families to learn music appreciation and concert etiquette. Past concerts have included performances by The Philharmonic Orchestra of Florida and The New World Symphony. Opera, jazz, classical, and other types of music are explored and performed for and by children. Concerts last about an hour, followed by light refreshments. Call for concert dates and ticket information. **Tip:** Recommended for children ages 6 and up.

□ **The Greater Miami Opera Association**
1200 Coral Way, Miami 33145. (305) 854-1643.

The Greater Miami Opera Association sponsors two auxiliary groups, The Young Patronesses of the Opera (YPO) and The Opera Guild, which provide activities that help children learn to enjoy opera. The YPO funds the "Opera Funtime" program and a program called "In-School Opera" that performs in elementary schools in Dade, Broward, and Palm Beach counties. The Opera Guild sponsors a similar program for high schools.

The Young Artist Program operas are free and open to the public. Watch local newspapers or call for information.

The YPO Opera Funtime program produces a series of outstanding activity/coloring books that introduce children to a dozen different operas. The books are available for a nominal fee through the Greater Miami Opera office or in the gift store at the Center for the Fine Arts, 101 West Flagler Street, Miami.

□ **Miami Choral Society**
536 Coral Way, Coral Gables 33134. (305) 443-7816.

The Miami Choral Society is a nonprofit organization composed of the Miami Youth Choir (for ages 8 to 12), the Boy Choir (ages 9 until the voice change), and the Girl Choir (ages 11 through high school). Auditions are held yearly, and children enter a three-year program to study music theory, voice, and ensemble participation. Public performances include annual concerts in May and December, and appearances at the Miami Youth Fair, civic events, and festivals.

□ **The New World Symphony**
541 Lincoln Road, Miami Beach 33139. (305) 673-3330.

"Family Concerts" are a great way for children to get a taste of classical music in a fun but formal atmosphere. "America's National Training Orchestra," led by artistic advisor Michael Tilson Thomas, was begun in 1988 to provide young musicians (ages 21 to 30) with the opportunity to gain professional performance experience. During their October to April season they present a series of three concerts for families. Children as young as age 5 are invited to learn about and enjoy classical music. A delightful program guide describes the music, orchestra, instruments, and concert etiquette. **Tip:** Concerts last about an hour, with no intermission, so plan accordingly.

□ **Performing Arts for Community and Education, Inc. (PACE)**
Mailing address is P.O. Box 40, Miami 33168-0040. (305) 681-1470 in Dade; (305) 764-4270 in Broward.

PACE is a nonprofit organization that supports and promotes local artists by presenting "concerts on the beach, dance in the streets, theater in the malls, and music in the museums, hospitals, community centers, schools, and

*New World Symphony Family Concerts
include performances such as "Mozart
Live!" and make classical music fun for
kids.*

businesses." Artists include classical, jazz, reggae, country, and other
musicians; puppeteers, mimes and jugglers; and ballet, modern, and
flamenco dancers. Check local newspapers for concert dates and locations,
or call the PACE offices for information.

☐ **South Florida Youth Symphony, Inc.**
555 NW 152nd Street, Miami 33169. (305) 238-2706.

Founded in 1963, the 70-member nonprofit South Florida Youth
Symphony aims to "promote symphonic music among young people,
encourage musical growth and appreciation in young people, enhance
music appreciation in the community through quality public performances,
and support the musical development of young musicians through a
substantial scholarship fund." Free "Young People's Concerts" and "Family
Day Concerts" are offered. Call or write for concert dates and locations;
concerts are offered from Coral Springs to Homestead.

Broward County

☐ **Viva Opera! The Opera Guild, Inc.**
333 SW Second Avenue, Fort Lauderdale 33312. (305) 728-9700.

Each year Viva Opera! sponsors a delightful performance written especially for children. Operas have included: "The Toy Shop," "Hansel and Gretel," "The Serpent Who Wanted to Sing," and "Little Red Riding Hood." Performances last about an hour, and are appropriate for children ages 5 to 12. They are sometimes presented at the Parker Playhouse, but check with the Guild for concert dates, location, and other information.

☐ **Philharmonic Orchestra of Florida**
1430 North Federal Highway, Fort Lauderdale 33304. For concert and ticket information, call (305) 945-5180 in Dade, (305) 561-2997 in Broward, (407) 392-5443 in Boca Raton, or (407) 659-0331 in Palm Beach.

Tiny Tots Concerts, which are geared to children ages 3 to 8, are presented in preschools, elementary schools, and at special events throughout Dade,

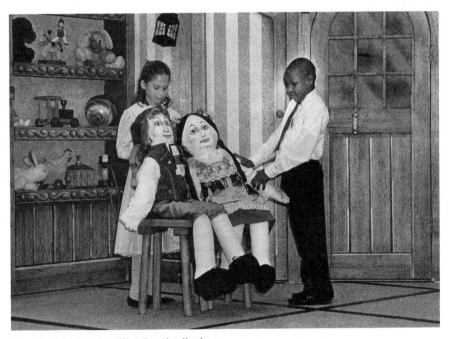

Young opera-goers will enjoy the lively music and the clever props of performances sponsored by Viva Opera!

Broward, and Palm Beach counties. A 45-minute version of "Peter and the Wolf" was presented during the 1988–89 season; other performances have included "The Circus Parade." Music for Youth Concerts are presented in the public schools for children in grades 3 to 6, and feature special guest soloists chosen from local high schools. Young People's Concerts are presented at major auditoriums throughout Broward and Palm Beach counties. They are designed for children ages 6 to 12.

Palm Beach County

☐ **The Greater Miami Opera Association**
(305) 854-1643.

See listing under Dade County.

☐ **Philharmonic Orchestra of Florida**
500 East Spanish River Road, Suite #27, Boca Raton 33431.
(407) 392-5443; (407) 659-0331 in Palm Beach.

See listing under Broward County.

Theater

Dade County

☐ **Actors' Playhouse Children's Theatre**
8851 SW 107th Avenue, Miami 33176. (Located in the Kendall Mall.)
(305) 595-5515.

Four plays per year are offered for children ages 5 and up. Productions have included "Puss 'n' Boots," "The Stone-Age Cinderella," and "Mr. Crinkle's Magic Spring." The theater seats approximately 300, and also presents performances for adults. Performances last one hour, followed by a 15-minute question-and-answer session with the actors. For party information, see listing in "Celebrate in Style."

☐ **Alphabet Theatre Productions**
14411 South Dixie Highway, Miami 33176. (305) 232-2628.

"What's It All About?" presents the U.S. Constitution in a multi-media program designed for children. A play, songs, "Sparkles the Magnificent" (a clown), puppets, and audience participation bring this basic element of U.S. government to life in a way that children not only understand but enjoy. Ask your child's school PTA or principal about bringing the show to their school.

☐ **Carousel Players**
Cavalier Theatre, 1401 Westward Drive, Miami Springs 33166. (305) 885-9883.

Professional performances for children have included "Robin Goodfellow" and "Cinderella." Call for schedule information.

☐ **Coconut Grove Children's Theatre**
3351 Matilda, Coconut Grove. Mailing address is P.O. Box 331002, Coconut Grove 33133. (305) 442-0489.

Creative director Corky Dozier presents "theatre by children, for children." Seminars in dance, music, film and television, makeup, and drama are available for students in grades K through 12 in Dade and Broward counties.

☐ **Fantasy Theatre Factory**
Mailing address is P.O. Box 430280, Miami 33243. (305) 284-8800.

A professional touring company, they call themselves new vaudevillians and buskers (strolling entertainers). They are featured at, and often co-produce, festivals throughout South Florida. Their children's theater delights kids in grades K through 12. Workshops in creative movement, improvisation, mask making, mime, clowning, circus skills, and creativity development are provided in the classroom. If they can't provide the performers themselves, they know where in the world to find someone who can do the job. Call for information about performance schedules.

☐ **Florida Shakespeare Festival**
Minorca Playhouse, 232 Minorca Avenue, Coral Gables 33146. (305) 858-6501; (800) 328-7638 (Florida WATTS). Discount tickets are available for children.

Innovative performances of classics, such as a '50s rock 'n' roll version of "Taming of the Shrew," will entertain older children.

□ **Kaleidoscope—A Young Show-Goers Series**
% Dave and Mary Alper Jewish Community Center, 12401 SW 102nd Avenue, Miami 33176. (305) 251-1394.

Kaleidoscope brings the best nationally known children's performing groups to Miami. Productions usually appeal to children ages 4 to 10, and can accommodate groups of up to 1,000 children. Call for program and ticket information.

□ **Locomotion Children's Theatre**
Mailing address is P.O. Box 161392, Miami 33116-1392. (305) 382-3246.

Locomotion Children's Theatre is a traveling theater that performs in parks, libraries, festivals, and other public places. Their original plays, which encourage audience participation and use of imagination, are excellent for children. Some of their titles include "Alphabet Soup and Gobbledy-Goop," "Dinosaur Eggs in My Lunchbox," "Moon Voyager," and "It's O.K. to Be Nice in Botswana." The Miami-Dade Community College South Campus offers the plays through their community education program—watch for performance information in your local newspapers, or give the theater a call. For information on party performances, see listing in "Celebrate in Style."

□ **Model City Cultural Arts Center**
6161 NW 22nd Avenue, Miami 33142. (305) 638-6770.

The center provides training for performing, visual, and media arts; it trains and develops in-house performing groups and provides performers for community events. A gallery features new exhibitions every six weeks of local and noted African-American and minority artists, and tours of the center are available.

Some of the programs offered through the center include "After School in the Arts" and "Saturday Creative Art Day Camp," which are open during the school year for children ages 5 to 15, and include classes in dance, drama, piano, guitar, drawing, and painting. Art day camps for spring break and summer are also offered.

"Magic City Monday Variety Show" at the Caleb Auditorium takes place twice monthly on Monday evenings throughout the year. Performances are appropriate for children ages 3 and up. The Cultural Arts Center (CAC)

Dance Troupe operates out of the Model City Cultural Arts Center. June is Black Music Month, and a talent search and music festivals are held. In August the annual Youth Talent Show showcases performers ages 5 to 21.

□ New Theatre for Children
At New Theatre, 4275 Aurora Street (one block south of Bird Road, three blocks east of Le Jeune Road), Coral Gables 33146. (305) 595-4260. Performances on Saturdays, 1 P.M. Adults, $5; children, $3.

In the summer of 1988 the New Theatre began presenting special plays based on classic stories for children. Recent performances include "Fabulous Fables," "Stories Not So Grimm," and "The Mark Twain Storybook." The plays use the "story theater" style, which combines narration, acting, and audience participation. The theater itself uses the "black box" format, in which the stage and seats are flexible and can be moved according to the needs of the play. Call for information about performances and special rates for parties and groups.

□ Pied Piper Players
Ruth Foreman Theatre, Barry University, 11300 NE Second Avenue, Miami Shores 33161. (305) 940-5902. Performances on Saturdays at 11 A.M. Adults and children, $3.50.

Ruth Foreman created the Pied Piper Players in 1949, and they've been performing children's theater ever since. Four performances are presented each year, including plays such as "The Frog Prince," "King Midas and His Golden Touch," and "Scrooge." Workshops for children are also available. Performances are recommended for ages 5 to 12.

□ The Puppet People
8705 SW 182nd Terrace, Miami 33157. (305) 253-3006.

Several full-length professional puppet shows, 14 different shows for holidays throughout the year, seven different preschool programs and puppet-making workshops for teachers, recreation leaders, and students— all these are available from The Puppet People. Excellent for children of all ages. Call for further information.

Broward County

□ Broward Community College Fine Arts Division
Lecture Theater, Building 6, BCC Central Campus, 3501 SW Davie Road, Davie 33314. (305) 475-6840. Ticket prices are very inexpensive.

Begun in 1970, this program is an excellent example of local drama students creating theater for children. Performances are presented to children in grades K through 6 during the week, and to the general public on weekends. Plays last about an hour, and refreshments and theme T-shirts are sold after some performances. Special admission is available for groups of up to 200 students.

□ Children to Children
7880 Wiles Road, Coral Springs 33067. (305) 753-7070. Performances on Friday evenings and Saturday mornings. Cost is under $5, but varies according to the play presented. Group rates are available.

This organization provides children interested in acting with an opportunity to learn as they rehearse for performances. Children from ages 8 to 14 perform in three children's theater presentations each year at the Opus Playhouse. Performances include revues, musicals, and plays based on children's books. Auditions are held for children throughout South Florida, and performers are given drama instruction during the production. Drama classes are also available.

□ Fort Lauderdale Children's Theater
640 North Andrews Avenue, Fort Lauderdale 33311. (305) 763-6901. Cost varies according to play; special rates are available for groups and schools.

This theater was founded in 1959, and continues to provide teaching and performance programs for children ages 3 to 18. Students produce and perform in the plays, which include titles such as "The Best Christmas Ever" and "Fool of the World." The auditorium seats 140, and season tickets are available for the four plays presented each year. From November to May the young actors tour in schools throughout Broward; during the summer they go as far south as Key West and north to Palm Beach County.

Saturday workshops in special-effects makeup, voice, puppetry, and clowning are offered throughout the year. Drama classes are available for children ages 3 to 18. Their Performing Arts Summer Camp teaches dance, drama, and music to children ages 5 and up.

□ Lauderhill Arts and Cultural Committee

Lauderhill Community Center, 1176 NW 42nd Way, Lauderhill 33313.
(305) 587-5720. Free admission.

Sponsored by the City of Lauderhill, this group has presented children's
musical theater productions annually since 1979. All children ages 8 and
up who are interested in participating will be included. Plays are performed
at the Community Center, and have been broadcast on local cable
television.

□ Lollipop Theater

Opus Playhouse, 7880 Wiles Road, Coral Springs 33067. (305) 753-7070.
Performances usually take place Saturday mornings; call for schedule. Cost
is under $5.

Marionettes and puppets, plays and other performances appropriate for
children ages 3 to 8, are a wonderful and very inexpensive alternative to
Saturday cartoons! See previous Children to Children listing for more
information about drama instruction.

□ Story Theatre Productions, Inc.

Mailing address is P.O. Box 4603, Fort Lauderdale 33338. Performances
take place at Parker Playhouse, 707 NE Eighth Street, Fort Lauderdale.
(305) 763-8813 in Broward, (305) 947-3790 in Dade.

These professional performances are excellent for mature 4-year-olds to
12th graders, depending on the play. Recent titles have included "The
Velveteen Rabbit," "The Further Adventures of the Potato People," and
"Susan B!" Refreshments, autograph sessions with the actors, and other nice
touches make this a very special event for children. When school groups
make reservations, they are sent teacher's guides prior to the performance.
Over 60,000 children enjoy these performances each year. **Tips:**
Subscriptions are available; ask about special rates for groups of 10 or more.

□ Theatre Company of Plantation

1829 North Pine Island Road, Plantation 33317. (305) 473-8100. Free
admission.

This is the resident theater company of the Broward Mall. Free
performances for children take place at the Center Court (in the middle of
the mall), and include titles such as "Cinderella" and "Rocking Around the

*Story Theatre Productions' performances
are often followed by autograph sessions
and other surprises.*

Christmas Tree." Children perform in the plays, and audience participation is encouraged. The company also sponsors face painting, clowning, and workshops in the mall.

Palm Beach County

☐ Gold Coast Mime Company
5151 Adams Road, Delray Beach 33445. (407) 495-1730.

This professional mime company offers performances such as "Pirate Game" that encourage audience participation. They also provide movement and theater training. Look for this group in libraries and parks throughout South Florida, or call for performance information. Recommended for children ages 4 and up.

☐ Little Palm Theatre for Young People
(Florida Academy of Dramatic Arts)
Mailing address is P.O. Box 1682, Royal Palm Dinner Theater, 303 Golfview Drive, Boca Raton 33429. (407) 394-0206. Performances take place on Saturdays at 9 A.M. Adults and children, $5; group rates available.

"Winnie the Pooh," "Arkansas Bear," and "Snow White and the Seven Dwarfs of the Black Forest" are among the performances offered since 1979 by this nonprofit regional theater for young people. They perform new and classic dramas on Saturday mornings at Royal Palm Dinner Theater. You can also plan to have a birthday party on their patio theater. For more information, see listing in "Celebrate in Style."

☐ Starmakers Production Children's Theatre Company
Delray Beach Playhouse, 950 Lakeshore Drive, Delray Beach. Mailing address is P.O. Box 1056, Delray Beach 33445. (407) 487-8722. Cost varies according to play.

A nonprofit children's theater company, Starmakers specializes in workshops that enhance children's self-confidence and self-esteem. Each year they present two or three major plays and musicals about and for children. Performances are appropriate for all ages, and performers, from 4-year-olds to teens, are chosen from auditions in Palm Beach, Broward, and Dade counties.

Monroe County

☐ **Red Barn Theater**
319 Duval Street, Key West. Mailing address is P.O. Box 707, Key West 33040. (305) 296-9911.

This theater is located in what was formerly the carriage house behind the Women's Association building; although it is small, it's great for kids because every seat is a good one. Three plays for children are presented each year, including titles such as "How to Eat Like a Child and Other Lessons on Not Being a Grown-up" and "Goldilocks and the Three Bears." The performances are produced by the Key West School of Performing Arts, and include young actors from ages 6 to 13. The school provides instruction in acting, music, fencing, and scene study; they also offer remedial classes for children with reading disabilities. Call for information about performances in other locations.

Miscellaneous

□ **Miami Book Fair International**
Miami-Dade Community College, Wolfson Campus, 300 NE Second Avenue, Miami 33132. (305) 347-3258. Free admission.

For eight days in the fall the Wolfson campus becomes a mecca for readers of all ages. The Miami Book Fair International, a nonprofit organization, has hosted this event since 1984. On the last three days (Friday through Sunday) you can take young readers to the Children's Alley section of the Book Fair—a wonderful place for kids to explore. Past fairs have included booths with children's book authors, illustrators, and publishers; as well as a petting zoo, a moon walk, train rides, face painting, puppet shows, arts and crafts, storytellers, mimes, and more.

The "Young People's Crossing" events, such as dance and karate demonstrations, take place in the atrium, and are appropriate for junior or senior high school students. For more information, see listing in "Mark Your Calendar."

□ **South Florida Juggling Academy**
3511 SW 35th Street, Hollywood 33023. (305) 966-3227.

This is not a place to go; rather, it's an event to request for your child's school, camp, or other community group. Juggling workshops can be geared to children of all ages and abilities. The proprietors estimate that since 1977 they have collectively taught over one million people throughout North America how to juggle. Call for more information.

Bytes, Kites, and Toy Delights

Watch as the sky fills with colorful kites and flying toy birds after browsing through a kite shop at the beach. Learn to create magical illusions from a pro. Wonder at the sight of life-size animals, such as kangaroos and camels, displayed beneath a brightly-colored carousel canopy. Choose tiny toys and candy to fill a party piñata. Try on hand-crocheted dresses imported from Spain and Latin America. Sit under a tree and listen to stories or meet characters from young readers' favorite books. Experiment with the latest computer software. Pretend you're at the Magic Kingdom in a store filled to the ceiling with official Disney products. These are just some of the things for children to do that we've discovered in our search for unique shops and services.

Children will enjoy visiting most of the stores included in this chapter. We've also slipped in a few special places where you'll find collectibles for both adults and children. Please call before you go to confirm the addresses, hours, and other information included here—the marketplace is full of changes!

Specialty Stores

Canastillas

Canastilla is a Spanish word for the straw baby baskets that are decorated with lots of lace, filled with baby supplies, and given to parents-to-be. It's also the generic term for stores found throughout South Florida (primarily in Dade County) that carry clothing, leather shoes, fancy socks, hair bows and ribbons, crocheted sweaters, and dresses imported from Spain. They usually have a selection of baby furniture and supplies, as well as gold baby jewelry. Check the yellow pages in the phone book for canastillas near you.

☐ **La Canastilla Cubana**
1300 West 49th Street, Hialeah 33016. (305) 557-5505. Monday through Saturday, 9 A.M.–8 P.M.; Sunday, 11 A.M.–5 P.M. AE, DIN, MC, V, personal checks accepted.

This is the largest canastilla in the country, maybe even in the world! You'll be overwhelmed by the selection in every department. There are numerous room displays that can be ordered the day the baby is born, and delivered and set up before you get home from the hospital. Prices range from inexpensive to very expensive—check out the leather strollers!

Dolls

Dade County

☐ **Enchantables**
26 NE 15th Street (east of Krome Avenue, off NE 15th Street/304th Street), Homestead 33030. (305) 248-0481. Monday through Saturday, 10 A.M.– 5 P.M.; Sunday, 11 A.M.–3 P.M. MC, V, local checks accepted; layaway available.

More than 100 limited-edition dolls fill one of the three rooms in this old house-turned-shop. Prices range from fifty to several hundred dollars for the artist originals, many of which have won awards. There is a small tea room at the back of the shopping area that serves lunch and wonderful desserts. It makes a nice stop for "grown-up boys and girls" (but they have high chairs, too). **Tip:** There are lots of things that children will want to pick up but shouldn't, so be prepared.

☐ **Heirlooms of Tomorrow**
2178½ NE 123rd Street (in the Causeway Shops, on south side of 123rd Street), North Miami 33161. (305) 899-0920. Monday, noon–5:30 P.M.; Tuesday, Wednesday, and Friday, 9:30 A.M.–5:30 P.M.; Thursday and Saturday, 9 A.M.–5 P.M. AE, DISC, MC, V, local checks accepted.

All types of dolls, made of porcelain, china, and other materials are available. The designer Cabbage Patch dolls with porcelain heads can cost over $500. This is not a good place for small children, but if you're looking for beautiful dolls, this is a great shop.

☐ Marlene's Almost New

2091 West 76th Street, Hialeah 33016. (305) 556-6119. Tuesday through Saturday, 10 A.M.–5 P.M.; Sunday, noon–5 P.M. AE, MC, V, personal checks accepted.

Antique and collectible dolls, dollhouse furniture, clothes, and related items are sold here. The store also carries stuffed animals.

☐ Pearl Artist and Craft Supply Corp.

13451 South Dixie Highway (across from Bloomingdale's), Miami 33156. (305) 251-5700. Monday through Friday, 10 A.M.–8:45 P.M.; Saturday, 10 A.M.–5:45 P.M.; Sunday, 11 A.M.–4:45 P.M. MC, V accepted.

In addition to its wide selection of arts and craft supplies, this large discount store carries doll-making supplies, dollhouse kits, miniature furniture, and accessories, including wallpaper.

☐ Rooms to Remember

1553 Sunset Drive (in Sunset Gates Arcade, behind Beverly Hills Cafe), Coral Gables 33143. (305) 665-9341. Tuesday through Friday, 11 A.M.– 5 P.M.; Saturday, 11 A.M.–4 P.M. MC, V, local personal checks accepted.

Scale-model (from one-inch to one-foot) dollhouses and miniatures fill this small shop. Imagine your favorite dolls in a Victorian mansion or a farmhouse, and surround them with the appropriate furniture. Dollhouse kits and assembled dollhouses are available. Dollmaking classes are scheduled during the year for adults.

☐ Wimpee's Wonders

13470 SW 129th Terrace, Miami 33186. (Take 137th Avenue to 128th Street, across from entrance to Tamiami Airport, and turn east.) (305) 252- 9782. Tuesday and Thursday, 9 A.M.–9 P.M.; Wednesday and Friday, 9 A.M.–5 P.M.; Saturday, 9 A.M.–noon. MC, V, local personal checks accepted.

Wimpee's Wonders include porcelain dolls, miniatures, dollhouse dolls, furniture, and stuffed animals, as well as supplies to make and dress dolls. Classes are available for adults to learn to make their own dolls.

Broward County

☐ **Dixie Doll Shop**
3553 North Dixie Highway, Oakland Park 33334. (305) 537-9325. Tuesday through Saturday, 11 A.M.–4 P.M. Local personal checks accepted.

New and antique dolls and related merchandise are available. Their doll hospital will treat your new and antique dolls in need of repair.

☐ **Dollhouses and Miniatures by Otilia Originals**
920 North Federal Highway (between Atlantic Boulevard and Copans Road), Deerfield Beach 33441. (305) 943-5737. Monday through Thursday, 9:30 A.M.–5 P.M.; Friday, 9:30 A.M.–3 P.M.; other times by appointment. Personal checks accepted.

All kinds of dollhouses and the tiny accessories that go in them (many of which are handmade originals) are available here. Miniature flower arrangements made by the proprietor are fascinating. Browse through a copy of the *Nutshell News* while you're in the shop to get an idea of the world of miniatures. Classes are available on request for older children; call for information.

☐ **The Paisley Bear**
3020 North Federal Highway, Suite 10, Plaza 3000, Fort Lauderdale 33306. (305) 563-5353. Monday through Friday, 9 A.M.–4 P.M.; Saturday, 9 A.M.– 2 P.M. Checks accepted.

This is a magical store, with life-size (and life-like!) toys and animals, mechanical toys, antique dolls, dollhouses, and furniture. The custom-made paisley or fur teddy bears and rabbits cost around $300 (the paisley cloth is at least 100 years old; the fur animals are fully jointed). Antique tin toys, old games, paper dolls, English Corgi vehicles, doll books, and teddy-bear greeting cards are also available. Doll repairs, costuming, and even teddy-bear weddings and operations can be arranged. In 1988 the proprietors provided the child's fantasy bedroom exhibit at the Museum of Art in Fort Lauderdale during the Festival of Trees, and presented a teddy bear display at the Children's Museum of Boca Raton. **Tip:** Children will want to touch, pick up, and otherwise play with many things here—keep an eye on what they get into!

☐ **Pearl Artist and Crafts Supply Corp.**
1033 East Oakland Park Boulevard, Fort Lauderdale 33334. (305) 564-

Antique toy treasures at The Paisley Bear charm young and old alike.

5700 in Broward; (305) 374-1622 in Dade. Monday through Saturday, 10 A.M.–5:45 P.M.

See listing under Dade County.

Palm Beach County

□ Ada's Cottage Antiques and Doll Hospital
810 Lake Avenue, Lake Worth 33462. (407) 582-9806. Tuesday through Friday, 10 A.M.–5 P.M.; Saturday, 11 A.M.–3 P.M. MC, V, local checks accepted; layaway available.

Come in and browse through the new and antique (including consignment) dolls and collectibles. If your new or antique doll needs an operation, this is an excellent hospital—the proprietor restored the dolls on display at the Flagler Museum.

□ Doll House Corner
Eight SE Fourth Avenue, Delray Beach 33444. (407) 272-7598. Monday

through Saturday, 10 A.M.–5 P.M.; other times by appointment. MC, V, personal checks accepted.

For over 20 years this shop has been creating dollhouse fantasies for the young and old. You'll find supplies and expertise to create everything from inexpensive cardboard dioramas to $65,000 custom-made dollhouses. Log cabins, forts, and gas station models will captivate boys and girls. Over 30 dollhouse models are available; prices begin at around $100. Serious hobbyists will want to see fascinating items such as the miniature sterling silver tea sets (around $250) and working electric lights.

Kites

□ **Key West Kite Company**
409 Greene Street, Key West 33040. (305) 296-2535. Daily, 10 A.M.– 6 P.M.; closed Christmas. AE, MC, V, personal checks accepted.

Florida's first kite store is still creating beautiful sky sculptures with kites, windsocks, and other flying toys. Greg Lavelle, Key West's "Kite Man," has the largest selection in the state, and sells good quality kites, handmade in the United States. He also sells Ornithopters (flying toy birds that flap their wings), beach and pool toys, and other outdoor recreation items.

The Kite Man offers kite-building classes for Girl Scouts, Boy Scouts, and area elementary schools, in which children make and fly their own kites. He also sponsors three kite festivals per year, free to the public: the Annual Kite Festival, at the end of April; the Summer Splash in June; and One Sky, One World in October (in conjunction with kite enthusiasts in 80 countries around the world).

□ **Peter Powell Kites Inc.**
1042 NE 43rd Court, Oakland Park 33334. (305) 565-5588. Monday through Friday, 7:30 A.M.–4:30 P.M. MC, V accepted.

In operation since 1979, this factory has a showroom open to the public, with kites and windsocks for sale. Their specialty is stunt kites.

□ **The Singer Island Kite Shop**
2407 Ocean Drive (in the Ocean Mall), Riviera Beach 33408. (Exit I-95 at Blue Heron Boulevard; go to Singer Island, and turn right at bottom of the

bridge.) (407) 848-9094. Daily, 10:30 A.M.–6 P.M. AE, MC, V, local
personal checks accepted.

An amazing visual experience, this small shop will make children want to
run out the door to the beach in front and fly a kite NOW! Windsocks,
kites, and supplies are on display, and you'll need to hold onto little hands
as you browse. Call to find out when the proprietor will perform his next
demonstration of kite sculptures on the beach.

Magic Supplies and Costumes

Magicians frequent these shops, and often provide spontaneous demonstrations for young fans and aspiring magicians. All the stores listed here provide complete instructions on how to use the products when you buy them.
Note, however, that these stores can be very scary for young children, especially in the weeks leading up to October 31.

☐ Annie's Costume & Holiday Shop
801 South University Drive, The Fountains, Building B, Suite #136 (north
side of mall), Plantation 33324. (305) 474-7474. Monday through
Wednesday, 10 A.M.–6 P.M.; Thursday through Saturday, noon–4 P.M.;
Sunday, noon–4 P.M. (From mid-September until October 31, hours are
Monday through Saturday, 10 A.M.–9 P.M.).

Open since 1982, Annie's moved to this new location during the summer of
1989. You'll find over 3,000 costumes in stock during most of the year, and
over 5,000 during September and October. Rental costumes are available
throughout the year. They also carry party supplies and at least 200 styles of
balloons. Staff will play videos in the store to teach you how to apply
costume makeup and how to use some of the magic tricks sold in the store.

☐ Biscayne Magic and Joke Shop/A & J Collectibles
and Party Goods
1680 NE 123rd Street, North Miami 33181. (305) 891-7224. Monday
through Friday, 11 A.M.–8 P.M.; Saturday, 10 A.M.–6 P.M. AE, MC, V
accepted.

On the magic side of the store you'll find an excellent selection of magic and
joke supplies, masks, makeup, and costumes (bunny and Santa Claus
costumes are available for rental). The other side of the store has fascinating

things like gumball machines, juke boxes, lobby cards and inserts, and autographs for sale.

☐ La Casa de los Trucos

1343 SW Eighth Street, Miami 33135, (305) 858-5029; 8590 SW 40th Street, Miami 33135, (305) 553-3553. Monday through Saturday, 10 A.M.– 7 P.M. AE, MC, V accepted.

In addition to the magic and joke supplies, both of these stores carry a large inventory of rental costumes. The staff is happy to demonstrate, in English or Spanish, how to use tricks that you purchase.

☐ Land of Magic and Novelties

450 NE 20th Street, Boca Raton 33431. (407) 393-7352. Monday through Saturday, 10 A.M.–5 P.M. AE, MC, V, personal checks accepted.

Excellent family-oriented store (no "adults only" merchandise), with a wonderful collection of illusions on display. Costumes, makeup, and juggling equipment are available. The tricks and illusions can cost up to $4,000 each.

☐ Miami Magic & Joke Shop

9728 Bird Road (SW 40th Street), Miami 33165. (305) 223-0927. Monday through Saturday, 10 A.M.–6 P.M. MC, V, personal checks accepted if you're a regular customer.

Large illusions and photographs of famous magicians provide the visual background for the merchandise. Costumes are available for sale or rent. From September to October 31, the store becomes a costume shop, with very few magic supplies.

Piñatas and Supplies

A *piñata* is a decorated clay or papier-mâché pot that is filled with candy, fruit, and toys, and suspended from a ceiling or tree branch. If it's a Mexican piñata, children are blindfolded and take turns trying to break it with a stick. A Cuban piñata may be better for very young children. It has multiple ribbons hanging from the bottom that the children pull to break it open. When either type of piñata finally breaks, everyone scrambles to collect as many goodies as possible.

□ **La Casa de las Piñatas**
1756 SW Eighth Street, Miami 33135. (305) 649-4711. Monday through Saturday, 10 A.M.–7 P.M. AE, MC, V, personal checks accepted.

This store specializes in Cuban piñatas, featuring all types of children's party themes, in all price ranges. They also sell party supplies as well as the goodies that go inside the piñata. Prices range from $19 to over $300. Special orders are available.

□ **La Piñata II**
8368 Mills Drive, Miami 33183. (Located in the Town & Country Mall), (305) 595-7701. Monday through Saturday, 10 A.M.–8 P.M.; Sunday, noon– 5 P.M. Personal checks accepted ($10 minimum).

If you plan to include a piñata in your child's birthday party, this store is a great place to start. This is also a good place to take kids when you want to give them a non-food treat that is cheap and fun. For under a dollar they can choose several tiny toys from row after row of barrels. Help small children choose things that don't have tiny pieces they could swallow. Piñata prices range from $25 to $40. (Note: La Piñata I is in Venezuela.)

Trademark Products

□ **The Disney Store**
The Fashion Mall, Plantation 33317, (305) 370-2301; The Gardens, Palm Beach Gardens 33410, (407) 624-0447. Monday through Saturday, 10 A.M.–9:30 P.M.; Sunday, noon–6 P.M. AE, MC, V, personal checks accepted.

A trip to this store is almost like a trip to Disneyworld. Disney characters frolic in large displays throughout the store, and a music video with clips from Disney cartoon movies plays continuously on a huge screen at the rear of the store. All kinds of Disney products (clothing, toys, stationery, and jewelry) are available.

□ **Dorissa Children's World Factory Store**
2850 NW Fifth Avenue, Miami 33131. (Take I-95 to North Miami Avenue exit; look for pink building on Fifth Avenue.) (305) 573-4293. Monday through Friday, 9 A.M.–5 P.M.; Saturday, 9 A.M.–2 P.M. MC, V accepted.

*La Casa de las Piñatas displays
beautifully decorated piñatas to fill with
party favors and treats.*

Take advantage of discounts on their own line of dresses and sportswear; they give good discounts on other designer labels for children.

□ The Gymboree Store
Broward Mall, Plantation 33317, (305) 370-3345; The Gardens, Palm Beach Gardens 33410, (407) 624-0577. Monday through Saturday, 10 A.M.–9:30 P.M.; Sunday, noon–6 P.M. AE, MC, V, personal checks accepted.

Part of a national chain related to the Gymboree gymnastic centers for children, these stores sell exercise clothing created for easy movement. They also carry exercise and music videos. For party information related to the Gymboree gymnastic centers, see "Celebrate in Style."

□ It's Showtime
401 Biscayne Boulevard (in Bayside Marketplace near food court), Miami 33132. (305) 375-0775. Monday through Friday, 10 A.M.–10 P.M.; Saturday, 10 A.M.–11 P.M.; Sunday, 11 A.M.–8 P.M. AE, MC, V, personal checks accepted.

Children will enjoy the yellow brick road that runs through the store, the dressing room that looks like a castle, and the Disney movies that play on a huge video monitor at the rear of the store. Licensed to sell Disney character products, you can find clothing and souvenir-type items in this shop.

□ McKids
Cutler Ridge Mall, 20505 South Dixie Highway, Miami 33189, (305) 251-9099; Coral Square, 9187 West Atlantic Boulevard, Coral Springs 33065, (305) 341-4000; Boynton Beach Mall, 801 North Congress, Boynton Beach 33426, (407) 369-1770; Palm Beach Mall, 1801 Palm Beach Lakes Boulevard, West Palm Beach 33401, (407) 684-5400. Hours vary according to location. DISC, MC, Sears, V.

Children will know this store was designed with them in mind from the moment they walk through the miniature door. Encourage them to head back to the wonderful play area while you shop. There's also a 48-inch screen and mini-bleachers where kids can preview educational videos. The store carries its own lines of children's clothes, as well as other popular brands, for infants to size 14. Accessories, toys, and books are also available. Special events include reading nights, game nights, and appearances by storytellers, jugglers, and, of course, the McDonald's characters.

□ **NBC Studio on the Air**
401 Biscayne Boulevard (at Bayside Marketplace on ground level under food court area), Miami 33132. (305) 577-3364. Monday through Saturday, 10 A.M.–10 P.M., Sunday, noon–5:30 P.M. AE, MC, V, local personal checks accepted.

If your favorite television programs are on NBC, this place will have something for you. They carry sweatshirts and pants, T-shirts, golf shirts, bibs, teddy bears, and baby jumpsuits, all displaying the NBC Peacock logo and your favorite television program's logo and characters. Call for new locations.

□ **National Football League Alumni Store**
4460 North Federal Highway, Fort Lauderdale 33308, (305) 491-4766; Aventura Mall, 19575 Biscayne Boulevard, North Miami Beach 33132, (305) 931-0575. Monday through Saturday, 10 A.M.–9:30 P.M.; Sunday, noon–5:30 P.M. AE, MC, V, personal checks accepted.

You can choose from a full line of NFL merchandise for all 28 teams. Helmets, mugs, key chains, posters, and sportswear (in child to adult sizes) are available.

□ **Polly Flinders Factory Outlet**
1521 East Las Olas Boulevard, Fort Lauderdale 33301. (305) 463-6807. Monday through Saturday, 9:30 A.M.–5:30 P.M. MC, V accepted.

Hand-smocked dresses are the specialty here, and you can get them for very reasonable prices. Watch the newspapers for special holiday sales.

Unexpected Surprises

□ **The Chosen Gift and Bookstore**
7146 SW 117th Avenue, Miami 33183, (305) 596-3639; 6350 West Atlantic Boulevard, Margate 33063, (305) 978-1716. Monday through Thursday, 10 A.M.–6 P.M.; Friday, 10 A.M.–4 P.M.; Sunday, 11 A.M.– 4 P.M. MC, V, personal checks accepted.

A wonderful place to browse through children's books or to select gifts for babies or adults. All merchandise reflects some aspect of Judaic history and beliefs. They also are one of the Southeast's largest suppliers of Judaic textbooks and materials. **Tip:** There are many breakable items, so it's best not to let small children wander around.

☐ A Christmas Place
401 Biscayne Boulevard (at Bayside Marketplace), Miami, (305) 358-3617; 800 NE 13 Street, Fort Lauderdale, (305) 763-1403. Monday through Saturday, 10 A.M.–5 P.M. AE, MC, V, personal checks accepted.

Christmas ornaments, trees, mechanical figures, and other holiday supplies are available all year at this store. Children never seem to tire of gazing at Christmas trees.

☐ "The Christmas Gallery" at Spauldings
7501 SW 100th Street, Miami 33156. (305) 666-6272. Monday through Saturday, 9:45 A.M.–6:45 P.M.; Christmas Gallery open from August to January. AE, DIN, MC, V, personal checks accepted.

Children and adults will enjoy browsing through the forest and looking at the animated Christmas scenes.

☐ Key West Hand Print Fabrics
201 Simonton Street (corner of Greene Street), Key West 33040. (305) 294-9535. Daily, 10 A.M.–6 P.M.

Older children might be interested to see how the designs get into plain cloth through the silk-screening process. Free guided tours of the printing factory are available.

☐ The Nature Company
2392 East Sunrise Boulevard (in The Galleria, on the upper level), Fort Lauderdale 33304, (305) 568-1945; 3101 PGA Boulevard (The Gardens, upper level), Palm Beach Gardens 33410, (407) 624-1066. Monday through Saturday, 10 A.M.–9:30 P.M.; Sunday, noon–6 P.M. Major credit cards, personal checks accepted.

Founded in 1973 in Berkeley, California, this is a visually beautiful and fascinating store that children and adults will enjoy. It "exists to provide fine quality products that contribute to observation, understanding, and appreciation of our natural world and the environment." They carry the country's largest selection of natural history books, and at least one-third of the inventory is devoted to material that provides learning experiences for children. A monitor is available to preview natural history videos and

Toys that help children explore and understand the world around them are a specialty of The Nature Company.

nonverbal documentary videos accompanied by ambient music. There is usually a pot of herbal tea brewing for visitors to sample as they browse. Nature discovery events are scheduled at various locations in the community; check their calendar for information.

□ Sea Store

614 Greene Street, Key West 33040. (305) 294-3438. Monday, Tuesday, and Thursday through Saturday, 11 A.M.–5 P.M. MC, V, personal checks accepted.

Pieces of old boats, old coins ("pieces of eight" from the Atocha), old bottles, cannonballs and musketballs, and handmade wooden objects made from native tropical hardwoods are fascinating for older children and adults. Tell children not to touch, but encourage them to ask all the questions they have about what they see. **Tip:** Be sure to call before you go to be sure the store is open—the schedule is somewhat irregular.

☐ **The Sharper Image**
401 Biscayne Boulevard (at Bayside Marketplace), Miami 33132, (305) 374-8539; Dadeland Mall, Miami 33156, (305) 667-9970; The Galleria, Fort Lauderdale 33304, (305) 566-2772; The Gardens, Palm Beach Gardens 33410, (407) 775-0021; Town Center, Boca Raton 33431, (407) 392-1977. Hours vary according to mall hours. Major credit cards, personal checks accepted.

Older children will be fascinated by the electronic and futuristic items on display. The numerous salespersons will keep an on eye on their merchandise and your children, but they don't seem to mind even young children sitting in the musical vibrating chair for a few minutes.

☐ **Southern Ornamental**
2419 10th Avenue, North Lake Worth 33461. (At Waterside Plaza, three stoplights west of I-95.) (407) 969-2662. Monday through Saturday, 10 A.M.–6 P.M. AE, MC, V, personal checks accepted.

Open since 1977, this store carries Christmas goods all year long, in addition to costumes for sale and rent.

Educational Books, Toys, and Supplies

Teachers, child development specialists, child psychologists, and most kids agree that a good toy provides the most opportunities for the child to imagine, create, invent, and discover. A quick tour of the big toy stores and warehouses, especially if accompanied by a child who has spent any time at all watching television cartoons and commercials, can be overwhelming and even discouraging. Many toys seem to do little more than briefly entertain the child. "What is the best product for my child's age, developmental needs, and skills?" is a question often asked by conscientious parents. The stores listed in this section have done some of the research for you, and the staffs seem happy to help find the perfect gift. Some of the stores carry only books or only toys, but most carry a selection of both.

Most of the stores listed here are small, and at holiday time there may not be much space to get through the aisles with strollers. The staffs will be happy to move things to help you get through, so don't hesitate to ask.

Dade County

☐ A Kid's Book Shoppe

1849 NE Miami Gardens Drive, North Miami Beach 33179. (305) 937-BOOK. Monday through Saturday, 9:30 A.M.–5:30 P.M. MC, V, personal checks accepted.

This is a store that children will enjoy as much as their parents. There are all kinds of books (including a large selection of ethnic and religious books) for and about children, plus toys, videos, cassettes, and computer software. Younger children will enjoy hiding in the playhouse. Special events are planned throughout the year, including concerts, author appearances, workshops, and poetry contests. Sign up for their birthday club and newsletter. **Tips:** Professional discounts, free gift-wrapping available. Purchases can be shipped if necessary.

☐ A Likely Story

5740 Sunset Drive, South Miami 33143. (305) 667-3730. Monday through Saturday, 10 A.M.–5 P.M. MC, V ($10 minimum), personal checks accepted.

One of America's largest selections of fiction and nonfiction titles for and about children. The staff really knows the field and is happy to help you find exactly what you need. There is a play area for children in the store. Call for information about special events and storytelling on Saturdays for children around 9 years old and younger. Pick up their quarterly newsletter with book reviews and join the reading club to receive discounts on purchases.

☐ Afro-In Books & Things

5575 NW Seventh Avenue, Miami 33127. (305) 756-6107. Wednesday through Saturday, 10 A.M.–5 P.M. MC, V accepted.

Children of all ages will enjoy looking through the many books and other fascinating items for sale. There is also a gallery area in the store that specializes in Haitian, African, and African-American art. Owners Dr. Earl

Wells and his wife Ursula write a column in *The Miami Times*. **Tip:** The owners are happy to host field trips to the store; call to make arrangements.

□ **Books and Books**
296 Aragon (between LeJeune Road and Ponce de Leon Boulevard), Coral Gables 33134. (305) 442-4408. Monday through Friday, 10 A.M.–8 P.M.; Saturday, 10 A.M.–7 P.M.; Sunday, noon–5 P.M. AE, MC, V, personal checks accepted.

A large selection of children's books in a separate room, with a couch and tables set up to help children browse through books, and an excellent book selection for everyone else combine to make this a nice place for a family outing.

□ **ChildRead**
13619 South Dixie Highway (in Colonial Palms Plaza), Miami 33176. (305) 378-8503. Monday through Saturday, 9:30 A.M.–9:30 P.M.; Sunday, 10 A.M.–6 P.M. MC, V, personal checks accepted.

This huge two-story store, opened in 1989, has a great selection of books for and about children. They offer many special events (reading contests, nutrition parties, seasonal events) in addition to regularly scheduled activities (computer classes and demonstrations, birthday parties, storytimes, playgroups, reading contests). Computer software and educational videos are available. Be sure to ask to be on their mailing list to receive discounts, newsletters, and information about special events. Staff will make up gift baskets for any occasion, and will deliver to hospitals. **Tip:** There are several play areas in the store for younger children. For party information, see listing in "Celebrate in Style."

□ **Early Learning Centre**
Aventura Mall, North Miami 33180, (305) 932-7552; Cutler Ridge Mall, Cutler Ridge 33189, (305) 232-5429; Miami International Mall, Miami 33172, (305) 477-1290; The Gardens, Palm Beach Gardens 33140, (407) 627-0369. Check individual mall hours. AE, MC, V, personal checks accepted.

Part of an English chain, the store's design and most of its products are imported. Several toys are set up to give kids a chance to try them out, and the staff is trained to direct you to age-appropriate products. Ask for a copy of their catalog if you can't decide what to buy. **Tip:** In the rear of these

Attractive displays of books and educational toys make shopping a pleasure for both parents and kids at ChildRead.

stores you will find absolutely wonderful, clean, fully-equipped rooms for changing diapers—probably the best ones in South Florida!

□ FAO Schwarz

Bal Harbor Shops, Bal Harbor 33154, (305) 865-2361; 318 Worth Avenue, Palm Beach, (407) 832-1697. Monday, Thursday, and Friday, 10 A.M.– 9 P.M.; Tuesday, Wednesday, and Saturday, 10 A.M.–6 P.M.; Sunday, noon– 5 P.M. AE, DIN, MC, V accepted.

The classic toy store still has all the classic toys. Be sure to look up at the train that circles around above the customers. **Tip:** Free gift-wrapping and shipping available.

□ Get Smart

13724 SW 84th Street (one block east of Kendale Lakes Mall), Miami 33183. (305) 387-0834. Monday through Friday, 10 A.M.–9 P.M.; Saturday,

10 A.M.–6 P.M.; Sunday, noon–5 P.M. DISC, MC, V, personal checks accepted.

This store is teacher-oriented but "mother friendly," and has a great selection of toys, books, records and tapes, art and teaching supplies. Most staff members are former teachers, so they know how to match customers to products. A Brio train is set up for children to play with while adults shop. Birthday, get-well, and holiday baskets are available; they will deliver baskets to hospitals. **Tips:** Free gift-wrapping, shipping, teacher discounts available. Orders taken by phone.

□ **Smartland Educational Toys, Inc.**
18553 West Dixie Highway (in Rodeo Shops, southeast corner of intersection), North Miami Beach 33160. (305) 932-7593. Monday through Friday, 10 A.M.–6 P.M.; Saturday, 10 A.M.–5 P.M. AE, MC, V, personal checks accepted.

This small shop opened in 1983 and specializes in early childhood books, toys, games, videos, and records. There are a few toys set up to entertain the children while parents shop. **Tip:** Discounts available for teachers. Free gift-wrapping provided.

□ **That's Clever**
8742 Mills Drive (in Kendall Town & Country Mall), Miami 33183. (305) 274-5019. Monday through Friday, 10 A.M.–7:30 P.M.; Saturday, 10 A.M.– 7 P.M.; Sunday, noon–5 P.M. AE, MC, V, local checks accepted.

Specializing in toys for infants and young children, this store carries most European lines of toys (such as Brio, Galt, Playmobil). Lumby dollhouses and Madam Alexander dolls are on display, and several toys are set up for kids to try out—and to keep them happy while you shop! Ask about their birthday club and the Clever Kids Club. **Tip:** Free gift-wrapping, free personalizing, and shipping available.

Broward County

□ **ABC Educational Supplies**
1255 South State Road 7, Plantation 33317. (305) 792-5650; (800) 432-1213. Monday through Friday, 10 A.M.–7 P.M.; Saturday, 10 A.M.–5 P.M. AE, MC, V, personal checks accepted.

Over 16,000 educational items fill this 4,500-square-foot store, making it the largest educational supplies store in Broward. Although it is a teacher-oriented store, parents are welcome to shop here. Educational toys, books, art supplies, classroom decorations, and other materials can be found here. The staff is made up of former teachers and parents who know the merchandise and their customers, the children. **Tips:** Shipping is available; you may place orders from their catalog.

☐ All Kids Bookstore
1947 North Pine Island Road (in Jacaranda Square), Plantation 33328. (305) 472-0002. Monday through Saturday, 9:30 A.M.–5 P.M. MC, V, personal checks accepted.

Here you can find books and toys for children and teens, as well as parenting and childcare books. Call for information about storytelling sessions for toddlers on Monday and Tuesday mornings.

☐ Bright Ideas
8698 Griffin Road (in Timberlake Plaza), Cooper City 33328. (305) 434-8801. Monday through Friday, 10 A.M.–6 P.M.; Saturday, 10 A.M.–5 P.M.; Sunday, noon–4 P.M. AE, personal checks accepted.

Bright Ideas provides "educational experiences and materials for moms, dads, kids, and teachers" through their educational books and toys, craft supplies, art and enrichment classes, and birthday parties. Products are divided into areas defined as "explore and discover," "look and listen," "read and learn," "educational materials," "classroom supplies," "toys and games," and "create and imagine." There are two large activity rooms in the rear of the store. For more information, see listing in "Celebrate in Style."

☐ The Creative Child
Corner of 441 and Sample Road (in the Peppertree Plaza), Margate 33063. (305) 968-7865. Monday and Saturday, 10 A.M.–5:30 P.M.; Tuesday and Wednesday, 10 A.M.–7:30 P.M.; Thursday and Friday, 10 A.M.–8:30 P.M. MC, V ($15 minimum), personal checks accepted.

These stores carry several lines of imported toys (Playmobil, Lego, Caspsela), books for all ages, and party supplies. **Tip:** Free gift-wrapping and personalizing available.

☐ Learn, Inc.
5493 North University Drive (in Modernage Plaza), Lauderhill 33321, (305) 742-6482; 4120 PGA Boulevard (Loehmann's Plaza), Palm Beach Gardens 33410, (407) 694-1939; 9907 West Glades Road, (Shadowood

Square Mall, corner of 441 and Glades Road), Boca Raton 33433; (407) 487-3170. Monday through Friday, 10 A.M.–8 P.M.; Saturday, 10 A.M.– 6 P.M.; Sunday, noon–5 P.M. AE, MC, V ($10 minimum), personal checks accepted.

These teacher-oriented stores carry a large selection of games, books, toys, and teaching materials (the store in Palm Beach Gardens has the largest supply of teaching supplies). The store in Loehmann's Plaza has a video-cassette player set up for previews, and several toys are on display for children to try out. A tutoring service is available through the store.

□ The Reading Tree
3514 South University Drive (in Feller's Plaza), Davie 33328. (305) 476-2163. Monday through Saturday, 10 A.M.–6 P.M. AE, MC, V, personal checks accepted.

The first thing you see when you walk in is a large and inviting tree that children can sit under to read or play. The store carries a variety of books, toys, puzzles, records, cassettes, and music videos for all ages. Equipment is available to preview video and audio cassettes. Storytelling and movies for preschoolers are offered on Saturday mornings; movies, arts and crafts classes for children as young as age 1, and other special activities are also available. Pick up a copy of their monthly events calendar when you stop by.

The "Creative Kids' Clubhouse" is located at the rear of the store. Activities include sing-alongs, reading, cooking, and science clubs, and more. Call or stop by for registration information.

Palm Beach County

□ Carousel of Playthings
3101 PGA Boulevard, Suite P-239 (The Gardens Mall, upper level), Palm Beach Gardens 33410. (407) 624-0101. Monday through Saturday, 10 A.M.– 9:30 P.M.; Sunday, noon–6 P.M. Major credit cards, personal checks accepted.

The centerpiece in this store is a huge carousel; there is a smaller working carousel in the middle of the store for young customers to ride on while their adult companions shop. There is also a life-size camel to greet you at the door, and a Brio train is set up to play with. Imported educational toys

Carousel of Playthings offers children a ride while parents shop.

and special collectibles are beautifully displayed. Free gift-wrapping is available.

□ Creative Child

7164 Beracasa Way (Del-Mar Shopping Center), Boca Raton 33434, (407) 395-0794; Forest Hill Boulevard and Jog Road (Riverbridge Center), West Palm Beach, (407) 439-1667. Call individual stores for hours. MC, V ($15 minimum), personal checks accepted.

See listing under Broward County.

□ The Curious Flamingo

5050 Town Center Circle (Crocker Center, on Military Trail south of Glades Road), Boca Raton 33432. (407) 394-7444. Monday through Tuesday, 10 A.M.–6 P.M., Wednesday through Saturday, 10 A.M.–9 P.M. AE, MC, V, personal checks accepted.

There are several toys set up to play with in this store. Neon flamingos serve as decorations, and rock music plays on the radio.

□ **Learn Inc.**
4120 PGA Boulevard (Loehmann's Plaza), Palm Beach Gardens 33410, (407) 694-1939; 9907 West Glades Road, (Shadowood Square Mall, corner of 441 and Glades Road), Boca Raton 33433; (407) 487-3170. Monday through Friday, 10 A.M.–8 P.M.; Saturday, 10 A.M.–6 P.M.; Sunday, noon–5 P.M.

See listing under Broward County.

□ **Storylines**
658 Glades Road, (Oak Plaza, one mile east of I-95), Boca Raton 33431. (407) 338-3094. Monday through Friday, 9:00 A.M.–6 P.M.; Saturday, 9 A.M.–5 P.M. MC, V ($15 minimum), local personal checks accepted.

A wonderful children's bookstore, Storylines carries the largest selection of books in the area. You'll also find many domestic and imported toys (such as Brio and Playmobil), party supplies, and tapes and videos. A large play area keeps little ones busy while adults browse.

Storytimes for toddlers (ages 2 to 4) take place on Mondays and Tuesdays; other special events include monthly dramatic storytelling, puppet shows, parenting and childcare seminars in the evenings, summer programs, and visits from children's book authors and characters. Call for a schedule. **Tips:** Free gift-wrapping and personalizing available. Personalized gift baskets for newborns and older children can be ordered.

Consignment and Resale Stores

Shopping for "twice-loved" items can provide a great way to save money on maternity and children's clothes, toys, shoes, baby equipment, and furniture. You can even make money by selling items your children have outgrown at a percentage of the proprietor's sale price. Most stores will accept only items that are in good shape (no stains, rips, missing parts). Call or visit stores first to find out about their policies. Most shops accept cash and local personal checks (with identification and major credit card); only a few accept credit cards. Keep these stores in mind as alternatives to new or rental baby equipment if you have a lot of guests. If you're planning a short winter trip, try these stores for coats, sweaters, ice skates, and hats.

Dade County

□ Children's Exchange
1415 Sunset Drive, Coral Gables 33143. (305) 666-6235. Monday through Friday, 9:30 A.M.–5 P.M.; Saturday, 10 A.M.–4:30 P.M. Local personal checks accepted.

This store has an excellent selection of clothes, sporting shoes, and winter items. They also carry bedding, some baby equipment, and toys. Note that there is no play area, and it is sometimes difficult to maneuver strollers through the aisles.

□ Cool Kids Clothes
18280 West Dixie Highway, North Miami Beach 33162. (305) 935-6126. Monday through Saturday, 10 A.M.–5:30 P.M. MC, V, personal checks accepted. One-week layaway available.

The "coolest kids' consignment shop" is a great place to save money and still buy the "cool" clothes that kids seem to crave. Clothes and shoes are available from newborn sizes up to size 32 pants for older boys. They also have a large selection of older boys' and girls' formal wear (suits and party dresses) for special events. Cribs, strollers, car seats, and other furniture are also available. Check out the painted floors and walls. There is a play area to keep young children entertained.

□ Lollipops & Rainbows
671 NE 125th Street, North Miami Beach 33161. (305) 891-5437. Tuesday through Saturday, 10 A.M.–5 P.M. Local personal checks accepted.

Items range from newborn to girls' size 14 and boys' sizes 16 to 18. They provide a selection of maternity clothes, and some equipment and toys. Look for the designer rack and special sales. There is a nice play area at the front of the store.

□ Painted Pony
992 NE 167th Street, North Miami Beach 33162. (If you take the 167th

Street exit off I-95, be aware that it becomes 163rd Street. Go north on 10th Avenue, and then turn right on 167th Street.) (305) 944-7669. Monday through Saturday, 11 A.M.–5 P.M. Personal local checks accepted. Three-week layaway available; ask about return policy.

You can find clothes, shoes, furniture, toys, and books in this small shop. This is a good place to find outfits for twins.

□ Twice Upon a Time
9939 SW 142nd Avenue, Miami 33183. (305) 385-7211. Monday through Saturday, 10 A.M.–5:30 P.M. Local personal checks accepted.

The castle theme decor and well-stocked play area make this a nice place to shop with the kids. Well-displayed clothing (newborn to girls' and boys' size 14), toys, bedding, and equipment can be found in this clean, cheery atmosphere. Some new clothing and crafts are available as well.

Broward County

□ Coral Springs Twice Upon a Time
9840 West Sample Road (west of University Drive), Coral Springs 33065. (305) 341-7053. Monday through Saturday, 9:30 A.M.–5:30 P.M.; Sunday, noon–5 P.M. AE, personal checks accepted.

New and "twice-loved" clothes are available here. All consignment items are laundered and ironed before being placed on the shelves. New items include customized bedding and clothing. This is also a discount outlet for Carter's, Healthtex, Lees, and Brittania, with new merchandise arriving every 15 days. Champagne and hors d'oeuvres are served during their discount sale every sixth Sunday (it's best to leave the children at home for this special event) and other special touches make this a fun place for moms, too.

□ Kinderbargain Resale Children's Apparel
333 SE 15th Terrace, Deerfield Beach 33441. (305) 429-0444. Tuesday through Saturday, 10 A.M.–5 P.M. Local personal checks accepted.

Kinderbargain's selection includes clothes for newborns up to girls' and boys' size 10 (check out the designer rack), ice skates and roller skates, toys, baby furniture, and equipment.

☐ **Kiss a Kid Consignment**
2171 Wilton Drive, Wilton Manors 33305. (305) 564-3497. Monday through Saturday, 10 A.M.–5 P.M. MC, V (4% surcharge), local personal checks accepted.

Here you'll find a huge selection of newborn, children's and maternity clothes, lots of toys, and a great selection of shoes (golf shoes, skis, and ice skates). This store is located among several other types of consignment stores.

☐ **Mommy & Me**
2300 NE Seventh Avenue, Wilton Manors 33305. (Take Sunrise exit off I-95.) (305) 564-2546. Tuesday through Friday, 10 A.M.–4 P.M.; Saturday, 10 A.M.–5 P.M. Personal checks accepted if you have an account.

Mommy & Me carries girls' and boys' clothes up to size 12, maternity clothes, toys, shoes, furniture, strollers, and car seats.

☐ **Passalongs Consignment**
771 South State Road 7, Plantation 33322. (305) 587-6013. Monday through Friday, 10 A.M.–5:30 P.M.; Saturday, 10 A.M.–5 P.M. Personal checks for under $25 accepted.

The play clubhouse filled with toys and surrounded by a fence will keep the children busy while their adult companions peruse the well-organized clothes, books, and toys. The store is very clean and prices are reasonable.

☐ **Young Folks Second Time Around**
2724 North State Road 7, Margate 33062, (305) 972-5040; 998 North Federal Highway, Pompano Beach 33062, (305) 941-2383; 4513 North State Road 7, Lauderdale Lakes 33313, (305) 739-6488. Monday through Friday, 9 A.M.–5 P.M.; Saturday and Sunday, 10 A.M.–4 P.M. MC, V, personal checks accepted.

Open since 1977, these shops provide an excellent selection of clothing that is well-organized and easy to get to. A play area is available to entertain youngsters while Mom and Dad shop.

Palm Beach County

□ **Almost New Kiddie Boutique**
*2602 North Federal Highway (near Hypoluxo Boulevard), Boynton Beach
33435. (407) 738-1133. Monday through Saturday, 10 A.M.–5:30 P.M.
Local personal checks accepted.*

Almost New sells clothing for newborn to girls' size 14 and boys' size 16.
Some baby equipment and toys are also available. A nice play area with a
football toy chest and table and chairs are set out for your children to enjoy.

□ **The Red Balloon**
*2201 NE Coast Street, Lake Worth 33461. (407) 588-7530. Monday through
Friday, 10 A.M.–5 P.M.; Saturday, 10 A.M.–4 P.M. Local personal checks
accepted.*

Childrens clothing, baby equipment, and toys are found here. A playhouse
and kitchen are set up in a play area to keep the kids entertained while you
shop.

□ **Togs for Tots**
*92 East 30th Street (behind the Island/Publix Plaza, east of Walgreens),
Riviera Beach 33404. (407) 863-8687. Monday through Saturday, 10 A.M.–
5 P.M. MC, V, local personal checks accepted.*

Newborn to size 8 clothes in "like-new" condition, baby equipment, and
furniture are available. They also have a large selection of new baby
equipment available for rent. There is a toy chest in the play area to keep
the kids busy.

Monroe County

□ **Kid's Closet**
*Mile Marker 91.9 (bay side), 91950 U.S. Highway 1, Tavernier 33070.
(305) 852-4710. Monday through Friday, 9:30 A.M.–4:30 P.M.; Saturday,
9 A.M.–3 P.M. Local personal checks accepted.*

This is one of the only places in the Keys to shop for newborn to junior
girls' clothes, maternity, and like-new baby furniture and equipment. They
also carry new children's clothing (including bathing suits), rental baby
equipment, and furniture. Call for information.

Malls

Very few places have town squares anymore, but it seems that malls are everywhere. Sometimes a stroll through an interesting shop, a ride on the kiddie toys, and a frozen yogurt cone, all in the air-conditioned comfort of your local mall, is a nice treat. What follows is a list of the major malls in South Florida, including their hours and major stores. Call the phone numbers listed to check on holiday events. Most malls have diaper-changing areas in the restrooms; first-aid centers, stroller rentals, and food courts provide for children's other needs.

The intrigue of mime offers entertainment at special events in South Florida malls.

Dade County

□ **Aventura**
19501 Biscayne Boulevard, North Miami Beach 33180. (305) 935-1110.
Monday through Saturday, 10 A.M.–9:30 P.M.; Sunday, noon–5 P.M.

JC Penney, Lord & Taylor, Macy's, Sears.

□ **Bakery Centre**
5715 Sunset Drive, South Miami 33143. (305) 662-4155. Open 9 A.M.,
Monday through Sunday; closing times vary.

Galleries, specialty stores, Miami Youth Museum.

□ **Bal Harbor Shops**
9700 Collins Avenue, Bal Harbour 33154. (305) 866-0311. Monday,
Thursday, and Friday, 10 A.M.–9 P.M.; Tuesday, Wednesday, and Saturday,
10 A.M.–6 P.M.; Sunday, noon–5 P.M.

Neiman-Marcus, Saks Fifth Avenue.

□ **Bayside Marketplace**
401 Biscayne Boulevard, Miami 33132. (305) 577-3344. Sunday through
Friday, 11 A.M.–10 P.M.; Saturday, 10 A.M.–8 P.M.

Not only a shopping area, this is also a popular South Florida attraction. There are several shops and restaurants that are appropriate and fun for children, but there are some shops that have too many breakable items in easy-to-reach places. The open-air market area might be best if you're bringing small children with you. Upstairs in the eatery section there are lots of different ethnic foods for children to try, and you can take your tray out to the patio and enjoy watching boats and birds in the bay while you eat. On that rare cool day or evening, try the hot chocolate served at the Cuban coffee counter—it's thick, chocolaty, and delicious (not made from a packet!).

□ **Cauley Square**
22400 Old Dixie Highway, Goulds 33170. (305) 258-3543. Monday through
Saturday, 10 A.M.–4:30 P.M.

Art galleries, boutiques, and antique shops fill this historic area. A tea room is open for lunch and dinner. For more information, see listing in "Tracing the Past."

☐ Cutler Ridge Mall

20505 South Dixie Highway, Cutler Ridge 33189. (305) 235-8562. Monday through Saturday, 10 A.M.–9 P.M.; Sunday, noon–5 P.M.

Burdines, Early Learning Centre, McKids, JC Penney, Jordan Marsh, Lord & Taylor, Sears.

☐ Dadeland Mall

7535 North Kendall Drive, Miami 33156. (305) 665-6226. Monday through Saturday, 10 A.M.–9 P.M.; Sunday, noon–5:30 P.M.

Major stores here include Burdines, JC Penney, Jordan Marsh, Lord & Taylor, and Saks Fifth Avenue. The eating emporium offers lots of interesting treats, including natural foods. In the center aisle of the mall you'll find carpeted pits, surrounded by benches, that are ideal for toddlers to run around in and work off excess energy. On the ground level of Burdines (in the middle of the mall) they sell frozen yogurt and fresh-baked cookies. Not far down the aisle, there is a gelato concession. It's a nice treat, but you have to go out into the mall to sit down and enjoy it.

☐ The Falls

8888 SW 136th Street, Miami 33176. (305) 255-4570. Monday through Saturday, 10 A.M.–9 P.M.; Sunday, noon–5 P.M.

You'll find Bloomingdale's, Laura Ashley, Oshmann's, Kidding Around (a children's clothing store with a wooden play area for children), and many other specialty stores and restaurants. Several events for children are scheduled during the year, and most children like to watch the outdoor waterfalls that fill the center of the mall.

☐ Kendall Town & Country

8505 Mills Drive, Miami 33183. (305) 598-0719. Monday through Saturday, 10 A.M.–9 P.M.; Sunday, noon–6 P.M.

Stores here include Sears, That's Clever, La Piñata, Pier 1, and other specialty stores and restaurants. The lake at the east end of this shopping area provides a nice place for a stroll.

☐ Mall at 163rd Street

1421 NE 163rd Street, Miami 33162. (305) 947-9845. Monday through Saturday, 10 A.M.–9 P.M.; Sunday, noon–5:30 P.M.

Burdines, Jordan Marsh, and lots of specialty stores.

□ **Mall of the Americas**
7795 West Flagler Street, Miami 33144. (305) 261-8772. Monday through Saturday, 10 A.M.–9 P.M.; Sunday, noon–5:30 P.M.

Luria's, Marshalls, TJ Maxx.

□ **Miami International Mall**
1455 NW 107th Avenue, Miami 33172. (305) 593-1775. Monday through Saturday, 10 A.M.–9 P.M.; Sunday, noon–5:30 P.M.

Burdines, Jordan Marsh, Lord & Taylor, Sears.

□ **Omni International**
1601 Biscayne Boulevard, Miami 33132. (305) 374-6664. Monday through Saturday, 10 A.M.–9 P.M.; Sunday, noon–5 P.M.

Stores include JC Penney and Jordan Marsh. Don't miss the carousel near the hotel entrance. For party information, see Omnibirthday listing in "Celebrate in Style."

□ **Westland Mall**
1675 West 49th Street, Hialeah 33140. (Exit the Palmetto Expressway at NW 103rd Street/NW 49th Street.) (305) 823-9310. Monday through Saturday, 10 A.M.–9 P.M.; Sunday, noon–5:30 P.M.

Built in 1971, the mall houses Burdines, JC Penney, Sears, and over 100 specialty shops. It was recently renovated to include several children's play areas, a permanent stage area, and more.

Broward County

□ **Broward Mall**
8000 West Broward Boulevard, Plantation 33317. (305) 473-8100. Monday through Saturday, 10 A.M.–9 P.M.; Sunday, noon–5:30 P.M.

Burdines, JC Penney, Jordan Marsh, Sears.

□ **Coral Square**
9469 West Atlantic Boulevard, Coral Springs 33065. (305) 755-5550. Monday through Saturday, 10 A.M.–9 P.M.; Sunday, noon–5 P.M.

Burdines, JC Penney, Jordan Marsh, Lord & Taylor.

☐ The Fashion Mall at Plantation
321 North University Drive, Plantation 33317. (305) 370-1884. Monday through Saturday, 10 A.M.–9:30 P.M.; Sunday, noon–6:30 P.M.

You'll find Macy's and Lord & Taylor among the 120 stores here.

☐ Galleria at Fort Lauderdale
2414 East Sunrise Boulevard, Fort Lauderdale 33304. (305) 564-1015. Monday through Saturday, 10 A.M.–9 P.M.; Sunday, noon–5:30 P.M.

Burdines, Jordan Marsh, Lord & Taylor, Neiman-Marcus, Saks Fifth Avenue, The Nature Company, The Sharper Image, and many boutiques and eating areas can be found here.

☐ Hollywood Fashion Center
101 South State Road 7, Hollywood 33023. (305) 966-1522. Monday through Saturday, 10 A.M.–9 P.M.; Sunday, noon–5:30 P.M.

Burdines, JC Penney, Jordan Marsh.

☐ Oceanwalk
101 North Ocean Drive, Hollywood 33019. (305) 925-2955. Monday through Friday, 10 A.M.–10 P.M.; Saturday, 10 A.M.–6 P.M.; Sunday, 11 A.M.–6 P.M.

Boutiques and specialty stores.

☐ Pompano Square
2001 North Federal Highway, Pompano Beach 33062. (305) 943-4683. Monday through Saturday, 10 A.M.–9 P.M.; Sunday, noon–5:30 P.M.

Burdines, JC Penney, Jordan Marsh, Sears.

☐ Shops of Las Olas
On Las Olas Boulevard from NE Seventh Avenue to NE 12th Avenue, Fort Lauderdale 33301. (305) 463-6713 (Las Olas Association).

You'll find 50 exclusive shops and elegant restaurants in this shopping area.

Palm Beach County

□ **Boynton Beach Mall**
801 North Congress Avenue, Boynton Beach 33435. (407) 736-7900. Monday through Saturday, 10 A.M.–9 P.M.; Sunday, noon–6 P.M.

Burdines, JC Penney, Jordan Marsh, Lord & Taylor, Macy's.

□ **The Gardens of the Palm Beaches**
3101 PGA Boulevard just east of I-95, Palm Beach Gardens 33410. (407) 622-2115. Monday through Saturday, 10 A.M.–9:30 P.M.; Sunday, noon–6:30 P.M.

Macy's, Burdines, Carousel of Playthings, The Disney Store, The Gymboree Store, The Nature Company, Sears, and over 200 shops, restaurants, and services can be found in this shopping center.

□ **Palm Beach Mall**
1801 Palm Beach Lakes Boulevard, West Palm Beach 33463. (407) 683-9186. Monday through Friday, 10 A.M.–9 P.M.; Saturday, 9 A.M.–10 P.M.; Sunday, noon–6 P.M.

Burdines, JC Penney, Jordan Marsh, Lord & Taylor, Sears.

□ **Town Center at Boca Raton**
6000 West Glades Road, Boca Raton 33431. (407) 368-6000.

Bloomingdale's, Burdines, Curious Flamingo, Jordan Marsh, Lord & Taylor, Saks Fifth Avenue, Sears.

Come and Get It!

South Florida's tropical environment, with its fresh seafood, colorful tropical fruits, and locally grown produce available year round, combines with the many cultural influences to produce great places to eat. From Jupiter to Key West, you can dine near the water on the catch of the day, or choose down-home country cookin' at family-style restaurants, or learn about different ethnic groups through their special dishes, or savor the flavor of fresh-picked fruits and vegetables, or just cool off with an ice cream treat.

This chapter describes a variety of unique eateries that will provide your children with culinary adventures. Most are reasonably priced, and can provide more for your money than the standard burger-and-fries meal. At the end of the chapter you'll find a glossary of Spanish terms often found on South Florida menus.

Two other options for family dining include chain restaurants, which usually provide children's menus, balloons, and high chairs. Popular chains in South Florida include Dalts, Red Lobster, Perkins, Bennigan's, Houlihan's, Raffles, El Torito, Morrison's Cafeteria, Wags, Tony Roma's, Gepetto's Tale of the Whale, Friday's, Piccadilly Cafeteria, and Denny's. The second eating option is hotel restaurants. These are often overlooked, but remember that since they have families staying as guests, they are usually equipped for and accustomed to children. The buffet meals are great for children; ask about special prices for kids' meals.

If you have young children, a few preparations will help make eating out more pleasurable for everyone.

☐ Bring a few finger foods that you know your child will like.

☐ Bring small activities (crayons, notepads, puzzles)

☐ If you go out for pizza, call to order first so that you don't have to wait when you arrive.

☐ Pack a wet cloth or wipes to clean sticky fingers during and after meals.

☐ Avoid the "restaurant rush hours" if possible. Friday and Saturday nights after 6:30 P.M., lunch hour in business areas, and Sundays at noon usually mean long waits that result in understandably squirmy children.

☐ When you order, be specific about your needs for drinks (large or small, with or without ice and/or straws), additional small plates for sharing meals, or cups to share soup. You may want to bring your child's own cup with lid/sipper seal, too.

When you visit Cuban/Latin restaurants, you may find that at 5 or 6 P.M. they're not very crowded; don't assume they're not popular. By 8 or 9 P.M. they're usually full of couples, three-generation families, and others who enjoy Latin cuisine. Restaurant staff in these places is usually very happy to accommodate your children! You also may find that regular patrons tend to dress a little more formally than in other family restaurants.

Restaurants

Dade County

☐ American Classics
8701 Collins Avenue (in the Quality Inn), Miami Beach 33139. (305) 865-6661. Daily, 7 A.M.–11 P.M. Major credit cards accepted.

Take a seat in one of the dining room's five 1959 Chevys and order up a burger-fries-shake combo. An old Wurlitzer jukebox plays '50s music to keep you in the mood. Very novel, and good food, too. **Tips:** There is no children's menu, but you can request half-orders for half price. Burgers are only available on the lunch menu, so plan accordingly. High chairs and booster seats are available.

☐ Angie's Place
404 SE First Avenue at South Dixie Highway (1/4 mile south of end of Florida Turnpike), Florida City 33034. (305) 245-8939. Daily, 5 A.M.–2 P.M. Cash payment only.

Angie's is run by sisters Angie, Tina, and Joyce, who were born and raised in Florida City. They serve up home-style breakfasts and lunches, using locally grown fresh vegetables. Ask about the daily specials.

☐ Beverly Hills Cafe
1559 Sunset Drive, Coral Gables 33134, (305) 666-6618; 7321 Miami Lakes Drive, Miami Lakes 33014, (305) 558-8201; 17850 West Dixie Highway, North Miami 33161, (305) 935-3660. Monday through Thursday, 11:30 A.M.–10 P.M.; Friday and Saturday, 11:30 A.M.–11 P.M.; Sunday, 11:30 A.M.–9 P.M. (the Miami Lakes location opens at 11 A.M.). AE, DIN, MC, V accepted.

A large variety of hamburgers and over-sized salads are the specialties at this family-style restaurant. Children's menu, high chairs, and booster seats are available.

☐ Big Fish Restaurant

55 SW Miami Avenue Road, Miami 33161. (Take Second Avenue south from East Flagler Street, cross bridge over Miami River, turn right at foot of bridge, turn right again at first street, follow sign to restaurant.) (305) 372-3725. Monday through Saturday, 11 A.M.–3 P.M. AE, MC, V accepted.

Children will enjoy this view of the Miami River, complete with tug boats, pelicans, and a bridge that opens and closes for the riverboat traffic. Try to get a table in the back. The seafood here is reasonably-priced—try the fish fingers and fries for the kids.

☐ Biscayne Miracle Mile Cafeteria

147 Miracle Mile, Coral Gables 33134. (305) 444-9005. Lunch: 11 A.M.–2:15 P.M., dinner: 4–8 P.M.; Sundays, 11 A.M.–8 P.M. Cash payment only.

This restaurant provides a delicious selection of salads, vegetables, meats, and fresh-baked breads and desserts. Children seem to love to put together their own meals. Waiters will carry high chairs and trays to the table, and bring coffee refills or additional food if you need it. They'll also bring doggie bags if anyone's eyes are bigger than their stomachs.

☐ Cami's Seashells

6272 South Dixie Highway, South Miami 33143, (305) 665-1288; 869 SW 107th Avenue (across from Florida International University), Miami 33152, (305) 227-2722. Sunday through Thursday, 5–10 P.M.; Friday and Saturday, 5–11 P.M. MC, V accepted with $20 minimum.

The paper plates and plastic forks will make the kids think they're at a picnic. If they like shrimp, scallops, and other seafood, this a great place to try. For dessert, try the mini sundaes or the fresh strawberries with whipped cream.

☐ Richard Accursio's Capri Restaurant

935 North Krome Avenue, Florida City 33034. (305) 247-1542. Monday through Thursday, 11 A.M.–11 P.M.; Friday and Saturday, 11 A.M.–midnight. Closed Sundays, except Mother's Day. AE, MC, V accepted.

Pizza, stuffed shells, antipasto, conch chowder, and delicious Key lime pie are specialties. No children's menu, but you may request half-orders of entrees. Booster seats and high chairs are available.

□ **Captain Bob's**
326 SE First Avenue, Florida City 33034. (305) 247-8988. Daily, 6 A.M.– midnight. Major credit cards accepted.

Bob's lists 800 ways to prepare seafood. And be sure to get the Key lime pie for dessert—it's great. Ask to sit in the room with the aquarium that houses a shark. There's no children's menu, but a selection from the "lite bites" menu would do. Booster seats and high chairs are available.

□ **Casita Tejas**
10 South Krome Avenue, Homestead 33030. (305) 248-8224. Monday through Thursday, 11 A.M.–9 P.M.; Friday, 11 A.M.–10 P.M.; Saturday, 8 A.M.–10 P.M.; Sunday, 8 A.M.–9 P.M. MC, V accepted.

The high ceilings and hardwood floors make you feel like you're in old Homestead, but the Mexican music, Tex-Mex food, and staff take you elsewhere. The portions are plentiful, and children always seem to enjoy the fresh tortilla chips that appear on your table as soon as you're seated. This is a popular place for family celebrations, and staff are happy to accommodate children. Take-out is available.

□ **Chuck Wagon Restaurant**
7628 SW 117th Avenue, Miami 33173. (305) 274-2263. Saturday through Thursday, 6 A.M.–3 P.M.; Friday, 6 A.M.–9 P.M. Cash payment only.

The food is good here anytime, but it seems to be one of the most popular places in the Kendall area to take children for breakfast. During the week you can get two fresh-baked hot biscuits, two eggs, and home fries for around a dollar, and waiters are happy to bring extra plates if you want to share your meal with your toddler. Another breakfast favorite is the special plate of home fries covered with melted cheese, with two eggs on the side. High chairs and booster seats are available.

After your meal, wander through the feed store located at the front of the complex. This part of town used to be Dade County frontier—children might enjoy a drive through the area known as Horse Country (go north one block to Sunset Drive, turn left to drive under the Florida Turnpike). There are several ranches along this route that offer horse boarding and pony rides—look for them on your drive. For more information, see horseback riding in "Under the Sun."

□ **Coopertown Restaurant**
22700 SW Eighth Street (Tamiami Trail, in the Everglades), Miami 33929. (305) 226-6048. Daily, 8 A.M.–6 P.M. Cash payment only.

If your children simply must try alligator meat or frogs' legs, and you don't mind looking at the stuffed alligator heads and skulls, and other such trophies on the walls, then this is the place to dine. The above-mentioned specialties are available morning, noon, or night.

□ **David's Cafeteria**
8288 Biscayne Boulevard, North Miami 33161. (305) 751-0631. Sunday through Friday: lunch, 11:30 A.M.–2 P.M.; dinner, 4–8 P.M. Cash payment only.

The home-style cooking at David's will appeal to young and old alike, and they usually have several children's selections. High chairs and booster seats are available.

□ **East Coast Fisheries**
360 West Flagler Street, Miami 33131. (305) 373-5516. Daily, 10 A.M.– 10 P.M. AE, MC, V accepted.

This dockside fresh-fish market and restaurant provides good food at fairly reasonable prices. Try the crab cakes and crabmeat salad on crackers. The best part is watching the boats come in loaded with fresh fish.

□ **El Cid**
117 NW 42nd Avenue, Miami 33126. (305) 642-3144. Sunday through Thursday, noon-midnight; Friday and Saturday, noon–1 A.M. Major credit cards accepted.

For all the young princesses and princes who dream of living in a castle, a meal here is a wonderful treat. The restaurant is inside a medieval castle, only a few miles south of Miami International Airport. As you enter, be sure to take time to admire the grilled and roasted food on display, as well as the whole dressed pigs, hams, and sausages hanging from the ceiling. The food is medieval Spanish-style (try the roast goose or lamb), and the servings are generous. Ask if you can climb the winding stone staircase to see the upper rooms. **Tip:** It's best to take children for late lunch or early dinner.

□ **El Pub**
1548 SW Eighth Street, Miami 33130. (305) 643-2651. Daily, 8 A.M.–1 A.M. AE, DISC, MC, V accepted.

Serving delicious Cuban food in the heart of Little Havana, this is a popular place with the who's who in Miami's Latin circles. The staff is very helpful with children, and is happy to provide extra plates, crackers, or whatever you need. There's no children's menu, but kids might like to try the black bean soup with white rice (you pour the soup over the rice), or the *caldo gallego*. High chairs and booster seats are available.

□ **Firehouse Four**
1000 South Miami Avenue, Miami 33131. (305) 379-1923. Lunch: Monday through Saturday, 11:30 A.M.–2 P.M.; dinner: Monday through Thursday, 5:30–10 P.M., Friday through Sunday, 5:30–11 P.M. Bar and grill open daily, 11:30 A.M.–midnight, for soups and sandwiches. Major credit cards accepted.

Listed on the National Register of Historic Places, Miami's oldest surviving fire station, built in 1923, houses this American cuisine restaurant. The original tile and pine floors remain intact, and the firehouse poles and other decorations appeal to children's imaginations. **Tips:** No children's menus, but sandwiches are available. No high chairs; just boosters. The "happy hour" here is popular, so plan your visit accordingly.

□ **Granny Feelgood's Natural Foods Restaurant**
190 SE First Avenue, Miami 33131, (305) 358-6233, Monday through Friday, 7:30 A.M.–6 P.M., Saturday, 11 A.M.–3 P.M.; Metrofaire, 111 NW First Street (2nd floor of Government Center), Miami 33128, (305) 579-2104, Monday through Friday, 7 A.M.—5 P.M.; Cultural Center Plaza, Miami, Monday through Saturday, 10:30 A.M.–3:30 P.M. Major credit cards accepted ($10 minimum) at the downtown (First Avenue) location; cash payment only at other locations.

The food is good at all three locations, and they're the only places we've seen children enjoy spinach (in lasagne)! The salads and fresh-fruit juices and shakes are delicious. Granny's is a good place to stop for lunch if you're on a downtown outing on Saturday—not many places are open. No high chairs, but booster seats are available at the downtown location.

□ **Gyro King**
18315 West Dixie Highway, North Miami Beach 33180. (Look for a hot-pink

and green building on the east side of West Dixie Highway.) (305) 935-9544. Daily, 10 A.M.–7 P.M. No credit cards accepted; checks accepted only when they get to know you.

This open-air eatery has a long counter with stools that older children will enjoy. Whether you eat in or take out, the Greek food and fruit drinks are delicious. Choose from *falafel* (a combination of chick peas, herbs, and spices, deep fried in sunflower oil, served in pocket bread), *gyros* (barbecued spiced lamb, served in pocket bread), stuffed grape leaves, *baklava*, or other specialties. The smoothies (chunks of pineapple, banana, and strawberries blended with apple juice) are wonderful.

□ Island Delight
12618 North Kendall Drive, Miami 33186. (305) 598-0770. Monday through Saturday, 10 A.M.–9 P.M. Cash payment only.

Enjoy a meal of delicious Jamaican food at one of the several small tables at the back of this grocery store, or take some home with you. Children will enjoy trying the jerk chicken or pork (the meat is shredded and served in a spicy sauce)—just be sure to ask them to serve the hot Scotch Bonnet peppers on the side on your first trip! The food gets good reviews from the large Jamaican population in Miami, and if you choose to eat in, your children will hear English spoken with a different accent.

□ Las Tapas
401 Biscayne Boulevard (near flag entrance to Bayside Marketplace), Miami 33132, (305) 372-2737; 7497 North Kendall Drive (in Dadeland Mall), Miami 33156, (305) 662-8616; 3850 SW Eighth Street, Coral Gables 33134, (305) 447-0730. Sunday through Thursday, 11:30 A.M.–midnight; Friday and Saturday, 11:30 A.M.–1 A.M. Major credit cards accepted.

Little dishes (*tapas*) of Spanish-style foods can make a wonderful meal for both children and adults. Spicy sausages, fried calamari, Spanish omelettes, and seafood sauteed in garlic butter are favorites. You can choose several *tapas* from the menu to make a meal everyone shares. The black bean soup comes with a dish of white rice—children can make a meal of this by adding a few bits of what the adults order.

□ Latin American Cafeteria
9608 Sunset Drive, Miami 33173, (305) 279-4353; 11366 SW 184th Street, Perrine 33157, (305) 255-6840; 2940 SW 24th Street, Miami 33155, (305) 448-6809; 1750 West 68th Street, Hialeah 33014, (305) 556-0641; Bayside

Marketplace, 401 Biscayne Boulevard, Miami 33132, (305) 381-7774. Daily, 7 A.M.–11:30 P.M. Major credit cards accepted.

This is a wonderful family-oriented restaurant that welcomes children at any hour. Children might enjoy a meal of a *batido de mamey* and an Elena Ruiz sandwich (made of sliced turkey breast, cream cheese, and strawberry jam on a Cuban roll). The sandwiches are huge; children may want to split one. Take-out and doggie bags are available. There's no children's menu, but high chairs and boosters are available.

☐ Los Ranchos

135 SW 107th Avenue (original location), Miami 33165, (305) 221-9367; 8430 Mills Drive (near cinema at Kendall Town & Country Mall), Miami 33183, (305) 596-5353; 401 Biscayne Boulevard, in Bayside Marketplace (North Pavillion), Miami 33132, (305) 375-0666. Monday through Thursday, 11:30 A.M.–11 P.M.; Friday, 11:30 A.M.–midnight; Saturday, noon–midnight; Sunday, 1–11 P.M. AE, DIN, MC, V accepted.

Los Ranchos serves excellent Nicaraguan-style food, such as marinated beef, thinly sliced fried plantains, thickly sliced and fried sweet plantains, black beans and rice, special sauces (try the parsley-garlic *chimichurri* sauce on your meat!), all in huge portions. Mondays through Fridays they feature two-for-one specials from 5 to 7 P.M., and live entertainment begins at 7 P.M. There's no children's menu, but waiters are very willing to provide extra plates and even extra rice and beans for toddlers. They do have plenty of booster chairs and high chairs.

☐ Miccosukee Restaurant

North side of Tamiami Trail (near Shark Valley entrance to Everglades National Park, about 30 miles west of the Florida Turnpike SW Eighth Street exit). (305) 223-8380. Daily, 8 A.M.–4 P.M. AE, CB, DIN, MC, V accepted.

Children will enjoy trying out the specialty foods served here, including Indian fry bread (dough deep-fried in peanut oil), Indian burgers (fry bread stuffed with ground beef and deep-fried), and breaded catfish and frogs' legs deep-fried in peanut oil. The murals of Indian scenes are interesting.

After you eat, don't miss spending some time looking for alligators, turtles, freshwater otters, and several species of birds and waterfowl in the canal north of the restaurant, or in the large pond on the south side of the Trail. Remember to pack the binoculars!

☐ **Muffin Tin**

12655 South Dixie Highway (in South Park Centre, former site of Miami Serpentarium), Miami 33156. (305) 235-9020. Daily, 7 A.M.–2:30 P.M. Personal checks accepted.

Here's a good stop for breakfast, lunch, or a midmorning snack of muffins and hot chocolate. For the best service and shortest wait, avoid arriving between noon and 1 P.M.

☐ **Mutineer**

U.S. 1 and SW 344rd Street (in Gateway Village at end of Florida Turnpike), Florida City 33034. (305) 245-3377. Daily, 11:30 A.M.–4 P.M. Major credit cards accepted.

This upscale restaurant offers a children's menu, and provides high chairs and booster seats. In addition to the Mutineer, Gateway Village offers a snack bar with fruit shakes, hot dogs, and more in an outdoor café-like setting. There is a little pond outside (complete with ducks and a turtle) between the dining room and café.

☐ **Natural Eats**

9477 South Dixie Highway (Dadeland Plaza), Miami 33156, (305) 665-7807; 8720 Mills Drive (Kendall Town & Country Mall), Miami 33176, (305) 271-7424. Monday through Saturday, 7:30 A.M.–9 P.M.; Sunday, 10 A.M.–9 P.M. Cash payment only.

If you or your child are on a restricted diet, or if you just prefer a more natural, wholesome meal, you'll enjoy this place. The menu of delicious salads, sandwiches, soups, breads, desserts, and juices includes an analysis of the calories, carbohydrates, protein, fiber, and grams of fat per serving. It also provides meal suggestions based on specific diet restrictions ("stress control," "sugarless," "low calorie," or "for a healthy heart").

☐ **94th Aero Squadron**

1395 NW 57th Avenue, Miami 33126. (305) 261-4220. Monday to Friday, 11 A.M.–3 P.M., 5–11 P.M.; Saturday, 5–10 P.M.; Sunday, 11 A.M.–3 P.M., 4:30–10 P.M. AE, MC, V accepted.

Children can watch the airport activities while they eat. They will enjoy putting together their own meals at the lunch buffet and Sunday brunch.

□ Pineapples

530 Arthur Godfrey Road, Miami Beach 33140. (305) 532-9731. Monday through Friday, 11 A.M.–10 P.M.; Saturday, 11 A.M.–11 P.M.; Sunday; 4–10 P.M. AE, MC, V accepted.

Even junk food junkies will enjoy the Chinese egg rolls and most desserts at this health food restaurant and store. Weekend brunches include Belgian waffles and overstuffed omelettes.

□ Potlikker's

591 Washington Avenue, Homestead 33030. (305) 248-0835. Daily, 7 A.M.– 9 P.M. MC, V accepted.

The name comes from "pot liquor," which is the broth left over from boiled greens. Try the "Bahama Mama Sausage" and "Flap Jacks" for breakfast. For dinner, tempt your children with fried Okeechobee catfish, or chicken and dumplings, or fresh vegetables and sweet potato pie. Let the Key lime pie thaw a bit before you eat it.

□ Shorty's

9200 South Dixie Highway, Miami 33156. (305) 665-5732. Daily, 11 A.M.– 10 P.M. Cash payment only.

Huge servings of finger-licking good food, served on long wooden tables, have made this a great place to take the family for barbecue for many years. Children's menu and booster seats that attach to the tables are available.

□ Sundays on the Bay

10880 Collins Avenue, (Haulover Park, Intracoastal side), Miami Beach 33141, (305) 945-6065; 4000 Crandon Boulevard, Key Biscayne 33149, (305) 361-6777. Monday through Saturday, 11:30 A.M.–midnight; Sunday, 10:30 A.M.–midnight. Major credit cards accepted.

The most interesting area for children to eat at the Haulover location is the patio area on the water. Beware when you first go through those doors to the patio, though, because there is no protective railing to keep the kids from falling into the water! There is no children's menu, but the appetizers here make good children's meals. There are lots of boats, pelicans, fishermen, and people to watch during your meal. Sunday brunch is usually crowded, but the food is good, and the live music is entertaining. Reservations are suggested. There are several high chairs and booster seats.

☐ Tokyo Rose

134500 Biscayne Boulevard, North Miami 33181. (305) 945-7782. Sunday and Monday, 5 P.M.–midnight; Tuesday through Thursday, 5 P.M.–1 A.M.; Friday and Saturday, 5 P.M.–2 A.M. (Hours change slightly during the summer.) Reservations recommended for Fridays and Saturdays.

Children will enjoy cooking their own food on the little tabletop stoves. They'll get a chance to try some new flavors and will enjoy the grownup atmosphere. Brochettes of sirloin, chicken, or vegetables, served on wooden sticks, are one of the many favorites. No high chairs or boosters, but the tables and chairs are low enough for toddlers to manage.

☐ Uncle Tom's Barbecue

3988 SW Eighth Street (near corner of Tamiami Trail and LeJeune Road), Coral Gables 33134. (305) 446-9528. Wednesday to Monday, 10 A.M.–10 P.M. Cash payment only.

Uncle Tom's has been serving barbecued ribs, chicken, and other delicious "down-home" meals since before 1948. Seat yourself in this small, informal, inexpensive eatery. There are booster seats and high chairs, but older children may enjoy sitting at the counter. There is no children's menu, but hot dogs and hamburgers, served in a basket with french fries, are available, and corn on the cob and baked beans can be ordered à la carte.

☐ Unicorn Village

16454 NE Sixth Avenue, North Miami 33162. (305) 944-5595. Monday through Thursday, 11 A.M.–9:30 P.M.; Friday and Saturday, 11 A.M.– 10 P.M.; Sunday, 4–9 P.M. MC, V accepted.

Unicorn Village contains a health food store, delicatessen, and restaurant. The menu includes such healthy food as tofu lasagne, vegetables, poultry and fish, and several daily vegetarian specials. There is no children's menu, but many of their side dishes would be suitable. High chairs and booster seats are available.

☐ Versailles

3555 SW Eighth Street, Miami 33135. (305) 445-7614. Monday through Thursday, 8 A.M.–2 A.M.; Friday and Saturday, 8 A.M.–3 A.M.; Sunday, 9 A.M.–2 A.M. Major credit cards accepted.

When you visit Little Havana, you might want to plan a meal at what has been called the most famous Cuban restaurant in the country. Lots of mirrors, lights, noise, and delicious food characterize this unique place. *Mariquitas* in *mojo* sauce, pork chunks, black beans and rice, and *batidos* are specialties. High chairs and boosters are available.

Broward County

□ **Brasserie Max**
321 North University Boulevard, Plantation 33317. (305) 424-8000. Daily, 11:30 A.M.–11 P.M. Cash payment only.

Dennis Max created some of the best restaurants in the area (Max's Place, Café Max, and Maxaluna), and he now has developed a family dining bistro. Don't be afraid to try it out with the kids—they're probably not as afraid to taste new things as you think they are.

□ **Cami's Seashells**
Corner of University and Hollywood boulevards in the Phar-mor Plaza, Pembroke Pines 33024. (305) 987-3474.

See listing under Dade County.

□ **Cap's Place**
2765 NE 28th Court, Lighthouse Point Yacht Basin. (Take North Copans Road exit off I-95; drive east to Federal Highway, turn left; turn right at NE 24th Street [first stoplight] and drive toward the ocean. Follow the restaurant signs. After you park, wait for a boat that will take you to Cap's Island. You can dock your own boat at the restaurant, turning at Marker 69, just north of Hillsboro Inlet.) (305) 941-0418. Sunday through Thursday, 5:30–10 P.M.; Friday and Saturday, 5:30–11 P.M. Major credit cards accepted.

This is a fun place to take children for a special occasion (the prices are somewhat higher than most restaurants listed here). Tell them that Marilyn Monroe, Franklin D. Roosevelt, Winston Churchill, Jack Dempsey (and other famous folk that they may never have heard of) have eaten here. If that doesn't impress them, the adventure of getting there will. The food is good, too!

□ **Hooper's Choice**
1100 Federal Highway (corner of Sunrise Boulevard and Federal Highway),

Fort Lauderdale 33309. (305) 760-4393. Open daily, 24 hours a day. AE, MC, V accepted.

Everything is fresh (as opposed to frozen), including the burgers, fries, pizza, roast beef, and other choices.

□ Joe Bel-Air's
1717 Eisenhower Boulevard (across from Ocean World), Fort Lauderdale 33309. (305) 463-5637. Daily, 6 A.M.–midnight. Cash payment only.

The atmosphere is from the '50s, with a game room, jukebox, and waitresses who look and act like characters from a '50s diner. It's a fun place for families. Burgers, Sloppy Joe Bel-Airs, Double Decker Peanut Butter and Jelly sandwiches, fresh-baked fruit pies, and other old favorites for a new generation are on the menu.

□ Jungle Queen
801 Seabreeze Boulevard (Route A1A), docked at Bahia Mar Yacht Basin, Fort Lauderdale 33316. (305) 462-5596. Departs at 7 P.M. for long cruise, 10 A.M. and 2 P.M. for shorter cruises. Adults, $6.50/day, $18.95/barbecue dinner cruise; children under 10, $4.50/day, $12.95/barbecue dinner cruise. Major credit cards accepted. Rainchecks available.

Cruise up the New River, where you'll see everything from plush homes to a bit of the Everglades. The four-hour dinner cruise includes a vaudeville show, a singalong, and an "all you wish to eat" dinner of shrimp, chicken, and barbecue, served on their own Tropical Isle. On the island you'll tour the Jungle Queen Indian Village where you can see rare trees and birds, as well as watch professional alligator wrestlers in action. Birthday parties may be held during the daytime cruise. **Tips:** Reservations recommended. Stroller and wheelchair access provided. The dinner cruise may not be appropriate for small children. Gifts, film, and restrooms available.

□ Lou's Pizza and Subs
1547 East Commercial Boulevard, Fort Lauderdale 33316. (305) 491-5600. Monday through Thursday, 11 A.M.–midnight; Friday and Saturday, 11 A.M.–1 A.M.; Sunday, 1 P.M.–midnight. AE accepted.

This small, family-oriented restaurant provides good Italian-style food and live entertainment. On Sunday evenings, from 6 to 8 P.M., Chuckles (a clown/magician) performs tableside one-on-one magic tricks and creates balloon animals. Kids really enjoy it!

□ **Mai-Kai**
3599 North Federal Highway, Fort Lauderdale 33316. (305) 563-3272. Sunday through Thursday, 5–10 P.M.; Friday and Saturday, 5 P.M.– midnight. Major credit cards accepted.

Children enjoy the Polynesian decor, and especially like watching the waterfalls. On Sunday nights the children of the Polynesian dancers perform, and kids eat for a special price. Sundays through Thursdays the dance performance is free for children ages 12 and under. Adult tickets to the performances are $5.95 on Mondays through Thursdays, and $6.95 on Saturdays and Sundays. Booster seats are available.

□ **Sadie's Buffet and Grill**
3500 University Drive (in Feller's Plaza), Davie 33315. (305) 476-0205. Sunday, 11 A.M.–8 P.M.; Monday through Thursday, 11 A.M.–3 P.M., 4– 8:30 P.M.; Friday and Saturday, 11 A.M.–3 P.M., 4–9 P.M. MC, V accepted. Children ages 3 to 10 are charged 44¢ per year of age to eat at buffet; children under 3 eat free.

Many factors combine to make this a great place to eat with children. The "all you care to eat" buffet with a good selection of not-too-spicy food (the salad section includes jello), the make-your-own-sundae in the dessert section, the unlimited refills of drinks, and the reasonable prices will encourage you to come here often. **Tips:** This is a very popular, crowded place to eat at the peak lunch and dinner hours. Try to come for late lunch or early dinner to avoid a long wait. Also, bring your own baby spoons— they only supply soup spoons.

□ **Shorty's**
5989 South University Drive, Davie 33328. (305) 680-9900.

See listing under Dade County.

□ **Spiced Apple**
3281 Griffin Road, Fort Lauderdale 33312. (305) 962-0772. Lunch: Monday through Friday, 11:30 A.M.–3 P.M.; dinner: Monday through Saturday, 4– 10 P.M.; Saturday and Sunday brunch, 11:30 A.M., regular hours 1–9 P.M. AE, MC, V accepted.

Fried chicken, country ham, corn fritters, and deep-dish peach cobbler are a few of the country-style dishes offered in this restored country house full of antiques. They have a license to sell alligator meat, so you'll also find

*A variety of things to look at and eat
makes a trip to Spiced Apple a treat.*

"Cross Creek Gator Tail" on the menu, along with "Frog Legs from the Glades." A children's menu is available for lunch and dinner. Be sure to make reservations, and take time before or after your meal to browse in the country store at the back of the parking lot, but beware if you have small children—there are lots of "If you break it, you pay" signs.

□ **Who Song & Larry's**

3100 North Federal Highway, Fort Lauderdale 33306. (305) 566-9771. Monday through Thursday, 11:30 A.M.–11 P.M.; Friday and Saturday, 11:30 A.M.–midnight; Sunday, 10:30 A.M.–11 P.M. Major credit cards accepted.

Part of the El Torito chain of Mexican restaurants, Who Song & Larry's is set up to entertain kids. The tablecloths are large squares of brown butcher paper, and each table has a can of crayons—instant entertainment! It's even okay to draw on the walls! Mariachis play typical Mexican music nightly at 7 P.M.

The food at Who Song & Larry's is bountiful and good—try the lunch buffet that includes chicken and steak fajitas, enchiladas, make-your-own tacos, rice and beans, salad, and tortillas. You can even watch the tortillas being made. Lunch is probably the best time to take small children—there

A can of crayons and walls to draw on provide entertainment at Who Song and Larry's.

are less people and service is faster, but you won't see the mariachis. **Tip:** Reservations are suggested for dinner and on weekends (the wait can be up to an hour).

Palm Beach County

☐ Bones Family Barbecue

3500 North Federal Highway, Boca Raton 33487. (407) 368-5515. Monday through Thursday, 11 A.M.–9 P.M.; Friday to Saturday, 11 A.M.–10 P.M.; Sunday, noon–9 P.M. MC, V accepted.

Open in Boca since 1983, the original location in Illinois opened in 1930, and they're still making good barbecue. There's no children's menu, but high chairs and booster seats are available.

☐ **Boston's Restaurant Hotel and Lounge**

40 South Ocean Boulevard (just south of Atlantic Boulevard), Delray Beach 33483. (407) 278-3364. Daily, 11 A.M.–2 A.M. AE, DIN, MC, V accepted.

Here's a great place to watch the boats and feel the ocean breeze (the Atlantic Ocean is just across the street!) as you eat fresh seafood or a grilled cheese sandwich. Children will prefer to eat on the outdoor patio, and may want hot dogs instead of fish, but there's something here for everyone. The staff really seems to enjoy having children stop by. **Tip:** This is a very popular eating place, so plan meal time accordingly in order to get an outside table.

☐ **Fat Boy's**

10875 Congress Avenue, West Palm Beach 33407, (407) 964-0619; 630-2 Royal Palm Beach Boulevard, West Palm Beach 33411. (407) 793-8844. Sunday through Thursday, 6:30 A.M.–9 P.M.; Friday and Saturday, 8 A.M.– 10 P.M. Cash payment only.

This barbecue restaurant is informal and inexpensive, and welcomes families with a smile. The food is delicious—try their wonderful baked beans. Nightly specials and children's meals are available.

☐ **Hamburger Heaven**

314 South County Road, Palm Beach. (407) 655-5277. Daily, 7:30 A.M.– 9 P.M. Closed from August 1 to September 15. Cash payment only.

Everyone in town comes by to enjoy the fresh ground beef burgers. You can also find sandwiches and salads here.

☐ **Island Queen**

900 East Blue Heron Boulevard, Riviera Beach, 33404. (407) 842-0882. Lunch cruises depart Wednesday through Sunday, 11 A.M. and 1 P.M. Dinner cruises depart the same days at 7 P.M. Cost varies according to cruise; children under 12 pay half price. MC, V accepted.

Enjoy a narrated sightseeing cruise along the Intracoastal Waterway as you dine in an authentic Mississippi paddlewheel steamboat. Cruises depart from the Phil Foster Steamboat Landing on Singer Island. **Tips:** Reservations recommended a week in advance. Sightseeing tours also available Wednesdays at 3 P.M. and at other times on Mondays and Tuesdays.

☐ Log Cabin Restaurant
631 North Route A1A, Jupiter 33477. (407) 746-6877. Daily, 7 A.M.–10 P.M. Breakfast served Monday through Saturday, 7–11 A.M.; Sunday, 7 A.M.–noon. Major credit cards accepted.

The Log Cabin has been serving barbecue and other specialties (baskets of frog legs or catfish, hush puppies) for a long, long time. High chairs, sassy seats, and boosters are available, and the menu has several things that children will like, such as the "Chili Jack," a bowl of french fries covered with homemade chili. Daily "all you can eat" evening specials are available from 4:30 P.M. The breakfast menu includes homemade sausage, biscuits, and pan gravy.

☐ Rizzo's
5990 North Federal Highway, Boca Raton 33487. (407) 997-8080. Open Monday through Friday, 4:30–10 P.M. for dinner. Saturday and Sunday, 11:30 A.M.–10 P.M. Early dinner specials, 4:30–6:30 P.M. Major credit cards accepted.

Rizzo's is Boca's oldest restaurant (opened 1966). The atmosphere is casual but very nice, and a children's menu is available. Meat, fish, fowl, and pasta are their main specialties. Reservations are encouraged.

☐ Scarlett O'Hara's
Northeast corner of Linton and Federal Highway (Old Harbor Plaza), Delray Beach. (407) 272-6239. Monday through Saturday, 11:30 A.M.– 2 A.M.; breakfast served on Sunday. Major credit cards accepted.

All the American favorites, such as burgers, chicken, salads, and pot roast, as well as a few Southern specialties, are served up at Scarlett's. A children's menu is available. Call ahead for live music performance times. If there is a waiting list and you don't want to be on it, there are several other eateries at this intersection.

☐ Spiced Apple
2700 North Federal Highway, Boca Raton 33483. (407) 394-3100.

See listing under Broward County.

☐ Valmaron County Stores
16891 Jupiter Farms Road, Jupiter, 33458. (407) 746-8229. Monday

through Saturday, 11 A.M.–8 P.M.; Sunday, 11 A.M.–3 P.M. Cash, local personal checks accepted.

Located just north of the entrance to Burt Reynolds' Ranch, this would be a good stop for a quick meal or to pick up something to snack on in the car. There is a store here, too, so you can pick up diapers, snacks, and juices if you need to. They have one booster seat but no high chairs. Children might enjoy ordering the frogs' legs. For more information, see Valmaron Equestrian Center listing in "On Your Mark, Get Set, Go!"

□ Waterway Café
2166 Barnard Drive, Palm Beach Gardens 33410. (West side of the Intracoastal Waterway on the south side of PGA Boulevard. Turn east off I-95 at PGA Boulevard, turn right just before you cross the bridge on the Intracoastal.) (407) 694-1700. Monday through Saturday, 7–11 A.M., 11:30 A.M.–10 P.M.; Sunday, 7 A.M.–11 A.M., noon–10 P.M. Major credit cards accepted.

A view of the Intracoastal makes this a fun place for children and adults alike. The outside patio is nice, especially if your child likes to see bridges, boats, and pelicans while eating. Buffet breakfasts are served from 7–11 A.M. Kid's menu, high chairs, and boosters are available. A reggae band plays on Sunday afternoons from 4 to 9 P.M.—it's fun to listen to, but be sure to make reservations to avoid a long wait.

Monroe County

□ Angler's Seafood House
3618 North Roosevelt Boulevard, Key West 33040. (305) 294-4717. Daily, 11 A.M.–10 P.M. AE, MC, V accepted.

Here you'll find fresh seafood and delicious Key lime pie. There are special prices for children's portions, and booster seats and high chairs are available.

□ BJ's Bar-B-Q Family Restaurant
Mile Marker 102.5, Key Largo 33037. (305) 451-0900. Daily, 11 A.M.– 9 P.M. Personal checks accepted.

As the name says, the specialty here is barbecue. Chicken and fish are also served. A children's menu is available, but side orders (chili, barbecue beans, conch fritters) are good choices for children, too. High chairs and booster seats are available.

□ Brian's in Paradise
11050 Overseas Highway, Marathon 33050. (305) 743-3183. Daily, 6 A.M.–10 P.M. Cash payment only.

This is a casual, reasonably-priced family restaurant. Children's menu, booster seats, and high chairs are available.

□ Don Pedro Restaurant
Mile Marker 53, Marathon 33050. (305) 743-5247. Open Friday through Wednesday, noon–9 P.M. AE, MC, V accepted.

In this Cuban restaurant, children will enjoy the *picadillo,* chicken chunks, and black beans and rice. High chairs and booster seats are available.

□ The Eatery
1405 Duval Street, Key West 33040. (305) 294-2727. Breakfast buffet: daily, 8–11:30 A.M.; lunch buffet: daily, noon–4 P.M.; dinner buffet: 5–10 P.M.; early bird prices from 5–6 P.M. MC, V accepted.

The waterfront location is entertaining in itself, but this restaurant also gives children a special price, and they love to put their meal together from the buffet. Prices are moderate for breakfast and lunch, higher at dinner ($13 for buffet).

□ Perry's of the Keys
Mile Marker 102.5, Key Largo 33037, (305) 451-1834; Mile Marker 82, Islamorada 33036, (305) 664-5066; Mile Marker 52, Marathon 33050, (305) 743-3108; 3800 North Roosevelt Boulevard (Mile Marker 2), Key West 33040, (305) 294-8472. Sunday through Thursday, 11 A.M.–10 P.M.; Friday to Saturday, 11 A.M.–11 P.M.; Upper Keys locations also serve breakfast, 7–11 A.M. Major credit cards accepted.

This local restaurant chain offers delicious, moderately priced food, including a menu of "Lite-Bites" (for children and light appetites), as well as a raw bar and lots of fresh seafood dishes. **Tip:** Lunch is served here until 5 P.M., which is rare throughout the Keys—most places close from 2 to 5 P.M.

□ Sugarloaf Lodge
Mile Marker 17, Sugarloaf Key 33044. (305) 745-3741. Daily, 7 A.M.–
9:30 P.M. AE, MC, V, local checks accepted.

This is one of the few family-style restaurants in the Key West area. The
dining room overlooks a bay where a dolphin (named "Sugar") entertains
visitors with spontaneous tricks. There are special discounts for children on
the dinner menu, and high chairs and booster seats are available.

□ The Sunset Café
In the Buccaneer Lodge, Mile Marker 48.5, Marathon 33050. (305) 743-
9071. Daily, 11 A.M.–9:30 P.M. Major credit cards accepted.

Meals are reasonably priced, and the restaurant has a Gulf view. If you're
there at the right time, you can join in the nightly sunset celebration. High
chairs and booster seats available

□ Turtle Kraals
Land's End Village (where Margaret Street meets the Gulf), Key West
33040. (305) 294-2640. Monday through Saturday, 11 A.M.–11 P.M.,
Sunday, noon–11 P.M. MC, V accepted ($15 minimum).

This is an informal eatery where kids can eat, learn, and have fun at a very
reasonable price (unlike most area restaurants!), for it's a place where
injured sea turtles are brought for recovery. Live loggerheads are kept in
tanks and in a small, enclosed bay—your young ones may enjoy watching
these creatures more than eating their sandwiches (the fresh seafood and
imported beer will appeal to the adults in the group). Don't miss the touch
tank as well.
    By the way, *kraal* comes from a Dutch/South African word that originally
meant "enclosure for livestock." The enclosure here was once used as a
holding pen for turtles before they were shipped off and slaughtered for
soup. Now it serves the opposite purpose. For more information, see listing
in "On Safari in South Florida."

□ Whale Harbor Inn
Mile Marker 83.5 (at the Whale Harbor Docks), Islamorada 33036. (305)
664-4803. Tuesday through Saturday, 4:30–9:30 P.M.; Sunday, noon–9 P.M.
MC, V accepted.

The menu features delicious fresh seafood and Key lime pie. A buffet is served upstairs; the regular menu is available downstairs, where a children's menu and high chairs are available.

☐ **The Wharf and Shucker's Raw Bar**
Mile Marker 24, Summerland Key 33042. (305) 294-8882. Dolphin shows at 10:30 A.M. and 12:30, 2:30 and 4:30 P.M.; adults, $4; children, $2.50. MC, V accepted.

Formerly the home of Flipper's Sea School, this is now a great place for a meal with children. There are two restaurants here: The Wharf, open for fine dining in the evening, and Shucker's Raw Bar, with an inexpensive lunch and dinner menu. There's no children's menu, but hot dogs and other snack foods are available for kids to eat as they watch the sea lions (dolphins can only be seen during the show). There are no high chairs, but booths are located inside and picnic tables and umbrella tables are outside.

Frozen Specialties and Bakeries

Dade County

☐ **Andalusia Bake Shop of Coral Gables**
248 Andalusia Avenue, Coral Gables 33134. (305) 445-8696. Monday through Saturday, 6 A.M.–6 P.M. Local personal checks accepted.

Here's a popular and delicious Kosher bakery with all kinds of treats to tempt you—makes a nice stop during a tour or shopping trip in Coral Gables.

☐ **Baptiste Bakery**
7488 NE Second Avenue (in Little Haiti), Miami 33138. (Park in the lot in front of the offices and bakery. Walk down a few steps to the window on left to order and pick up baked goods.) (305) 756-1119. Daily, 8 A.M.–8 P.M. Cash payment only.

Fresh coconut biscuits, creole rolls, and bread make this a popular place to stop and buy a snack to take home (it's not a sit-down place to eat).

□ King's Ice Cream

1831 SW Eighth Street (Calle Ocho and Tamiami Trail) in the Tamiami Plaza, Miami 33135. (305) 643-1842. Daily, 10 A.M.–11 P.M. Cash payment only.

Open since the 1960s, this is a wonderful place to get kids to try new tropical fruit flavors. The ice creams and sorbets here are made with natural ingredients. Try their thick, homemade hot chocolate and crunchy *churros*, or the half coconuts filled with coconut sorbet. There are no tables, so plan to walk around or take your treats home. **Tip:** This is a great place to practice your Spanish, but English is also spoken.

□ Knauss Berry Farm

15980 SW 248th Street (across from Redlands Junior High School), Homestead 33031. (305) 247-0668. Open from Thanksgiving to last week of April, Monday through Saturday, 8 A.M.-5:30 P.M. Cash payment only.

Don't miss a delightful trip to this countrified bakery. They've been selling delicious homemade pies and bread, all kinds of beautiful fresh vegetables, and huge fresh strawberries since 1956. Children may be interested in the staff's clothing (the women all wear long dresses and bonnets); explain that they are members of a Protestant denomination called German Baptists or "Dunkers." **Tip:** Stop here for cinnamon rolls and a fresh strawberry shake, then travel west to the Preston B. Bird and Mary Heinlein Fruit and Spice Park. For more information, see listing in "Exploring Science and Nature."

□ La Mexicana

Half block east of Krome Avenue on Mowry Street, behind small Mexican restaurant (El Toro Taco) on corner. Monday through Saturday, 8 A.M.– 4:30 P.M. Cash payment only.

Freshly baked *pan dulce* and giant Mexican-style cookies make this a tempting stop. The sweet rolls are not really that sweet, but they are delicious with a hot chocolate or a cup of *café con leche*.

□ La Rosa Bakery

4259 West Flagler Street, Miami 33134. (305) 443-2113. Monday through Saturday, 7 A.M.–8 P.M.; Sunday, 7 A.M.–5 P.M. Cash payment only.

This is an excellent bakery where you'll find all kinds of Cuban and Latin goodies.

□ **Nature's Garden Bakery**
600 Collins Avenue, Miami Beach 33139. (305) 534-1877. Sunday through Thursday, 8 A.M.–5 P.M.; Friday, 8 A.M.–2:30 P.M. Cash payment only.

Children will enjoy trying out different health food selections. Kosher and special diet meals are available.

□ **Sycamore Farms Bakery**
19110 SW 177th Avenue (Krome Avenue, inside Botanical Garden Center), The Redland 33031. (305) 232-4646. Tuesday through Saturday, 8 A.M.– 5 P.M. Cash payment only.

You can watch the bread, cinnamon rolls, and other baked goods being prepared. Pick up something to munch on as you browse through the Botanical Garden Center, then stop on your way back to the car to take more home.

□ **Steve's Ice Cream Parlor**
3434 Main Highway, Coconut Grove 33133. (305) 448-0848. Sunday through Thursday, noon–11:30 P.M.; Friday and Saturday, noon–1 A.M. Cash payment only.

Delicious ice cream and indoor/outdoor seating make this a fun place to stop when you visit Coconut Grove.

□ **Whip 'n' Dip**
1407 Sunset Drive (across from Audubon House), Coral Gables 33143. (305) 665-2565. Monday through Thursday, 11 A.M.–10:30 P.M.; Friday and Saturday, 11 A.M.–11:30 P.M.; Sunday, 1–10:30 P.M. Local personal checks accepted.

Ice cream and frozen yogurt creations are served here. One specialty whips fresh frozen fruit with frozen yogurt for a refreshing treat. A few tables and chairs are available.

Broward County

□ **Grandma's**
3404 North Ocean Boulevard (Galt Ocean Mile), Fort Lauderdale 33308. (305) 564-3671. Daily, noon–11 P.M. Cash payment only.

Indoor seating is available at this typical, old-fashioned ice cream parlor.

□ **The Ice Cream Club**
3702 North Ocean Boulevard, Fort Lauderdale 33308. (305) 563-4713. Daily, noon–11 P.M. Cash payment only.

The ice cream served in this popular parlor is made fresh in their own Palm Beach factory. It's delicious, but it's not for dieters (14% butterfat). Ask about their members club, as well as birthday parties and their weekly drawings for free cones.

□ Nunzio's
4475 North University Drive, Lauderhill 33313. (305) 749-6090. Monday through Saturday, 11:30 A.M.–9 P.M. Cash payment only.

Serves *spumoni*, *tortoni*, *tartufi*, *sorbetto*, and Italian ice. Inside seating is available.

□ Skipper's Ice Cream Café
1600 East Hillsboro Boulevard, Deerfield Beach 33441. (305) 421-5876. Sunday through Thursday, 10:30 A.M.–10:30 P.M.; Friday and Saturday, 10:30 A.M.–11:30 P.M. AE accepted.

This café has a nautical theme, and serves soup, salads, and sandwiches. The specialty is homemade ice cream; their plant in Boca Raton makes over 250 flavors, with 32 available at any given time. A very popular place with young and old alike.

□ The Sugar Plum
10137 West Oakland Park Boulevard (Welleby Plaza), Sunrise 33304. (305) 748-6447. Daily, noon–10 P.M. Cash payment only.

This small, old-fashioned ice cream parlor has a few benches to sit on while you enjoy your treat. You can order ice cream cakes to go.

Palm Beach County

□ The Ice Cream Club
Plaza del Mar, 278 South Ocean Boulevard, Manalapan 33460. (407) 582-0778.

See listing under Broward County.

□ Scoops Ice Cream Parlor and Restaurant
9919 Glades Road (Shadowood Square, corner of 441 and Glades Road), West Boca Raton 33434. (407) 487-3155. Monday through Thursday, 11 A.M.–11 P.M.; Friday and Saturday, 11 A.M.–midnight; Sunday, 4 P.M.–11 P.M. AE, personal checks accepted.

For party information, see listing in "Celebrate in Style."

□ **Skipper's Ice Cream Café**
Corner of Linton Road and Federal Highway in Old Harbor Plaza, Boca Raton. (407) 750-7145. Monday through Thursday, 11 A.M.–10:30 P.M.; Friday and Saturday, 10:30 A.M.–midnight; Sunday, noon–10:30 P.M.

See listing in Broward County.

Fresh off the Vine

Take a trip to the country and bring home some of that just-picked freshness. Tourists and natives alike will enjoy picking their own strawberries, tomatoes, peppers, and squash in the winter months. For information about tours to agricultural areas, see listing in "By Land, Sea and Air." See listings in "Exploring Science and Nature" for information about working citrus groves. The fields are open mostly on weekends during the winter. Bring your own baskets or plastic containers, one for each member of the family. The field operators are most helpful as to the picking techniques and ripeness of the vegetables and fruits. Remember that Florida state law prohibits children under 10 years of age from entering the fields.

□ **Robert Is Here Fruit Stand**
19900 SW 344th Street, Homestead 33034. (305) 246-1592.

In existence for nearly 30 years, this fruit stand has it all: unusual and delicious tropical fruits, a snack area, and plenty of good advice from Robert himself. Try a Key lime milkshake or taste a Monstera Deliciosa. Also, pick up a brochure and check out the handy chart on the back that tells when fruits are in season.

Fruit and vegetable stands offer pumpkins galore during October.

Glossary of Spanish Terms

If you don't speak Spanish, you and your children may want to look over this list of foods before trying out one of the many Latin American eateries described in this section. Some of the restaurants provide English menus, and occasionally there is an English description of the dish, but it's fun to try to order in Spanish.

arroz con pollo a mixture of saffron-seasoned rice and chicken decorated with peas and pimentos

batido a milkshake, often made with fresh tropical fruit

bollos similar to hush puppies, but made with ground black-eyed peas instead of cornmeal

brazo gitano jelly roll-type dessert filled with liqueur-laced whipped cream

café cubano strong black coffee, sweetened with lots of sugar and served in tiny cups. Usually served with a glass of water—drink that first to prepare your stomach, and be prepared to feel very awake (it's delicious, but don't order two—you'll be awake all night!). This is what you see people selling and drinking in little plastic cups at take-out windows outside many Cuban restaurants and newsstands.

café con leche "coffee with milk," usually comes with a cup of hot milk and a small pitcher of Cuban coffee

caldo gallego thick Basque soup made with white beans, sausage, and ham

carambola yellow star-shaped fruit, usually served in slices

chimichurri sauce made with garlic, parsley, vinegar, basil, and other spices. Served on grilled meat in many Central and South American restaurants.

churros deep-fried lengths of dough made of yuca (a potato-like vegetable), sprinkled with sugar and served hot. *Delicioso!*

coquitos macaroon-type pastries found in Cuban bakeries (*pastelerias*)

cortadito half a cup of hot milk mixed with half a cup of Cuban coffee

empanada turnover filled with meat, potatoes, or other ingredients; varies according to nationality

fabada asturiana thick Basque soup made with white beans and sausage—can be a meal in itself

granizados snowcones flavored with tropical fruit syrups

lechón pork roast, usually seasoned with garlic and sour oranges

maduros very ripe, sweet plantains, sliced and fried

mamey large brown fruit with sweet, rose-colored, avocado-like flesh; delicious in a *batido*

mariquitas thinly sliced plantains, deep-fried and lightly salted

medianoche sandwich made with sliced ham and cheese on a Cuban roll and heated until cheese melts

mojo a sauce made with sour orange, garlic, and other spices

moros black beans, sometimes served in a thick soup along with white rice. You can pour the beans over the rice or eat them separately.

moros con cristianos literally "Moors and Christians," a mixture of black beans with white rice

paella a mixture of saffron-seasoned rice, seafood, sausage, chicken, rabbit, and vegetables

palomilla thinly sliced steak (sometimes called "minute steak") that fills your plate, usually served with french fries

pastelito a flaky pastry filled with cream cheese (*queso*), guava paste, coconut (*coco*), or a meat mixture

picadillo mixture of ground beef, capers, raisins, and spices in a sauce; served with white rice

ropa vieja meaning "old clothes," the shredded beef looks like rags (ask your kids why they think it's called "old clothes"), and is mixed with vegetables in a stew

tostones thick slices of plantain, flattened, fried, and lightly salted

Tres Leches rich dessert made with a sponge cake base soaked in a sweetened condensed milk mixture and topped with merengue and maraschino cherries

Under the Sun

The great outdoors is one of South Florida's primary attractions. Parks, nature centers, and beaches abound in South Florida, and you will see from the listings that follow that each facility has its own personality. There are theme parks and recreational parks; parks just for kids and parks that have something for each member of the family; large regional parks and cozy neighborhood parks; garden parks and beach parks; but they all have one thing in common—they're ours to enjoy.

Many of the parks in this part of Florida are designated as wildlife or historic preserves. They provide wonderful places to teach young children respect and compassion for our environment and its wildlife and rich history.

There are a few hints to keep in mind when visiting outdoor areas in South Florida:

☐ First of all, never forget the power of the Florida sun. You must respect its strength and be aware of its potential harm. Please take care of yourself and your children, especially infants and toddlers, by using sunscreen, not only at the beach, but any time you are outdoors. Even in the winter months the sun's rays can produce severe burns and long-term side effects.

☐ When visiting beaches, always swim near a lifeguard and check out the water's condition. In the spring you may find the ocean waves to be rough, and the undertow may be too dangerous for children. Lifeguards are helpful and can give good advice on swimming conditions.

☐ Remind children to be cautious around jellyfish and other sea creatures.

☐ South Florida weather is unpredictable—if you see lightning or a storm approaching, always find shelter.

☐ Watch out for biting insects. Mosquitoes are year-round pests, but are especially prevalent in the summer months. Keep insect repellant handy. Effective and inexpensive choices include vinegar, yeast tablets, and, believe it or not, Avon's Skin-So-Soft bath oil. Bug-proof netting is great when camping and for placing over baby playpens and carriages. On the ground, look out for fire ants—their bites can be extremely bothersome and some people have terrible allergic reations. It's a good idea to carry ammonia dabbers (available in pharmacies) to get the sting out of bug bites.

☐ If you visit parks often you may want to keep a box of outdoor toys in your car for those unplanned trips.

☐ Always check out the condition of playground equipment before your children begin to play. For guidelines on minimum safety standards, and playground equipment that has been recalled, contact the Consumer Products Safety Commission at (800) 638-CPSC.

There are many wonderful parks, nature centers, and beaches within the counties listed here. National, state, county, and city parks have programs for all interests. Observe the safety rules and regulations at each of the places you visit. Also, many parks change their hours and prices during the summer months, so be sure to call ahead for up-to-date information. Concessions and rental policies may also fluctuate with the seasons.

Dade County
Dade County has one of the largest parks systems in the nation. Over 100 staffed parks and 450 park sites are open to the public—this only includes county parks! Each city and neighborhood has its own parks as well.

☐ A.D. Barnes Park
3701 SW 72nd Avenue, Miami 33155. (Look for the tall trees on Bird Road!) Mailing address is 3701 SW 70th Avenue, Miami 33155. Park and pool, (305) 665-1626; naturalist services, (305) 662-4124. Daily, 7 A.M.–7 P.M. (until 8 P.M. in summer months). Free admission.

There's something here for everyone to enjoy. From the "tot lot" play area to a wheelchair-accessible "tree house," you'll have a fun outdoors experience in this nature area tucked away from the busy city. Within the 62-acre park you'll find picnic facilities, a jogging and biking path, and a solar-heated swimming pool with a hydraulic floor that is raised and lowered to accommodate wheelchairs. The tree-house facility is actually a 200-foot ramp that extends about 12 feet above ground into a cluster of trees.

Children will enjoy the Sense of Wonder Nature Center and Trail, which offers hands-on activities and animal exhibits. (This area is not open to the public on a daily basis, but field trips can be arranged, and families can enjoy Saturday morning nature walks during the school year.) The unique trail is made up of outdoor exhibits that teach children to use their five senses to learn about the wonders of nature. One stop on the trail focuses on the Seminole and Miccosukee Indian cultures—touch and smell the dried palm fronds that make up an Indian home. At the pond, listen to a waterfall as it splashes on the rocks, or watch fish and turtles as they are fed. Smell different fragrances in an herb garden and watch as beautiful butterflies dance around the plants. The trail is wheelchair-accessible.

Previously called Bird Drive Park, A.D. Barnes Park (newly-named for Doug Barnes, the first director of the Dade County parks system) often hosts special-needs camps and programs. Call for information about their annual camps for asthmatic and ventilator-dependent children.

□ Alice Wainwright Park

2845 Brickell Avenue, Miami. (From Bayshore Drive turn east on side street north of entrance to Vizcaya. Follow around until it becomes Brickell Avenue [you can't get there directly on Brickell Avenue south from downtown]; park on street near entrance.) (305) 856-6794. Daily, sunrise to sunset. Free admission.

This native hardwood hammock has shady picnic sites and a view of Biscayne Bay that make it especially peaceful. (A hammock is a fertile land area made up of densely-grown hardwood trees.) You'll need a watchful eye for young children here, as there is no barrier at the water's edge. Two play areas (with jungle gym and spring toys) and a nature trail through the hammock are located within the park. **Tip:** Restrooms are near entrance.

□ Amelia Earhart Park

401 East 65th Street, Hialeah 33013. (305) 685-8389. Daily, 9 A.M.-sunset. Cars, $2 on weekends and holidays, and daily from June through August. Beach and waterslide additional fee.

The new Farm Village at this park is a hit with children. From the authentic red barn (complete with goats, chickens, horses, and sheep) to the farm-type play equipment, they'll never be bored. Plus, Mom can browse in the General Store!

Not all of the 515 acres are developed at Amelia, but you already can find bike paths, picnic facilities, a playground, and a jogging trail. If water's your preference, try out the beach, waterslide, and rental items, such as boats and canoes. The Tom Sawyer Play Island can be reached by a suspension bridge and has plenty of play equipment for children. Young children should be supervised on the island—rock structures for climbing and easy access to water can make this area a bit dangerous for adventurous children.

□ Arch Creek Park

1855 NE 135th Street, North Miami 33181. (305) 944-6111. Daily, 9 A.M.–

5 P.M. Park admission is free, small fee for naturalist group activities (make reservations).

This historical park dates back to prehistoric times, and offers a unique opportunity to study history, archaeology, and nature. There is a museum on the grounds modeled after a pioneer home. In it you'll find a treasury of artifacts dating back to the Ice Age, as well as relics from the prehistoric Tequesta Indians and early pioneers. Shell tools, vertebrae fossils, and pottery are housed in the museum.

Many children are introduced to Arch Creek Park through school field trips; however, families can participate together in such activities as an archaelogical dig, held periodically throughout the year. The dig takes about three hours and you just might find Tequesta Indian artifacts dating back 3,000 years.

Teachers may inquire about classes visiting the site during the week. A very popular field trip is called "Indian Pow Wow," where children become Indians for a day and trace the history of the Seminole and Tequesta tribes by walking the nature trail, studying edible plants, and digging for artifacts. **Tips:** Children should wear old clothes when participating in the programs. Bring your own drinks and treats. Trails are not accessible for strollers or wheelchairs. Restrooms, drinking fountains, and picnic areas are available. Self-guided tours run 45 minutes to an hour—best time to visit is in the afternoons or on Saturdays at 1 P.M. for a free nature walk. For party information, see listing in "Celebrate in Style."

☐ Bill Baggs/Cape Florida State Recreation Area

1200 South Crandon Boulevard, Key Biscayne 33149. (305) 361-5811. Park: daily, 8 A.M.–sundown; lighthouse: tours Wednesday through Monday at 10:30 A.M. and 1, 2:30, and 3:30 P.M. Florida residents: driver, $1; passengers, 50¢; children under 6, free. Nonresidents: driver, $2; passengers, $1; children under 6, free. Lighthouse: $1; children under 6, free. Rickenbacker Causeway toll: $1.

At the tip of famous Key Biscayne you'll find a wonderful blend of beach and woods with bike and nature trails, making a picturesque setting for a family outing. There are picnic areas with lots of shade, but watch for raccoons who are ready to "mooch" your lunch if given the opportunity.

Within the park is the Cape Florida Lighthouse, built in 1825. It is the oldest structure built in South Florida and is open for tours (see beginning of listing for times). You'll have to climb 122 steps to reach the top, so you may not want small children to attempt this.

A full-service concession stand is located on the beach. Rentals, including bikes, lounges, umbrellas, windbreakers, and fishing equipment are available here. Take a few moments to sit on the seawall at the tip of the island to watch the sunset and the many boats that are finding their way back to port. There goes the sun . . . down . . . down . . . oops! . . . back to reality! **Tip:** Outside showers are available. For more information, see listing of Cape Florida Lighthouse in "Tracing the Past."

□ **Biscayne National Park**
9700 SW 328th Street (Herbert W. Hoover Drive), Homestead 33030. (Nine miles east of Homestead at Convoy Point—from the Florida Turnpike take Tallahassee Road [SW 137th Avenue] south to North Canal Drive [SW 328 Street] and head east.) Mailing address is P.O. Box 1369, Homestead 33090-1369. Visitors' Center, (305) 247-7275; boats, (305) 247-2400. Daily, 8 A.M.–sunset. Visitors' Center hours vary with seasons. Free admission.

America's largest aquatic national park, comprising 181,500 acres of islands and reefs, gives a picture of what South Florida looked like hundreds of years ago. Approximately 45 small keys, including Elliott Key and Sands Key, are within the park's boundaries, and are accessible only by boat. Ninety-five percent of the park is water and contains part of the only living coral reef in the United States. Tales of ancient shipwrecks and fascinating islands make it a legendary place.

The park's headquarters and information area are located on the mainland at Convoy Point. Here you'll find exhibits and schedules of park activities. There's a 13-minute slide show to enjoy, as well as a touch table and displays of sponges, turtles, and coral samples. There's an aquarium set up to view.

Picnic areas are available here with tables, grills, and restrooms. There is a short trail to follow that allows you a view of the marine life and birds of Biscayne Bay. A trip on a glass-bottom boat (call ahead for departure times), as well as canoeing, snorkeling, and scuba diving (rental equipment is available) can give you a first-hand look at the scenic underwater reefs. **Tips:** There are no lifeguards on duty. Some of the Keys have recreation facilities, but Elliott Key is the only one with drinking water. The park puts out a wonderful map and information guide—write or call for a copy.

□ **Camp Owaissa Bauer**
17001 SW 264th Street, Homestead 33031. (305) 247-6016. Weekdays, 8 A.M.–4 P.M.; weekends open to groups of 40 or more, or to the public

Stories told by park rangers at Biscayne National Park help children understand the environment and its wildlife.

from 8 A.M.–4 P.M. if not already reserved. Cost starts at $200 per night for a minimum of 40 people.

This is a dormitory-style camp facility that caters to youth groups and organizations, but because of its popularity, you need to make reservations almost a year in advance. There's lots to do in this secluded park, like swimming, hiking, organized sports, and arts and crafts. There's a campfire area and meeting rooms are available, but you must plan your own programs.

☐ **Castellow Hammock**
22301 SW 162nd Avenue, Goulds 33170. (From Florida Turnpike take Quail Roost Drive [starts as 186th Street and becomes 200th Street] west to SW 162nd Avenue, then turn left.) (305) 245-4321. Daily, 9 A.M.–5 P.M. Free admission.

A nature trail loops through this 60-acre tropical hammock; a self-guided tour gives children a chance to find interesting species of plants and birds. The interpretive building has restrooms and drinking fountains, as well as a display area with snakes and a native plant arboretum. Picnic tables are found at the front of the property.

□ Charles Deering Estate

16701 SW 72nd Avenue, Miami 33157. (305) 235-1668. Weekends only, 9 A.M.–5 P.M. Adults, $4; children ages 6 to 12, $2; children under six, free. (Cost includes tour of houses and hammock.) Canoe trips: adults, $10; children, ages 6 to 12, $5.

The history at the Charles Deering Estate is rich with human presence dating back 10,000 years, when Paleo-Indians lived on the site as hunters and gatherers. To learn about the grounds, you must tour the Deering home and the Richmond Inn, as well as take a tram tour of the hammocks. The entire trip back in history lasts about 90 minutes.

Special programs at the 350-acre estate include evening hammock walks, when you can seek out night creatures. Bring your flashlight and be ready for an exciting adventure. Birdwatching is also popular here.

For early risers, try a sunrise canoe trip across Biscayne Bay to Chicken Key. Canoe trips take place on Saturday and Sunday at 9:30 A.M. and 1 P.M., and last 2½ to 3 hours. Reservations are needed. **Tips:** Best time to visit is in the morning. Access is restricted for strollers and wheelchairs. No drinking fountains, but picnic tables are available here. For more information, see listing in "Tracing the Past."

□ Chekika State Recreation Area

24200 SW 160th Street, Homestead. (Take Krome Avenue to SW 168th Street, go west to SW 237th Avenue. Signs are posted.) Mailing address is P.O. Box 1313, Homestead 33030. (305) 252-4438. Daily, 8 A.M.–sunset. Florida residents: driver, $1; passengers, 50¢; children ages 6 and under, free. Nonresidents: driver, $2; passengers, $1; children ages 6 and under, free. Annual memberships available.

This 640-acre area of the Everglades was named after Chekika, an Indian chief of the early 1800s who played a major role in the Second Seminole War. While walking the nature trail here (about a 20- minute walk), you can almost visualize the Indians behind the trees. The trail will give you a feel for a true tropical hammock—signs posted along the way tell brief, interesting stories about the vegetation and hammock characteristics. Rangers give guided tours upon request if staffing allows.

From the parking lot, walk along a boardwalk to the picnic and swimming areas. You may see a number of alligators along the way—remember that these are dangerous reptiles and must be treated with caution. Never approach or try to feed them.

Picnic areas are shady and equipped with grills. There's a small sandy beach at the swimming hole, which used to be a natural depression in the hammock. The swimming area was built by diking and directing artesian water into the depression from a nearby well that was discovered in 1943, when prospectors were trying to strike oil.

Campsites are located within the park, along with a primitive camp for youths available by reservation. **Tips:** There are no concessions on the grounds, so be sure to bring along what you need, including bug spray. Best time to visit is in the winter months. Pets may come along on a six-foot leash. Showers are available.

□ Crandon Park

4000 Crandon Boulevard, Key Biscayne 33149. (305) 361-5421. Daily, sunrise to sunset. Cost is $2 per vehicle, plus $1 toll on the Rickenbacker Causeway.

Famous Key Biscayne is just moments from downtown Miami, but oh, what a few moments can do! An ideal spot for beach-goers, Crandon Park has three miles of scenic beach. You'll find cabana rentals, picnic areas, lifeguards on duty, restrooms, grills, and concessions. Snorkeling is popular at the Bear Cut area north of the park. Discover a unique black mangrove fossil reef here—one of only two such reefs in the world.

Within Crandon Park is Calusa Park (across the street next to the fire station). This unusual play area has climbing equipment, a hippo for children to crawl through, and a giant turtle to sit on.

□ Douglas Park

2755 SW 37th Avenue, Miami 33145. (305) 442-0374. Daily, 8 A.M.–sunset. Free admission.

This city park, with its "Friendship Playground" or "Parque de la Amistad," is a wonderful find for anyone with imaginative children. You and your child will be enchanted by the wooden castle, built by the Kiwanis Club of Little Havana (with assistance from Frito-Lay). There is a fenced-in section for toddlers that allows them to climb around and peek through the

*The castle and wooden playset at
Douglas Park become a stage for
imaginative children.*

windows of their own castle. This play area is floored by gravel, not sand—
while you won't have to worry about Junior's shoes being filled with sand
when you get home, you may want to enforce the "no-eating-the-gravel"
rule. There is a large multipurpose field and a small picnic area; food is not
allowed in the castle area. Birthday parties are popular here on the
weekends, so come on weekday mornings or other nonpeak periods.
Tip: The park's playing surface is gravel, so be sure to wear appropriate
shoes. For party information, see listing in "Celebrate in Style."

☐ **Greynolds Park**
*17530 West Dixie Highway, Miami 33160. (305) 945-3425. Daily, 7 A.M.–
7 P.M. Car, $1.50; RV, van, or bus, $6.*

You'll almost believe you're out in the country when you enter Greynolds
Park. The lush tropical landscaping and rolling land are a welcome site in
an otherwise busy part of town. This 160-acre park is a good place to picnic
in the shade and have the children close by in a playground. (Try the
Mahogany picnic area past the golf course, around the corner on your left.)
There's a castle on a hill for young children to play in—it may be dangerous
for toddlers, as the path leading up to it is rocky and steep, but sure-footed
and imaginative kids will love playing in this storybook dwelling.

Greynolds is famous for its bird rookery (a bird colony or breeding place), home to almost 3,000 long-legged wading birds. Every Thursday evening there is a free birdwatching program. Call for times, as they vary throughout the year.

Also within the park are bike paths, several nature trails, and a coral rock boathouse that is now a concessions area. **Tips:** Concessions area at park's golf course is open seven days a week.

☐ **Homestead Bayfront Park**
9698 North Canal Drive, Homestead 33030. (305) 247-1543. Daily,
7 A.M.–sundown. Cars, $2; boats, $5.

You don't have to be on Miami Beach to get close to the water! The beach here is a favorite for young and old alike. All the ingredients—an ocean view, clean sand, and nice playground equipment—make this a good family stop. Restrooms, showers, and concessions are available.

☐ **Kendall Indian Hammocks Park**
11395 SW 79th Street, Miami 33173. (305) 596-9324. Daily,
7 A.M.–sunset. Free admission.

This neighborhood park (the first regional park in the Kendall area) is especially nice, with lots of shade and land. You'll be amazed at the open space, picnic areas, and play equipment that you will find at the end of the winding road that takes you back into the park.

There are lots of ways to picnic here; tables, shelters, barbecue pits, a chickee hut, and a picnic "platform" set among the trees provide all the options you need. After lunch, visit the play area (the climbing apparatus may be too advanced for small children, but a scaled-down tot lot is planned for the future). Two kinds of slides, a swinging bridge, and a tire swing make the wooden jungle gym a fun spot for kids. (The little ones will want to play in the sandy area underneath!). This is a good place to meet other parents and children. **Tips:** Shelter rentals available for parties. Inquire about summer camp programs for children ages 7 to 10.

☐ **Larry and Penny Thompson Park**
12451 SW 184th Street, Miami 33177. (305) 232-1049. Park open daily,
7 A.M.–sunset. Call for hours of waterslide and beach. Park admission is
free; beach: $1 per person, children under age 3, free; waterslide: weekdays,
$3; weekends, $4 (must meet height requirement).

Located south of the Miami Metrozoo, this park offers a peaceful country setting for a picnic. The tall pine trees allow for plenty of shade, but the play area is situated in a sunny spot. After your meal in the shade, head over to the swimming lagoon or waterslide for a sure way to cool off. Canoe, paddleboat, and sailboat rentals are available in the summer months.

Also within these 200 acres is a campground for RVs, trailers, and tents. The camping area is accessible for handicapped travelers. If you bring your own horse, you'll find a quiet bridal path to explore.

□ **Matheson Hammock Park**
9610 Old Cutler Road, Miami 33156. (305) 666-6979. Daily, 6 A.M.–sunset. Cars, $2; boats, $5.

The swimming lagoon here, with its calm and shallow water, is quite ideal for small children. There is a lifeguard on duty from early morning to near closing seven days a week. Showers, dressing areas, concessions, picnic shelters, and tables are all near the beach.

A marina is situated within the park, and a nature trail winds through the hammock. The land was donated to the county in 1930 by William Matheson, a philanthropist and pioneer of the south Dade area.

□ **North Shore Park Beach**
From 79th to 87th streets, along Route A1A (Collins Avenue), Miami Beach.

The wooden boardwalks along this stretch of beach are great for walks. Showers, pavilions, snack stands, restrooms, and lifeguards make this a convenient place for parents with young children.

□ **Old Cutler Hammock Nature Center**
17555 SW 79th Avenue (½ mile west of Old Cutler Road on SW 176th Street), Miami 33157. (305) 255-4767; "Nature Zone" program information, (305) 235-1668. Daily, 9 A.M.–5 P.M.; nature center open weekends only, 9 A.M.–5 P.M. Free admission.

A surprise awaits you as you head down SW 79th Avenue! This nature center is hidden in the trees and is an excellent find for mothers of young children. The play area, with swings and equipment, is good to visit on weekday mornings, when you can have the whole playground to yourselves. There's a picnic table and shelter here, along with a nature trail that winds through a tropical hammock.

The interpretive building contains a collection of reptiles, amphibians, fish, and insects. There are programs here for children on Saturday mornings, as well as in the summer. Call for information on "Nature Zone," a program for young children that uses games, arts and crafts, and songs to teach them about ecology, archaeology, and wildlife. There's something for children of all ages, from toddlers on up, including summer camps and preschool co-ops. Class fees are minimal.

On Saturday nights you can go star-gazing here from 8 to 10 P.M., with the help of the Southern Cross Astronomical Society. It's free! For more information, call (305) 661-1375, or see listing in "Exploring Science and Nature."

□ **Oleta River State Recreation Area**
3400 Sunny Isles Boulevard, North Miami. Mailing address is P.O. Box 601305, North Miami 33160. (305) 947-6357. Daily, 8 A.M.–sunset. Florida residents: driver, $1; passengers, 50¢; children under 6, free. Nonresidents: driver, $2; passengers, $1; children under 6, free.

The main attraction here is the man-made sandy white beach (not a common sight for South Floridians!), but the primitive camping facility is also a big draw for Scouts and other youth groups. There's also plenty of swimming, saltwater fishing, and boating.

□ **Tamiami Park**
11201 SW 24th Street, Miami. (305) 223-7072; pool, 223-7077. Recreation building: 8 A.M.–5 P.M.; park: 8 A.M.–11 P.M. Free admission.

The park's solar-heated swimming pool may be the largest of its kind in the U.S., so you might guess that this is a popular spot for kids when the temperatures soar. There's also baseball, football, soccer, and multi-purpose playing fields, as well as tennis courts, to give children plenty of opportunities to get involved in some kind of a game. Many events throughout the year are held at this busy 265-acre park, including RV shows, dog shows, circuses, and the Dade County Youth Fair in March. For more Youth Fair information, see listing in "Mark Your Calendar."

□ **Tropical Park**
7900 SW 40th Street (Bird Road), Miami 33155. (305) 226-8315. Daily, 7 A.M.–10 P.M. Free admission.

Over two million people a year visit this busy county park, where there is an array of activities to choose from, including tennis, racquetball, baseball, boxing, swimming, soccer and basketball, to name a few. There are four lakes for sailing, paddleboating, and fishing during the summer. Children enjoy the two large play areas located within the park.

At one time a popular racetrack, the park is now equipped with an equestrian center, an 8,400-seat stadium for sporting events, and a vita course. In December, the east side of the park becomes Santa's Enchanted Forest, a magical-lighted paradise for children. For more Enchanted Forest information, see listing in "Mark Your Calendar."

Broward County
Call the Special Events Hotline, available 24-hours a day, at 563-PARK for information about Broward County parks. The message changes weekly.

□ Brian Piccolo
901 Sheridan Street, Cooper City 33024. (305) 437-2600. Call for costs and hours.

Broward's newest county park, Brian Piccolo, is action-packed with playing fields, racquetball and tennis courts, a canoe/kayak course, and a jogging/ bike path.

□ C.B. Smith Park
900 North Flamingo Road (just north of Hollywood Boulevard), Pembroke Pines 33026. (305) 435-2500. Daily, 8 A.M.–sundown. Weekends and holidays: driver, $1; passengers, 50¢; children ages 5 and under, free. Daily beach admission: adults (ages 13 and up), $1; children, 50¢; children ages 3 and under, free with parent. Waterslide and other attractions extra.

If your family enjoys water sports, they'll enjoy this 320-acre park situated around an 80-acre lake. You might start your day at the beach, where paddleboats, canoes, and aquacycles can be rented to provide exercise and fun. Try out the 700-foot waterslide (you can't miss it!) and tube ride that provides a new challenge around every turn. Next, move on to the 2.5-mile bike and skate trail, where rentals are also available. You might even be game for 18 holes of miniature golf.

Depending on the size of your group, picnic shelters are available in three sizes: small, medium, and large. There is also a meeting cabin that will accommodate over 300 people. For a breezy ride, try the nine-station tram route that runs through the park. There are 11 restrooms and 15 drinking fountains available!

☐ Colohatchee Natural Park
1975 NE 15th Avenue, Wilton Manors 33305. (305) 390-2130. Daily,
9 A.M.–6 P.M.; closed Tuesdays. Free admission.

Named by Indians after William C. Collier, the first white settler of the area,
this natural park is a peaceful find in a relatively busy area. Just off a main
street, you will walk along a boardwalk that is nestled among mangrove
trees (tropical trees with spreading branches and thick roots) that are very
interesting to look at; they're even eerie at certain times of the day. Small
children should be confined to strollers, as wiggly toddlers may find it too
tempting to stray from the trail (it's not solidly fenced on either side). At the
end of the trail there is a fenced-in area with play equipment, a basketball
court, and a sand pit for volleyball or castle-building. There's a nice picnic
pavilion with a stone fireplace in the center. Restrooms and soda machines
are available, and a boat ramp is across the street. Groups of 25 or more
need a permit to use the park facilities.

☐ Cypress Park
*1300 Coral Springs Drive, Coral Springs 33071. (South of Sample Road at
Lakeview Drive. Park extends east and west of Coral Springs Drive.) (305)
345-2100. Daily, 7:30 A.M.–10 P.M.; hours for pool vary. Free admission to
park; fees for tennis and swimming.*

This new 42-acre recreational facility straddles both sides of Coral Springs
Drive. To the west, visitors will find a swimming pool, clubhouse (a real
beauty!), tennis courts, nature trail, and picnic area. A tot lot, multipurpose
fields, and basketball courts can be found on the east side of the park.

☐ Deerfield Island Park
*One Deerfield Island, Deerfield Beach 33441. (Go east on Hillsboro
Boulevard. Turn left [north] across traffic onto Riverview Road just before
Intracoastal Waterway bridge.) Mailing address is P.O. Box 966, Deerfield
Beach 33441. (305) 428-5474. Open daily at 8 A.M.; closing hours vary.
Nature tours on Wednesdays and Saturdays at 8:30 A.M. Free admission.*

This heavily-wooded island serves as home to many animals, including grey
foxes, raccoons, gopher tortoises, and armadillos. It is also the roosting and
feeding place for many sea birds. It's hard to believe the hustle and bustle of
city life is just moments away from this unique place.

Nature walks are available Wednesdays and Saturdays at 8:30 A.M.—you
can check in at the park office for these walks. A 1,500-foot boardwalk will
lead you through winding mangroves, while another trail gives you a view

of the Intracoastal Waterway. A special event, "Show and Tell," teaches about the care and feeding of park animals. It is usually scheduled on the first Wednesday of every month, but call for information and reservations. **Tips:** Be sure to bring a picnic lunch; there is a shelter on the island that accommodates 60 people. Vending machines and restrooms are located near the picnic and playground area. Transportation to the island is free (it is accessible only by boat), and parking is available near the shuffleboard courts.

□ **Easterlin Park**
1000 NW 38th Street, Oakland Park 33309. (From I-95 take Oakland Park Boulevard east to NW Ninth Avenue [Powerline Road]. Turn north on NW Ninth Avenue to NW 38th Street, then go west across railroad tracks. Park entrance is on the left.) (305) 776-4466. Daily, 8 A.M.–7 P.M.; closing time varies with seasons. Weekends and holidays only: driver, $1; passengers, 50¢; children ages 5 and under, free.

This 46-acre park is a nice setting for a picnic lunch in the shade. There is a children's playground and a lake where ducks and other wildlife gather. Some of the cypress trees here are 250 years old and 100 feet tall.

□ **Everglades Holiday Park**
21940 Griffin Road, Fort Lauderdale 33332. (Eastern entrance to the Everglades, west of U.S. 27, 30 to 45 minutes west of Fort Lauderdale.) (305) 434-8111 in Broward; (305) 621-2009 in Dade. Park open 24 hours a day; airboats run daily, 9 A.M.–5 P.M. Park admission is free; airboat rides: adults, $11; children ages 3 to 11, $5.50; children under 3, free. Group rates and private airboat tours available.

You'll feel like you're on a safari in this 750,000-acre portion of the Everglades. Fish, camp, picnic, birdwatch, and tour the park by airboat. Boat rentals and guided fishing tours are available. (They say that more fishing licenses are sold here than anywhere else in South Florida!)
Chickee huts are available for picnicking. There are no grills, but if you bring your own you will be charged 50¢ per person. **Tips:** Don't forget your mosquito repellant. Snack bar available.

□ **Fern Forest Nature Center**
201 Lyons Road South (1/2 block south of Atlantic Boulevard), Pompano Beach 33068. (305) 975-7085. Daily, 8:30 A.M.–6 P.M. Free admission.

Fern Forest has three nature trails that wind through a scenic forest—on weekend afternoons you can join a park naturalist for free guided walks that will delight young and old alike. The half-mile Cypress Creek Trail has a raised boardwalk, accessible for wheelchairs and strollers. The one-mile Prairie Overlook Trail explores an open prairie, while the Maple Walk, the shortest of the three trails, winds through a red-maple swamp.

Be sure to stop in the interpretive building; a covered amphitheater, which seats 125 people, is on one side of the building, and an assembly hall with displays and exhibits is on the other. It is available for rent and is complete with a full buffet counter and kitchen. A nice facility for a special function! **Tips:** Restrooms are in the nature building. There are a few tables north of the parking lot available for picnickers.

□ **Fort Lauderdale Beach**
Stretches along A1A from East Sunrise Boulevard to East Las Olas Boulevard. (305) 523-1407.

This beach is famed for its "Spring Break"—look at your calendar before venturing out here or you may not find any sand to put your blanket on! Lifeguards are on duty from 9:30 A.M. to 5:15 P.M. Restrooms, picnic tables, and metered parking are nearby. (Bathroom facilities are also available across the street at Burger King and McDonald's.) Forgot your beach chairs? You can rent one here!

□ **Hampton Pines Park**
7800 Hamptons Boulevard, North Lauderdale. (305) 726-0274. Daily, 10 A.M.–6 P.M. Weekends and holidays only: adults, $1; children ages 3 to 12, 75¢.

Hampton Pines is a 32-acre park with nature trails, a nature center, playground, and biking paths. On weekends and holidays you can rent paddleboats, rowboats, canoes, and bikes.

□ **Hollywood North Beach Park**
3501 N. Ocean Drive (Route A1A and Sheridan Street), Hollywood 33019. (305) 926-2444. Parking fee only; walk-in admission is free.

At this facility you will have access to the City of Hollywood's public beach, as well as the park's food concessions, picnic area (with tables and grills), and 2.2-mile boardwalk used for biking and jogging. There is a 60-foot-high tower, which you can enter for free and observe what's happening in the area.

There is also a sea turtle hatchery and holding tank area for this endangered creature. During the summer months (nesting season) you may want to take part in one of the educational programs offered here about the sea turtles. **Tips:** Metered parking is available on the Intracoastal side of Route A1A. Lifeguards are on duty along the beach; play areas are located within the park.

□ Hugh Taylor Birch State Recreation Area

3109 East Sunrise Boulevard (north side of Sunrise Boulevard, west of A1A and east of the Intracoastal Waterway), Fort Lauderdale 33304. (305) 564-4521. Daily, 8 A.M.–sundown. Florida residents: driver, $1; passengers, 50¢; children ages 5 and under, free. Nonresidents: driver, $2; passengers, $1; children ages 5 and under, free.

This 180-acre state park, located on a barrier island, is made up of beach, hammock, freshwater lagoons, and mangroves. Lots of shade can be found throughout the park, except at the children's play area. Picnic areas, ball fields, hiking, biking, and canoeing can all be enjoyed here. Call ahead to see if the concessions are open for rental equipment, and to get a schedule of nature walks. Children will enjoy walking through the tunnel to Fort Lauderdale Beach.

□ John U. Lloyd State Recreation Area

6503 North Ocean Drive, Dania 33004. (East of Dania Beach Boulevard on Route A1A—from I-95, take Sheridan Street east to Route A1A; go north on Route A1A to entrance.) (305) 923-2833. Daily, 8 A.M.–sunset. Florida residents: driver, $1; passengers, 50¢; children ages 5 and under, free. Nonresidents: driver, $2; passengers, $1; children age 5 and under, free. Annual pass available.

A large park with over 300 picnic tables, 60 grills, and lots of shade make for a fun picnic area. There's a nice beach with dunes, and a lifeguard is on duty every day. Boating and fishing are also popular here.

□ Markham Park and Range

16001 West State Road 84, Sunrise 33326. Park, (305) 389-2000; target range, (305) 389-2005. Park: daily, 8 A.M.–sundown; range: hours vary, call for an update. Weekends and holidays only: driver, $1; passengers, 50¢; children ages 5 and under, free. Annual pass available.

One of the largest parks in Broward County, Markham encompasses 665 acres. Located on the edge of the Everglades Conservation Area, it offers a wide variety of activities—you'll find everything from a target range to nature trails, and more facilities are expected to be added in the near future. Picnicking and youth-site camping are popular here.

The regional target range is the park's most unique feature. (Juniors, ages 10 through 17, must be accompanied by an adult at the range.) It is equipped with rifles, pistols, skeets, and traps. There are a number of classes available, including one on home protection techniques taught by the National Rifle Association. A complete set of rules and regulations is available through the park office. A model airplane field is also located in the park, and serves as the gathering place for regularly scheduled meets.

□ Plantation Heritage Park

1100 South Fig Tree Lane, Plantation 33317. (West of Florida Turnpike, just north of Peters Road—Davie Boulevard turns into Peters Road.) (305) 791-2225. Daily, 8 A.M.–7 P.M. Weekends and holidays: drivers, $1; passengers, 50¢; children ages 5 and under, free.

There are three children's playgrounds in this 90-acre park that was once the University of Florida's agricultural experimentation farm. The flowering trees that abound here give a brief hint of the park's past. There's also lots of open grassy area for organized (and unorganized!) play. Call the Rare Fruit and Vegetable Council at (305) 731-6959 for a permit to pick fruit in the designated areas.

Bicycles, tandems, funcycles, and paddleboats can be rented within Plantation Heritage. **Tips:** Free field trips by reservation. Picnic areas are scattered throughout the park; shelters can be reserved and a deposit is needed.

□ Quiet Waters Park

6601 North Powerline Road, Deerfield Beach 33073. (305) 421-3133; ski information, 429-0215. Daily, 8 A.M.–7 P.M. Weekends and holidays: driver, $1; passengers, 50¢; children ages 5 and under, free. Annual pass available.

Quiet Waters Park is known for its many activities in, on, and around the water. In the summer a freshwater swimming beach with lifeguard staff is always a nice place to cool off. If you like a bit more action, try cable water-skiing or kneeboarding (popular with the 10-to-12 year olds!). At the far northwest end of the park is a marina that is available for canoe, johnboat, and paddleboat rentals. Fishing is permitted in the various lakes and you'll find that bass, bream, and catfish are plentiful.

Sandy beaches give hours of fun playtime to kids of all ages.

Also located within Quiet Waters is a children's play area (look for the clown!), an 18-hole miniature golf course, picnicking and camping facilities, and over two miles of bikepaths (bike rentals are available). **Tips:** Best time to visit is weekends after 10 A.M. "Rent-a-Camp" equipment, a complete, preassembled camping package, is available for both novice and experienced campers. Ask for details when you register. Bring firewood, insect repellant, and quiet games for children. Rainchecks are available on boat and bike rentals and miniature golf.

□ Secret Woods Nature Center

2701 West State Road 84, Fort Lauderdale 33312 (½ mile west of I-95 on the north side of State Road 84). (305) 792-8528. Weekdays, 8:30 A.M.– 5 P.M.; Weekends and holidays, 8 A.M.–5 P.M. Free admission. Field trips by reservation.

Secret Woods Nature Center is an educational and relaxing recreation area. Its nature conservatory contains an active beehive exhibit and displays on the park's flora and fauna. Its 3,200-foot New River Trail is wheelchair and stroller accessible, and helps visitors explore the different environments within the park. A self-guiding tour book is available for a small fee.

☐ Topeekeegee Yugnee (T.Y.) Park
*3300 North Park Road (west off I-95 at Sheridan Street), Hollywood 33021.
(305) 961-4430. Daily, 6:30 A.M.–7 P.M. Weekends and holidays only:
driver, $1; passengers, 50¢; children ages 5 and under, free. Attractions
additional.*

T.Y. Park's name comes from the Seminole language, and means "meeting or
gathering place." So what better way to "meet or gather" than by having a
picnic near beautiful oak trees and a 40-acre lake! Shelters and tables can be
found throughout the 150-acre area, with food and snacks available
adjacent to the marina area and the beach. This is one of the most popular
picnic spots in South Florida.

Children's favorite park features include the Falling Waters Swimming
Lagoon and Twisting Waters Flume Ride. The lagoon has been designed so
that children can swim in a shallow area and play safely on the slides and
fountains and on the sandy white beach. The flume ride is 50 feet high and
has 700 feet of turns, drops, and tunnels.

Sailboats, paddleboats, canoes, and bicycles are available for rent.
Camping is another popular family activity at T.Y.

☐ Tradewinds Park
*3600 West Sample Road, Coconut Creek 33073. (Park, lake, and Butterfly
World on south side of Sample Road; stables on north side.) Park, (305)
968-3880; stables, (305) 973-3220. Park: daily, 8 A.M.–7 P.M.; stables
open weekends only. Guided tours for ages 9 and up (52" height
requirement) at 10 and 11:30 A.M., and 1 and 2:30 P.M. Pony rides for
children ages 8 and under (or less than 52"), 11 A.M.–3:30 P.M. Park
admission fees, weekends and holidays only: driver, $1; passengers, 50¢;
children ages 5 and under free. Annual pass available. Guided trail rides,
$12.50/hour; pony rides, $1 once around ring, $2.50 three times around
ring.*

There's so much to do at Tradewinds that you'll need a whole day to tour
and explore. This enormous facility is home to the famous Butterfly World,
where thousands of exotic and domestic butterflies live in an 8,000-square-
foot screened-in tropical rain forest. There is a separate entrance fee for this
attraction.

For photo opportunities, try a family classic in front of Tradewinds'
water-pumping windmill. Or have Junior pose with "Kimberly," a 700-
pound pig who calls the park's farmyard home. The Garden Area is also a
picturesque spot.

Tradewinds Park Stables offers trail rides through a wooded area and along lakes and pastures for a real country experience. Younger children can enjoy pony rides around a fenced-in ring. Hay rides in a tractor-pulled cart make a fun party idea.

If you enjoy water sports, try the rental paddleboats or canoes. Bikes can also be rented for the 1.75-mile path in the south end of the park. Other sporting opportunities include miniature golf, jogging, and ball-playing on one of the many fields. **Tips:** When horseback riding, wear long pants and shoes with closed toes and heels. The park's four concession areas are open weekends and holidays only. For more information on Butterfly World, see listing in "On Safari in South Florida."

□ **Tree Tops Park**
3900 SW 100th Avenue, Davie 33328. (Take University Drive to Orange Drive, across the canal from Griffin Road. Go west 1.6 miles to SW 100th Avenue. Turn right and go ½ mile to park entrance on right.) (305) 474-4650. Daily, 8 A.M.–7 P.M. Pavillions close at 6:30 P.M. Weekends and holidays only: driver, $1; passengers, 50¢; children ages 5 and under, free. Annual pass available.

Tree Tops' history has been traced to the time of the Tequesta Indians (circa 1565), and evidence shows that a Seminole Indian village and garden existed here almost 200 years ago.

Before venturing out on one of the three nature trails within the park, stop by the Tree Tops Center, a beautiful wood building available for rental. It is also equipped with lots of park brochures and literature about special events.

The 1,000-foot Sensory Awareness Trail offers everyone an opportunity to explore the park. The hard-surfaced path was donated by the Davie Kiwanis Club and is wheelchair accessible. Signs posted along the way are written in braille and explain the characteristics of the woodlands surrounding the trail.

Picnic areas and playgrounds are available here, as well as a 28-foot tower that lets you get a tree-top view of the area.

□ **West Lake Park**
1200 Sheridan Street, Hollywood 33019. (305) 926-2410. Daily, 8 A.M.–8 P.M. Weekends and holidays only: driver, $1; passengers, 50¢; children ages 5 and under, free. Annual pass available.

This park has a long future ahead of it, with only a portion of its 1,400 acres developed at this time. Plans are in the works for a nature conservation and education center, boardwalks, trails, and a viewing tower. Now you will find a children's playground, racquetball and tennis courts, picnic shelters, and a vita course.

Palm Beach County

□ Caloosa Regional
1300 SW 35th Avenue, Boynton Beach 33435. (407) 964-4420. Daily, sunrise to sunset. Free admission.

Here is a large, district-level facility with plenty of ball fields for all types of sports (including tennis and racquetball courts), bike paths, and walking and wheelcourse trails. After you play, enjoy a picnic near the lake.

□ Coral Cove Park
19450 State Road 707, Tequesta 33458. (407) 964-4420. Daily, sunrise to sunset. Free admission.

Coral Cove is a tranquil beachfront park with picnic facilities, a playground, and a nature trail. It's also a popular spot for snorkeling and fishing.

□ Dubois Park
19075 Dubois Road, Jupiter 33458. (407) 964-4420. Daily, sunrise to sunset. Free admission.

Toddlers can play in the water and swim in the inlet here, while the adults prepare a picnic (a popular spot for this!). On Sunday afternoons a small museum, the Dubois House, is open for tours. The home, built on an ancient Indian mound in 1898, demonstrates the lifestyle of the early pioneers. For more information, see listing of the Loxahatchee Historical Museum in "Tracing the Past."

□ John Prince Park
2700 Sixth Avenue, Lake Worth 33461. (407) 964-4420; boat rental information, 964-0178. Daily, sunrise to sunset. Free admission.

For a lakeside view, visit this 600-acre county park, complete with picnic facilities, softball fields, cycling routes, nature trails, wheelcourse, and concessions. Boat rentals include Sunfish, Hobie Cats, daysailers, and windsurfers. Call for rates and hours. With over 250 campsites here, many groups find this a prime meeting spot.

□ **Lake Ida Park**
West entrance: 2929 Lake Ida Road; south entrance: 950 Ninth Street; east entrance: 13369 Lake Drive, Delray Beach 33444. (407) 964-4220. Daily, sunrise to sunset. Free admission.

Two children's playgrounds are found at this park, situated on a 300-acre lake. Biking, fishing, picnics, boating, and hiking are common interests shared by its visitors.

□ **Lake Lytal**
3645 Gun Club Road, West Palm Beach 33406. (407) 964-4420. Daily, sunrise to sunset. Free admission.

Lake Lytal is home to a therapeutic day camp called "Little Bit of Leisure," a recreational program of games, arts and crafts, and storytelling open to children ages 2½ to 5. A playground, multipurpose playing fields, and picnic areas dominate the rest of the park. Call for information about pool activities available to the public.

□ **Loggerhead Park**
1200 U.S. Highway 1, Juno Beach 33408. (407) 964-4420. Daily, sunrise to sunset. Free admission.

This beachfront park has a boardwalk, tunnels to the beach, sand dunes for children to run on, and nature trails that will keep young ones busy. The Children's Museum of Juno Beach is located within the park, and offers children an in-depth look at sea turtles and other endangered marine life. Touch tanks outside house adult and baby turtles. **Tips:** No lifeguards on duty. For more information on the Children's Museum of Juno Beach, see listing in "Exploring Science and Nature."

□ **Meadows Park**
1300 NW Eighth Street, Boca Raton 33486. Pool, (407) 393-7851; park, 393-7806. Pool open daily, noon–5:45 P.M. Free admission.

A major renovation of the pool in 1989 made this a "like-new" facility. Classes and special swimming-related activities are provided to the public. The pool has a modern wheelchair lift that assists people into the water.

Also within the park are lighted little-league baseball fields, a children's playground, and tennis courts.

☐ Ocean Inlet Park

6900 North Ocean Boulevard, Oceanridge 33435. (407) 964-4420. Daily, sunrise to sunset. Free admission.

This beach has a shallow area for children to enjoy, plus a tot lot for some exercise.

☐ Okeeheelee Park

7715 Forest Hill Boulevard (north side, just east of Florida Turnpike), West Palm Beach 33463. (407) 964-4420. Daily, sunrise to sunset. Free admission.

A beautiful view and plenty of fun activities await you at Okeeheelee. The serene 200-acre lake is available for boating and fishing. A fine waterskiing course is located here and draws many fine skiers from around South Florida.

Picnic facilities, baseball and multipurpose playing fields, nature trails, and concessions are all located within the park. A popular BMX track is available for children and adults. Call for practice and racing schedules and fees.

☐ Patch Reef Park

2000 NW 51st Street (Yamato Road, just west of Military Trail), Boca Raton 33431. (407) 997-0791. Park: Monday through Saturday, 9 A.M.–10:30 P.M.; Sunday, 8 A.M.–sunset. Community Center: Monday through Friday, 8 A.M.–10 P.M.; Saturday, 9 A.M.–5 P.M. Free admission.

A city park with fields galore! Try any sport and you'll find the facilities you need at Patch Reef! A new tennis facility with 16 courts (plus a pro court, pro shop, and lockers) is available for tennis lessons and leagues. Softball, baseball, soccer, basketball, and football are played here during all seasons. Restrooms and concession facilities are conveniently located. The community center within the park offers a variety of classes (ballet, cooking, karate), activities, and special events.

☐ Red Reef Park

1400 North State Road A1A, Boca Raton 33431. (407) 964-4420. Daily, 8 A.M.–10 P.M. Weekdays, $5 per car; weekends, $7 per car.

An ocean boardwalk and pavillon, as well as grills, picnic facilities, restrooms, showers, and lifeguards are available at this 80-acre park. This is a delightful beach park for family outings.

☐ Spanish River Park
3001 North Route A1A, Boca Raton 33431. (407) 393-7810. Daily, 8 A.M.–sunset. Weekdays, $5 per car; weekends, $7 per car.

The shade at this popular park makes for a cool way to spend an afternoon. The children's playground is nestled in the trees near a picnic area that has grills and tables. A nearby nature trail, tunnels to the beach (with wheelchair access), and a 40-foot observation tower give you lots of choices for activities. For boaters, there's a lagoon boat dock near the tower. Lifeguards are on the beach from 9 A.M. to 5 P.M.

Monroe County
You'll find that the Keys are somewhat of a playground of their own! This tropical paradise is a haven for those who like to boat, fish, and snorkel. Keep in mind that there aren't too many sandy beaches for children to just swim and play. Encourage them to explore marine life in the shallow water of the reefs, examine the formations of rocks and coral, and view the wild-life native to the area—and they will be enriched by their visit to the Keys.

☐ Astro City Park
Across from Higgs Memorial Beach, Reynolds and White streets, Key West.

This popular kiddie park boasts a giant rocket ship that will certainly catch your children's eye! The fenced-in play area has extra-nice climbing equipment and the picnic area is equipped with chickee huts and plenty of shade! The beach is close by.

☐ Bahia Honda State Recreation Area
Mile Marker 38, U.S. 1, Box 782, Big Pine Key 33043. (305) 872-2353. Daily, 8 A.M.–sundown. Florida residents: driver, $1.50; passengers, $1; children ages 5 and under, free. Nonresidents: driver, $2.50; passengers, $1.50; children ages 5 and under, free. Individual and family passes available.

Bahia Honda, or "deep bay" in English, is an ancient coral reef now covered by beaches, dunes, hammocks, and mangroves. You'll find a variety of bird life (great white heron, reddish egret, and brown pelican), as well as rare plant species (satinwood tree, spiny catesbaea, and dwarf morning glory) within the park.

One of the best beach areas in the Keys, Bahia Honda's own Sandspur Beach lets you swim in the Atlantic Ocean to the south, and in the Florida Bay to the north. Many other water sports are offered here, such as snorkeling, fishing, and boating. Windsurfing lessons are provided, and rental equipment for all activities is available.

Camping facilities, including cabins, can be reserved for a special family outing. Regular campfire programs and guided nature walks are offered, but reservations should be made. Snacks and some grocery items are available at the concession area. **Tips:** Best time to visit is from September through November. If park gets extremely busy, it may close briefly at times to accommodate the crowds. Shade is limited, so bring sunscreen and other equipment. Men-of-war can be spotted in the water and on the beaches year-round. Stroller and wheelchair access is limited. Restrooms and drinking fountains available. Plan to spend about two hours to tour.

□ **Fort Zachary Taylor State Park**
End of Southard Street, Truman Annex, Key West 33040. (Follow the small signs!) Mailing address is P.O. Box 289, Key West 33030. (305) 292-6713. Daily, 8 A.M.–sunset. Florida residents: driver, $1.50; passengers, $1; children ages 5 and under, free. Nonresidents (IDs checked): driver, $2.50; passengers, $1.50; children ages 5 and under, free.

Travel back in time as you visit a Civil War-era brick fort. If weather and staffing permit it, take the free daily tour at 2 P.M. A museum and beach are also part of Fort Zachary Taylor. Picnicking here under Australian pine trees (with grills, tables, and showers) makes a lovely setting for a special day. For more information, see listing in "Tracing the Past."

□ **Harry Harris County Park**
Mile Marker 92.5, Beach and East Beach roads, Tavernier. Daily, sunrise to sunset. Free during the week; weekends and holidays only, cars, $2.

A popular swimming spot, with a rare white beach! The swimming lagoon is great for small ones, and the play equipment on the beach makes watching the children extra fun. Softball fields, boating and picnicking facilities, hiking trails, and basketball courts make this a fun-filled park.

□ **Higgs Memorial Beach**
Reynolds and White streets, Key West. Daily, sunrise–11 P.M. Free admission.

A lovely beach for the whole family, Higgs provides picnicking facilities, swimming and fishing areas, and tennis and racquetball courts. The playground area on the beach offers a view of the Atlantic Ocean.
Tips: Clean restrooms and a small restaurant with fast foods is right on the beach. There's also plenty of parking for RVs.

☐ **Indian Key**
Mailing address is % Long Key State Recreation Area, P.O. Box 776, Long Key 33001. (Off U.S. 1 near Islamorada; accessible by boat, which leaves from Mile Marker 78.5). (305) 664-4815. Daily, 8 A.M.–sundown; the park's boat leaves at 8:30 A.M. for a two-hour tour every day except Tuesdays and Wednesdays. Adults, $6; children ages 12 and under, $3.

An observation tower, boat dock, shelters, and nature trails will be found on the key. Tales of a colorful past are told on a narrated tour of the island—at one time it was occupied by Indians and later became the seat of newly created Dade County in the 1830s. **Tips:** Most facilities not accessible for wheelchairs. There are no restrooms.

The Atlantic Ocean serves as a backdrop for the playground at Higgs Memorial Beach.

☐ John Pennekamp Coral Reef State Park

Mile Marker 102.5, U.S. 1, Key Largo 33037. Park, (305) 451-1202; concessions, (800) 432-2871. Daily, 8 A.M.–sunset. Florida residents: driver, $1.50; passengers, 50¢; children ages 5 and under, free. Nonresidents: driver, $2.50; passengers, $1.50; children ages 5 and under, free.

This park was named for John Pennekamp, an associate editor of *The Miami Herald* who played an influential role in the establishment of the Everglades National Park; it is the only underwater state park in the continental United States. The coral reefs, located five miles offshore, can be reached by glass-bottom boats that depart from the concessions area. You'll get a once-in-a-lifetime view of brightly colored coral and fish.

Camping, picnicking, swimming, and boating can all be enjoyed here (rentals available). An excellent nature museum in the visitor center contains a huge (30,000-gallon) saltwater aquarium filled with dozens of species of sea creatures. Touch tanks also allow visitors a closer look at the underwater world. **Tips:** A few shaded picnic tables are available. Several aggressive raccoons are eager to take your food; don't let children get too close to them.

☐ Long Key State Recreation Area

Mile Marker 67.5, between Conch and Lower Matecumbe keys. Mailing address is P.O. Box 776, Long Key 33001. (305) 664-4815. Daily, 8 A.M.– sundown. Florida residents: driver, $1.50; passengers, 50¢; children under age 6, free. Nonresidents: driver, $2.50; passengers, $1.50; children under age 6, free.

Long Key was an important depot during the railroad days before it was destroyed by the "Hurricane of 1935." Nowadays, its nature and campfire programs, as well as boating and swimming, are popular with visitors. Picnic facilities are on the key, as is an observation tower that gives you a spectacular view. A nature trail at the base of the tower takes you along the beach and over a mangrove-lined lagoon. Be sure to look for the interpretive signs along the way.

☐ Smathers Beach

Along South Roosevelt Boulevard, Key West.

Here's a nice shady beach with equipment rentals. The water along this stretch is nice, but be careful of the rocky bottom when wading here. Vendors park along the beach and sell food and beverages. There are public

restrooms and plenty of parking on the beach side of the road (RVs can
park across the street).

□ Sombrero Beach Park
Mile Marker 50, Sombrero Beach Road, Marathon.

Sombrero is a free community park and beach that covers a long narrow
area along the Atlantic Ocean. Facilities include picnic areas, playground
equipment, and restrooms. A grassy area provides a good place for children
to run and play.

On Your Mark, Get Set, Go!

The thrill of watching athletes perform is always an exciting part of childhood. It seems that every baby grows up with a ball, and to see that ball in action often plants the seed for dreams of their own athletic ambitions.

In South Florida those dreams can surely come true. Not only is this a great place for spectator sports—football, baseball, basketball, soccer, rodeos, polo, and horse racing—but all year long, youngsters and their adult companions can enjoy their favorite recreational activities. From bowling to biking, horseback riding to fishing, swimming to skating—South Florida has it all!

Sports events are not only exciting to watch and healthy to participate in, but are usually affordable as well. Whether you buy season tickets to your favorite professional or college team, or attend local high-school games, the only thing that matters is that you're having fun and you're doing it with someone special. So—on your mark, get set, go! Have some fun!

Spectator Sports

South Florida is not only a host of international cultures, but home to a medley of sports as well. The Dolphins, the Heat, the 'Canes, the Miracle, the Sharks, the Strikers, and the horses all help make the sports scene here one of the best in the country.

In addition to seasonal sports, children may also enjoy annual sporting events such as the Doral/Ryder Open golf tournament, the Miami Grand Prix racing extravaganza, and the Orange Bowl Classic football game. For more information, see listings in "Mark Your Calendar."

Baseball

Although South Florida cannot claim a major league team as its own, there is a great following of the major league clubs that flock to the state for spring training camps. You can still get the feel and excitement of major league competition by attending a spring training game. Minor league and college-level teams also provide the area with plenty of spectator opportunities.

□ Atlanta Braves
West Palm Beach Municipal Stadium, 715 Hank Aaron Drive (at Palm Beach Lakes Boulevard and Congress Avenue), West Palm Beach 33409. (407) 683-6100. Ticket prices range from $3 to $7.

You can watch the Braves' games and practice sessions during March and early April at the West Palm Beach Municipal Stadium. This is also home to the West Palm Beach Expos summer baseball league.

□ Baltimore Orioles
Bobby Maduro Stadium, 2301 NW 10th Avenue, Miami 33127. Office, (305) 635-5395; ticket info, 633-9857.

This major league baseball team, with popular players on the roster year after year, brings exciting Grapefruit League games to Miami the entire month of March.

□ Miami Miracle Baseball
Mailing address is P.O. Box 650826, Miami 33265-0826; games are at Florida International University, SW Eighth Street and 107th Avenue. (305) 220-7040. Adults, $4; seniors and children ages 14 and under, $2.

This new minor league Class "A" team of the Florida State League is partially affiliated with the Cleveland Indians. Home games are played at Florida International University from April to August, and host such teams as the Fort Lauderdale Yankees, the Vero Beach Dodgers, and the West Palm Beach Expos.

Singer Jimmy Buffet and comedian Bill Murray, along with local businessmen, are part owners of the Miracle team. Groups planning to attend a Miracle contest can get special rates and will be recognized during the game.

☐ **Montreal Expos**
West Palm Beach Municipal Stadium, 715 Hank Aaron Drive (at Palm Beach Lakes Blvd. and Congress Avenue), West Palm Beach, 33409. (407) 689-9121. Mailing address is P.O. Box 2546, West Palm Beach 33401.

The Expos play about 15 exhibition home games from mid-March to mid-April in the West Palm Beach Municipal Stadium.

☐ **New York Yankees**
Fort Lauderdale "Yankee" Stadium, 5301 NW 12th Avenue, Fort Lauderdale 33309. (305) 776-1921. Ticket prices range from $6 to $8.

The famed Bronx Bombers play about 15 to 17 games at Fort Lauderdale Stadium in March. February practice sessions are open to the public as well.

☐ **University of Miami Hurricanes**
Hecht Athletic Center, 5821 San Amaro Drive, Coral Gables 33146. (305) 284-3822; ticket information, 1-800-GO-CANES.

Coach Ron Fraser's Hurricane baseball team entertains fans at Mark Light Stadium on the University's Coral Gables campus in the spring. In 1982 and 1985 the 'Canes were NCAA champions, and have been in the College World Series 11 out of the last 16 years. Besides watching superb baseball competition, fans also enjoy the exciting antics of the world famous Miami Maniac, and can take part in prize give-aways and between-inning fun.

Inquire about the Ron Fraser's Sports Camp, held each summer. For over 14 years this popular camp has offered kids a chance to participate in baseball, swimming, bowling, and more at the UM campus.

Basketball

Always a favorite fast-moving game, professional basketball is new to Miami, but is proving to be a fun family adventure. Try taking the Metrorail downtown for a Miami Heat or 'Canes game. Other college games provide kids a look at the campus scene!

☐ **Miami Heat**
Miami Arena, 721 NW First Avenue, Miami 33136. (305) 577-4328. Tickets range from $12 to $25.

*The Miami Maniac entertains fans at all
University of Miami Hurricanes' sporting
events.*

See Miami's entry in the National Basketball Association play against the best in an atmosphere second to none. A new arena and a new team made for an exciting first season in 1988–89. NBA stars like Larry Bird, Magic Johnson, and others come alive during basketball season. Children can anticipate all kinds of excitement at the games, including bands, cheerleaders, and prize give-aways.

□ University of Miami Hurricanes
Hecht Athletic Center, 5821 San Amaro Drive, Coral Gables 33146. (305) 284-3822; ticket information, 1-800-GO-CANES.

The Hurricane basketball team hosts some of the top collegiate teams in the country with all games played at the new Miami Arena downtown.

Football

There's nothing like the thrill of a football game, and South Florida offers some of the best in the nation. From parking the car and finding your seats to watching live gridiron action, every child will get caught up in the excitement.

☐ Miami Dolphins

Joe Robbie Stadium, 2269 NW 199th Street, Miami 33056. (sixteen miles northwest of downtown Miami; one mile south of Broward County). (305) 620-5000. Call the box office at (305) 620-2578 for ticket information.

In 1989, Miami's first professional franchise hosted Super Bowl XXIII in what is considered the best stadium in the country—Joe Robbie Stadium. The $100 million complex is home to Coach Don Shula and his Dolphin team. Watch for announcements about Family Day (in the summer), when the public is invited to a scrimmage and season ticket holders can select their seats for upcoming games. The stadium has hosted concerts, soccer contests, several major league baseball exhibition games, and Australian football matches. Call the Dolphin office for tour information.

☐ University of Miami Hurricanes

Hecht Athletic Center, 5821 San Amaro Drive, Coral Gables 33146. (305) 284-3822; ticket information, 1-800-GO-CANES.

Be sure to see the Miami Hurricanes, the most successful college football team in the 1980s. The 'Canes, winners of three national championships in the last seven years, play all home games at the famous Orange Bowl. **Tip:** You can see other great collegiate sports events hosted by UM, including the Doral Park Intercollegiate Golf Tournament, the Ryder Collegiate Tennis Tournament, the West Palm Beach Basketball Tournament, and the Burger King Women's Basketball Classic.

Horses

A 1988 state law granted permission for children under 18 years of age to attend parimutuel events when accompanied by an adult.

□ Calder Race Course

21001 NW 27th Avenue, Miami 33055. (305) 625-1311. Open for spring/ summer and fall/winter racing seasons; call for exact dates.

Watch thoroughbred racing at its best at this ever-popular racing facility. Calder opened in 1971 and has two racing seasons a year. The dates change yearly, so be sure to call or watch the newspaper for announcements. This glass-enclosed, air-conditioned facility is one of the largest of its kind in the South.

□ Davie Rodeo Grounds

Davie Arena, 6591 SW 45th Street (Orange Drive), Davie. (305) 797-1145. Cost varies with event (see listing).

Every Thursday night at 8 P.M. the Davie Arena offers a first-hand look at true rodeo action. Tickets are $4 for adults and $2 for children ages 12 and under. "Five-Star" rodeos are held once a month, when cowboys compete to increase points towards national ratings. This event is $7 for adults and $4 for children.

□ Gulfstream Park

901 South Federal Highway (U.S. 1 and Hallandale Beach Boulevard), Hallandale 33009. (305) 454-7000. Grandstand, $2; clubhouse, $4; children under age 18 admitted free with adult.

For over 50 years Gulfstream has been one of the most famous tracks in the country. In 1989 it was host to the Breeder's Cup, horse racing's top event, and throughout the year it entertains the most famous of horses. Two annual events, Family Day in January and Florida Derby in March, are always exciting for adults and children. Polo matches are also played on the grounds. **Tip:** Children are not allowed near betting area. For more event information, see listings in "Mark Your Calendar."

□ Hialeah Park

Corner of East Fourth Avenue and 79th Street, Hialeah 33011. (Metrorail Hialeah stop puts you right outside the gates.) (305) 885-8000; (800) 423-3504, in Florida. Off season: daily, 9:30 A.M.–4:30 P.M. for sightseeing, free; racing season: call for season schedule. Cost varies according to seat selection; children ages 17 years and under admitted to races free with adult.

Hialeah horse racing has been an exciting tradition since 1925. It's always a thrill to see a horse fly down the stretch during a close race. The historic building here is a charmer, with an antique fire engine and vine-covered walls. Sightseeing tours of this 220-acre park are available when the horses aren't running.

If you are an early-rising family on weekends, "Breakfast at Hialeah" is a fun adventure. Arrive at the track at 7:30 A.M. (plan to spend two hours), watch the horses work out, and chat with famous jockeys and trainers. Watching is free; breakfast (a nice treat) is $4 for adults and $2.50 for children. If the children should get restless, have them try counting the flamingos (there are over 600 of the salmon-colored birds here!) or any of the 100 species of birds that make Hialeah Park their home. Watch the sports page for dates and information regarding this popular family event. **Tips:** If the elevator at the Hialeah Metrorail station is working, you can go right down to ground level; if not, be prepared to walk up and down two flights of stairs. A free Metrorail return ticket is available from the gift shop or information booth. Call for updated information on the park's Flamingo Fest concert series for families. For more information about the park, see listing in "Tracing the Past."

☐ **Palm Beach Polo and Country Club**
13198 Forest Hill Boulevard, West Palm Beach 33414. (407) 793-1440. Winter season only. Adult general admission, $5; reserved, $10; box seats, $14 and $17; children under age 12 admitted free for general admission; reserved and box seats, regular price. Call for season ticket information. AE, MC, V accepted.

Enjoy polo matches from January through April at this world-famous facility. Sunday matches begin at 3 P.M. and feature top players from around the world, including Prince Charles of Wales. Occasionally there will be special entertainment before the Sunday afternoon matches, so call ahead to see what's planned. If you'd rather not sit in the grandstands, try a picnic on the sidelines. Just drive your car to a designated area 10 yards from the action and tailgate for a leisurely afternoon. The cost for a prime space is $20 for the driver and $5 for each additional passenger.

If you are polo fans, plan on attending the Annual Winter Equestrian Festival, which runs for about three weeks in February and March. This event is held at the Palm Beach Equestrian Club and features Olympic and world-class riders. Wednesdays through Saturdays during this time you can attend the events for free. There is an admission charge on Sundays. **Tips:** Rainchecks available for Sunday polo matches played during the same season. Wheelchair and stroller access in general admission and reserved seating only. Tours can be scheduled. Gift shop with souvenirs open during season. Drinking fountains and restrooms available. For more information on the Winter Equestrian Festival, see "Mark Your Calendar."

☐ **Pompano Harness Track**
1800 SW Third Street, Pompano Beach 33069. (305) 972-2000. Grandstand, $1.50; clubhouse, $3; children under age 18 admitted free to grandstand with adult.

Harness racing is fun for kids to watch. For more than 25 years Pompano Track has provided exciting racing seasons to local residents and tourists. Call during the season to see if barn tours are being conducted on Saturday mornings.

☐ **Royal Palm Polo Sports Club**
6300 Clint Moore Road, Boca Raton 33496. (407) 994-1876. Sundays, 1–3 P.M., January to April (call to confirm). Adults, $5; children under age 17, $2.

This 160-acre club hosts international competitions on Sundays during the season, which varies from year to year. Tailgating is a fun way to watch the matches, or try brunch at the club's restaurant and then head out to the polo grounds. Watch for special half-time events, celebrity week, the Annual Classic Car show, and arts festivals.

Soccer

Possibly the most popular game of the 1980s for kids, soccer is not only fun to play, but also fun to watch. With so many youngsters playing in youth leagues, watching professional soccer games is a great way to help them understand the game and to see professionals demonstrate their techniques.

☐ **Miami Sharks**
7855 NW 12th Street, Miami 33126. (305) 858-7477. Group discounts available.

Watch the sports section of your newspaper for information about the Sharks' home games. This American League soccer team plays about 10 games at home, and travels up to Fort Lauderdale for other local matches. Call for information on tickets and family specials.

☐ **Fort Lauderdale Strikers**
Games held at Lockhart Stadium, 5301 NW 12th Avenue (1/2 mile west of I-95), Fort Lauderdale 33309. (305) 735-4913. Mailing address is 2200 West Commercial Boulevard, Suite 305, Fort Lauderdale 33309. Season runs April through August. General admission: adults, $7; children, $3.

The Strikers, members of the American Soccer League, play about 12 home games, including exhibitions, at Lockhart Stadium. Tailgating parties, entertainment, and special events at the games are fun for children and adults.

Recreational Activities

There are many opportunities for children to participate in team sports like T-Ball, flag football, volleyball, softball, and soccer—call your neighborhood community center or parks and recreation department for information. Here are suggestions for other recreational activities and unusual facilities for specialized sports.

Amusements

☐ **Grand Prix Race-o-Rama**
1500 NW First Street (between Griffin and Stirling roads on I-95), Dania 33004. (305) 921-1411. Game room open 24 hours a day; go-karts open Sunday through Thursday, 10 A.M.–11 P.M.; Friday and Saturday, 10 A.M.– 1 A.M. Park admission is free; costs vary for activities.

Buy tickets to drive go-karts around this large and sophisticated race track just like the great racing stars. Almost a mile around, the curves and graded banks will give kids a thrill. The bumper cars are also exciting to drive. Birthday parties are fun here and you'll be able to take advantage of group rates. There's also an arcade with more than 400 games for everyone. **Tip:** Children ages 15 and under must be accompanied by an adult.

☐ Malibu Grand Prix
7775 NW Eighth Street, Miami 33126. (West of the Palmetto Expressway, just north of the Mall of the Americas.) (305) 266-2100. Monday through Thursday, 11 A.M.–11 P.M.; Friday and Saturday, 10 A.M.–2 A.M.; and Sunday, 10 A.M.–midnight.

This castle fun-house was remodeled in 1989 and has plenty of amusements for kids of all ages. Kiddie rides (for ages 6 and older), miniature golf, nine batting cages, 160 video games, and two new go-kart racetracks can be found here. For party information, see listing in "Celebrate in Style."

☐ Whirlyball
1779 NW 79th Avenue (off Palmetto Expressway), Miami 33126. (305) 593-0555. Open 11 A.M., with closing time depending on games in progress. $12.50 per person (minimum 10 people). Cash payment only.

This new sport is a cross between jai alai and basketball, but get this—you play the game in bumper cars! For adults and children ages 10 and older, the challenge is all coordination. You hold a racket called a *cesta* (the basket-type racket used in jai alai) and try to score points by throwing whiffle balls through a target.

Baseball

☐ Bucky Dent's Baseball School
490 Dotterel Road, Delray Beach 33444. (407) 265-0280.

For baseball players ages 8 to 23 who want to improve their knowledge and ability, this school teaches proper skills and playing habits through an organized and disciplined program. There's a special program for kids ages 12 and under—instructors work closely with these youngsters and give each student personalized attention.

☐ Red Berry's Baseball World
7455 SW 125 Avenue, Miami 33183. (305) 279-2668.

For over 20 years, Coach Red Berry has hosted baseball camps for boys and girls. With an emphasis on fun and player development, Berry and his staff run various programs throughout the year, including summer vacation camps, spring and fall instructional leagues, boy's baseball, and girl's softball. For more information, see listing in "Celebrate in Style."

Biking

This is a fun way to spend time with your family. Small children can ride in seats attached to the backs of bicycles, or in a "trailer" that attaches behind adult bikes. Older children can usually pedal a long way before tiring. Parks are good places to ride, and some have special trails for bikers. Call (904) 488-7950 for a handy free publication from the state called *Florida Bicycle Trails*. Also available through many bike stores is an important reference called *Bicycles Are Vehicles: Florida's Bicycle Laws*. Backpacks and canteens are great to bring on bike outings. Below is a list of places that rent bicycles.

☐ **The Bicycle Center**
523 Truman Avenue, Key West. (305) 294-4556.
Daily, 9 A.M.–6 P.M. $4/day.

The Bicycle Center offers children's 20″ bikes and adult bikes with carriers attached (will transport children weighing 40 pounds or less). Helmets are for sale in the store.

☐ **Broward Schwinn**
701 East Sunrise Boulevard, Fort Lauderdale. (305) 467-8181. Monday through Friday, 10 A.M.-8 P.M.; Saturday, 10 A.M.–6 P.M.; Sunday, 1–5 P.M. Children's bikes, $5–$7/day; adults, $10–$12/day with attachments.

Baby seats, BMX bikes, and locks are available. Helmets can be purchased for $25 to $30.

☐ **Dade Cycle**
3216 Grand Avenue, Coconut Grove 32133. (305) 443-6075. Monday through Saturday, 9 A.M.–6 P.M.; Sunday, 10:30 A.M.–6 P.M. Adult bikes: $3/hour, $15/24 hours, $46/week. Children's bikes: $2/hour, $1.50/day for baby seats. MC, V, personal checks accepted.

BMX, baby seats, and helmets are available.

□ Gary's Bike Shop
18151 NE 19th Avenue, North Miami Beach 33162. (305) 940-2912. Monday through Friday, 9:30 A.M.–8 P.M.; Saturday, 9 A.M.–6 P.M.; Sunday, 10 A.M.–4 P.M. Cost begins at $10/day. MC, V, personal checks accepted.

Rent a trailer that connects to adult bikes and carries children. Most of your biking needs can be met here, plus a seven-mile trail is nearby.

□ John's Mopeds Beach Rental
419 South Atlantic Boulevard, Fort Lauderdale. (305) 763-8789. Daily, 10 A.M.–6 P.M. $50 deposit required. $5/hour, $9/2 hours, $15/half day, $20/day, $35/week.

Children's bikes and attachments for adult bikes are available.

□ KCB Bike Shop
11518 Overseas Highway, Marathon 33050. (305) 289-1670. Weekdays, 9:30 A.M.–5 P.M.; Saturdays, 9:30 A.M.–2 P.M.; closed Sundays. Hourly, daily, and weekly rates. AE, MC, V, personal checks accepted.

All sizes of bikes can be rented here. Baby seat attachments can be rented, but helmets are not available. Call for current rates.

□ Key Biscayne Bicycle
260 Crandon Boulevard (middle of the village of Key Biscayne), Key Biscayne. (305) 361-5555. Daily 9 A.M.–6 P.M., closed Wednesdays. $7/2 hours, $10/day. AE, MC, V, personal checks accepted.

Since 1973, this has been a popular rental stop for people exploring Key Biscayne. This store is close to Crandon Park and Bill Baggs/Cape Florida State Recreation Area. Adult bikes with seat attachments, small bikes (12″) for young children, and 16″ bikes are available. Free baskets are provided with the bikes to carry your picnic lunch!

□ Key Largo Bikes
Mile Marker 99.5, Key Largo 33037. (305) 451-1910. Monday through Saturday, 9:30 A.M.–5:30 P.M. Closed Sundays and some Wednesdays. $20 deposit required. $8/day, $35/week, $10/baby seat. AE, MC, V, personal checks accepted.

Adult bikes, 16″ and 20″ children's bikes, and seat attachments are available at this Key Largo shop. Ask if helmets are available.

☐ **Palm Beach Bicycle Trail Shop**
223 Sunrise Avenue (at the Palm Beach Hotel), Palm Beach. (407) 659-4583. Daily, 9 A.M.–5 P.M. Deposit required; $6/hour, $15/half day, $20/day, $45/week. AE, MC, V, local personal checks accepted.

Palm Beach Bicycle Trail Shop can satisfy all your bicycle needs, from training wheels on up to adult bikes. Locks come with all bikes; helmets are available to buy.

Bowling

☐ **Don Carter's Kendall Lanes**
13600 North Kendall Drive, Miami 33186. (305) 385-6160. Open 24 hours a day.

Bumper Bowling is the lastest fad for 18-month-olds! This Saturday morning bowling league is especially for small children. Youngsters up to age 5 have the advantage of the gutters being blocked with plastic inserts called bumpers. This helps them build confidence and gives them a better chance at knocking down the pins. Coaches work with the children and parents are encouraged to watch. (Children ages 6 and up bowl without the bumpers!) Winter leagues run 30 weeks, summer leagues are about 10 weeks long. Look for other Don Carter lanes throughout South Florida.

Boxing

☐ **Metro Dade Amateur Boxing**
Tropical Boxing Center, 7900 SW 40th Street, Miami, (305) 221-0678; 27th Avenue Boxing Center, 6950 NW 40th Street, Miami, (305) 835-7816.

This amateur boxing program is sponsored by the Metro-Dade County Parks and Recreation Department. The facilities used are considered to be two of the finest in the country. Children must be at least 10 years old to participate. Most of the 4,000 participants in the program are using this training for fitness and conditioning purposes. Such world boxing champs as Roberto Duran, Trevor Berbick, and Alexis Arguello have trained at these centers. Call for more information.

Fishing

Fishing is available at many parks, beaches, rivers, and canals. If this is your hobby, contact the parks in your area for information. Remember that fishing licenses are required when fishing in fresh water. For information, write to the Florida Game and Fresh Water Fish Commission, Farris Bryant Building, Tallahassee 32301; for saltwater fishing, Florida Marine Patrol, Marjorie Stoneman Douglas Building, 3900 Commonwealth Boulevard, Tallahassee 32303.

□ **Anglin's Pier**
2 East Commercial Boulevard, Lauderdale-by-the-Sea. (305) 491-9403. Open 24 hours. Adults, $2.75; children ages 12 and under, $1.75; sightseeing, $1.

At Anglin's you'll find monthly fishing contests and a great view of the Atlantic. Rentals are available.

□ **Bill Baggs/Cape Florida State Recreation Area**
1200 South Crandon Boulevard, Key Biscayne. (305) 361-8487. Daily, 8 A.M.–sunset. Florida residents: driver, $1; passengers, 50¢. Nonresidents: driver, $2; passengers, $1. Extra charge for equipment rentals.

The park rents fishing rods, and has a seawall here where you can cast off. Snappers and jacks galore!

□ **Black Point Marina**
24777 SW 87 Avenue, Miami. (Take Old Cutler Road to SW 87 Avenue and head east.) (305) 258-3500.

This new bait and tackle shop is situated near Biscayne Bay. Trout and snapper are plentiful, and you'll see plenty of manatees, as this is a protected area attracting these friendly aquatic mammals. Fishing equipment and boats are available for rent, but call for prices and times of operation. A dockside restaurant is located here.

□ **Dania Beach Pier**
300 North Beach Road, Dania. (305) 925-2861. Open 24 hours. Adults, $2; children under 5, free.

Catch it all here—you'll find snook, grouper, mackerel, and more in these waters. Rental equipment includes rods and bait. A restaurant and a picnic area are available.

☐ **Deerfield Beach International Pier**
200 NE 21st Avenue, Deerfield Beach. (305) 480-4406. Open 24 hours.
Adults, $1.75; children ages 5 to 17, 75¢; children under 5, free.

Here's a popular snapper and barracuda spot. Rod rentals, bait, and tackle
are available, and a restaurant is nearby.

☐ **Haulover Pier**
10501 Collins Avenue, North Miami Beach. (305) 947-6767. Open 24
hours. Adults, $2; children under 16, $1; spectators, $1. Parking, $2.

Bait and tackle available to rent with a deposit. Types of fish include snook,
mackerel, barracuda, grouper, shark, snapper, and blue runners. **Tips:** Ask
about a 30-day pass. Snack bar open from 7 A.M. to 6 P.M.

☐ **Holiday Inn-Newport Beach Pier**
16701 Collins Avenue, North Miami Beach. (305) 949-1300 (ask for pier).
Open 24 hours. Adults, $2; children, $1; spectators, $1.

Rentals include rods, bait, and tackle. Cast off in the Atlantic Ocean and
catch mackerel, snapper, pompano, and bluefish. Snack bar available at the
pier.

☐ **Pompano Fishing Pier**
222 Pompano Beach Boulevard, Pompano Beach. (305) 943-1488. Open 24
hours. With gear: adults, $2.07; children ages 10 and under, $1; sightseeing,
80¢. Additional charges for rentals.

Catch snook, snapper, grouper, mackerel, cobia, sand perch, blue runner,
and bluefish varieties. Restaurant, playground, and bait and tackle shop are
all located right on the Atlantic Ocean.

Horseback Riding

☐ **Horses and the Handicapped, Inc.**
(305) 981-9075.

Sponsored by the Miami Kiwanis Club, this therapeutic program is
designed to teach basic horseback riding skills to handicapped children.
Students learn the English riding technique, which provides physical
therapy for the leg muscles and improves motor functions, concentration

level, self-image, confidence, muscle strength, and balance. Approximately 40 students, with disabilities such as cerebral palsy, scoliosis, and blindness, are involved in the program at several facilities in the county. Kiwanians, parents, therapists, and volunteers all help to make the program the success that it is. In addition, children learn responsibility by caring for the horses.

☐ Horses and the Handicapped of South Florida

417 NE Third Street, Delray Beach 33483. (407) 278-2441. Saturday morning sessions are free; call about costs for private classes during the week.

Children ages 4 and up with cerebral palsy, Down's syndrome, and other special needs ride at two facilities: Trails West Riding Academy in Palm Beach Gardens, and Triple Trails Ranch in Coconut Creek. Riders are matched to horses compatible with their needs. The skills learned here carry over to other parts of the students' lives. A physician's referral is necessary for admission to the program.

☐ Jimaguas Ranch

12201 SW 80th Street, Miami 33183. (305) 271-4289. Weekends and some holidays, 8 A.M.–5 P.M. Trail rides, $10 per hour; buggy rides (mornings only), $5 per person.

Even the natives don't realize that a unique place called "Horse Country" is nestled between some of the busiest streets of the suburbs. The Jimaguas Ranch is just one of many ranches that has remained untouched by suburban development in this area that is bounded by Bird Road and Kendall Drive between SW 118th and SW 127th avenues. The entire family can enjoy a relaxing trail ride directed by a guide, or a horse-drawn carriage ride through the Horse Country area. The horses here are all very gentle. The antique buggy may be rented for parties. Call for information.

☐ Rockin 'n' Ranch

NE 16th Avenue and 135th Street, North Miami 33161. (Look for signs to Enchanted Forest.) (305) 891-9512 or 891-7107. Tuesday through Friday, 10 A.M.–2 P.M.; Saturday and Sunday, 9 A.M.–5 P.M.; closed Mondays. 50¢ for one time around ring.

Children ages 8 and under will enjoy riding the ring with one of 11 ponies at the Enchanted Forest. A new stable area provides a country backdrop. The small park has a picnic area and bike and jogging trails. These ponies are available for parties, too.

□ Tropical Park Equestrian Center
7900 SW 40th Street, Miami 33155. (305) 554-7334.

See year-round shows for all breeds and classes of horses. The shows are usually held on the weekends and are free of charge. Call for a schedule.

□ Valmaron Equestrian Center
16891 Jupiter Farms Road, Jupiter Farms 33478. (Go west on Indiantown Road to Jupiter Farms Road. Valmaron is about 1¼ miles on right.) (407) 746-8229. Shows take place second Sunday of every month at 8:30 A.M.

A nice drive in the country will take you to Valmaron Country Store and Equestrian Center. There are small bleachers to sit on, and you can get a snack and watch the show from the deck of the Country Store. Inquire about classes for beginners and up. Parking is available behind the Valmaron Country Store under the trees.

□ Vinceremos Riding Center, Inc.
8765 Lake Worth Road (one mile west of Florida Turnpike), Lake Worth 33467. (407) 433-5800.

Sitting in the saddle wearing jockey silks is thrilling for children of all ages.

Fully accredited by the North American Riding for Handicapped Association, Vinceremos provides riding therapy for people with disabilities and special needs. Horses are specially selected and trained for this purpose. The programs teach riding skills and help students meet therapeutic goals by working on balance, muscle tone, posture, coordination, confidence, and concentration. A professional recreation therapist and certified riding instructor develop individual therapy plans for each student.

Ice Skating

□ Lighthouse Point Ice Skating Arena
4601 North Federal Highway, Pompano Beach 33064. (Located almost a mile north of Sample Road on Federal Highway.) (305) 943-1437. Open daily, hours vary. $4 to $5; skate rental, $1.50.

Dress warmly (it's about 50 degrees rinkside) and think winter when you visit this skating facility. Competitions and ice shows are held periodically throughout the year. For small children, try the "Tiny Tots" class on Saturday mornings.

□ Scott Rakow Youth Center Ice Rink
2700 Sheridan Avenue, Miami Beach 33140. (305) 673-7767. Call for schedule information. Miami Beach residents, $1.50; nonresidents, $3. Skate rental, $1.50.

Children in grades 4 through 12 can get a feel for the ice at this neighborhood youth center. Group and private lessons are available.

□ Sunrise Ice Skating Center
3363 Pine Island Road, Sunrise (south of Oakland Park Boulevard and west of University Drive). (305) 741-2366. Hours vary with sessions. $5.50 (includes skates).

Sunrise offers special family-discount nights, classes for all ages, and occasional spectator events, such as hockey games.

Roller Skating

□ Hot Wheels
12265 SW 112th Street (Devon-Aire Shopping Center), Miami. Hotline, (305) 595-3200; information, 595-2958. Call for schedule information. Admission, $5.25; shoes, 75¢.

Special scheduled events include tot skates, family skates, all-day skates, Christian music night, rock night, and sleep-overs. The facility is available for party rentals. **Tip:** Smallest shoe size is a child's size 8. For more information, see listing in "Celebrate in Style."

□ Roller Skating Center of Coral Springs
2100 University Drive, Coral Springs 33071. (305) 755-0011. Hours, cost vary depending on sessions. $1 skate rental.

A popular spot for the whole family, and a big hit for birthdays, this skating rink offers family discount night, tiny tot classes, all-day skates, and more. Inquire about special group rates for schools, camps, and religious organizations. For party information, see listing in "Celebrate in Style."

□ The Palace
6016 Old Congress Road (one mile west of I-95), Lantana. (407) 967-0311. Hours, cost ($3-$5) vary depending on sessions.

This popular spot hosts lots of special events. Private party rooms are available when you have your birthday bash here. Twins' nights, two-for-one nights, and family nights are great fun. For party information, see listing in "Celebrate in Style."

□ The Skating Center
255 NE Second Drive (off U.S. 1, just south of Campbell Drive), Homestead. (305) 246-0737. Call for schedule information. Cost ranges from $2 to $5, depending on sessions. Free skate rental; speedskates $2.

The Skating Center hosts special events, family skates, all-day skates, and children's sessions on Saturday mornings. Call for more information.

Sailing

◻ Coconut Grove Sailing Club
2990 South Bayshore Drive, Coconut Grove 33133. (305) 444-4571.
Monday through Friday, 10 A.M.–3 P.M. Booklet, $2.50; classes are free.

A Junior Pram program for children ages 9 to 12 offers free beginner lessons for kids who live in Miami. The week-long summer sessions teach children the essentials of sailing: tacking, water safety, general handling of the boat, basic seamanship, and rigging and unrigging. Sign up fast, because this popular summer class fills up in a hurry. If you don't get in, however, don't lose heart—this same beginners' class is available on weekends during the school year. The spring break program is also popular.

Swimming

◻ International Swimming Hall of Fame Pool
501 Seabreeze Boulevard (located one block west of the beach and one block south of Las Olas Boulevard), Fort Lauderdale 33316. (305) 523-0994.

The Hall of Fame Pool is open to the public daily, except during special swimming events and competitions. Many types of classes are offered, from infant water orientation to synchronized swimming. Summer camps are also offered. Call for a complete schedule.

◻ Mission Bay Aquatic Training Center
10333 Diego Drive South (441 and Glades Road), Boca Raton 33428. (407) 488-2001.

This state-of-the-art facility has two 50-meter Olympic pools and a diving well with five platforms. The highly experienced coaches give group and private lessons for children ages 6 months and up. Diving lessons, Saturday morning swim leagues, and group and private swimming and diving lessons for the handicapped are also offered at Mission Bay.

◻ University of Miami
One Hurricane Drive, Coral Gables 33146. (305) 284-3593. Half-hour private lessons daily for a week begin at $100.

For 40 years University of Miami swim coach Jack Nelson, a former Olympic coach, has been providing swim lessons to Miami's youngsters. Together with his staff of coaches from around the world, Nelson has created a top-notch program. Classes are held in the university pool or in your pool at home. Group and private lessons are available and are recommended for children ages 1 and up.

During the summer, UM hosts a swim camp for children ages 2 to 7. It is available three times a week in the afternoons and is primarily a confidence builder (or "organized chaos!") for small children.

□ Venetian Pool

2701 DeSoto Boulevard, Coral Gables 33134. (305) 442-6483. Weekdays (June through August): Monday through Friday, 11 A.M.–7:30 P.M.; weekdays (September, October, April, and May): Tuesday through Friday, 11 A.M.–5:30 P.M.; weekdays (November through March): Tuesday through Friday, 11 A.M.–4:30 P.M.; weekends (throughout year): 10 A.M.–4:30 P.M. Adult residents, $1.72; adult nonresidents, $2.88; children ages 12 and younger, $1.15. Call for updated class schedules and fees.

Kids will feel they're in another world when they swim here. Nearly $2.5 million was spent in 1989 to totally restore this historic gem listed in the National Register of Historic Places. The pool was carved from a rock quarry in the late '20s. The original coral architecture that was popular back then can still be seen. Swimming lessons for ages 5 and above are offered by the Venetian Aquatic Club during the summer months. Call for information. **Tip:** Accessible to handicapped. For party information, see listing in "Celebrate in Style."

Exploring Science and Nature

Children are fascinated with the world around them. By studying our earth's natural beauty, as it is revealed in botanical gardens, bodies of water, and tropical hammocks, we can see how our ancestors once lived off the land and used its resources to survive. By exploring the world beyond us—the stars, planets, and weather conditions—we can tap a child's imagination and curiosity. By observing the creatures that share our globe—mammals, reptiles, amphibians—we can learn about ourselves. By delving into our world each and every day, whether through a walk in our backyards or an afternoon in a museum, we can help our children create dreams—and hopefully, someday, fulfill them.

Dade County

□ Environmental Center
Miami Dade Community College South Campus, 11011 SW 104th Street (West Perimeter Road, opposite baseball diamond), Miami 33176. (305) 596-4113. Monday through Friday, 9 A.M.–4:30 P.M.

The Environmental Center was founded in 1977 in an effort to provide educational opportunities to the public. The children's programs focus on small critter care and hands-on science activities. Classes are recommended for children ages 5 and up and emphasize respect for the environment. A summer camp program is held annually and gives kids a chance to participate in nature-oriented activities in an outdoor suburban wilderness.

□ Fairchild Tropical Gardens
10901 Old Cutler Road, Miami 33156. (305) 667-1651. Monday through Sunday, 9:30 A.M.–4:30 P.M.; closed Christmas. Café open Saturday and Sunday, September through May, 10 A.M.–3 P.M. Adults, $4; children under 13 free when accompanied by an adult. Forty-minute, narrated tram rides: adults, $1; children, 50¢. Guided walking tours are free. Annual memberships available; personal checks accepted.

Walking the grounds of this botanical paradise is a peaceful and educational way to spend a day. There are over 5,000 plants from around the world here, with the various species labeled for easy identification. Its 83 acres make it the largest garden of its kind in the continental United States. Children may touch the plants, feel the trees, and smell the flowers, but remind youngsters not to pick or collect them.

The paved trail that winds around 11 lakes makes for a great stroller path, but keep on your toes—alligators inhabit some of the waters. Remind children not to approach or feed any wildlife.

For a lunch or snack break, visit the Rain Forest Café (see beginning of listing for hours). Sandwiches, hot dogs, salads, desserts, and beverages (including juices) make up the menu. Food is restricted to this area and no picnicking is allowed. However, you may wish to eat at an outdoor table here and enjoy the view from under a sprawling tree! Vending machines are nearby also.

The best time to visit is during the winter months, when the weather is beautiful and many of the tropical and subtropical plants are in bloom. The Garden's annual Ramble, held the first weekend in December, is a must.
Tips: Management reminds us that the Gardens are not a playground or park—please do not allow children to run freely without supervision. Wear sturdy walking shoes. Book shop sells souvenirs and nature video cassettes. For more information on the Ramble, see listing in "Mark Your Calendar."

☐ Miami Beach Garden and Conservatory
2000 Convention Center Drive, Miami Beach 33139. (Take MacArthur Causeway; turn north on Alton Road, then right on 17th Street; turn left at Meridian Avenue; go north to 20th Street, where you'll see the signs.) (305) 673-7720. Daily, 10 A.M.–3:30 P.M. Free admission.

This is a small but beautiful collection of exotic earth and air plants (a plant that grows on another) found around South Florida. There is a 32-foot-high domed conservatory that always fascinates children. "Take time to smell the roses" in the American Rose Garden, and look at the miniatures in the authentic Japanese Garden.

☐ Miami Museum of Science and Space Transit Planetarium
3280 South Miami Avenue, Miami 33129. (Across from Vizcaya—take I-95 south to exit 1 and follow signs to Museum/Planetarium, or ride Metrorail to Vizcaya Station.) (305) 854-4247; Cosmic Hotline, 854-2222. Daily, 10 A.M.–6 P.M.; closed Thanksgiving and Christmas. Museum: adults, $4; senior citizens and children ages 3 to 12, $2.50. Planetarium: adults, $5;

senior citizens and children ages 3 to 12, $2.50; Thursday nights, free. Combination tickets: adults, $7; senior citizens and children, $4. Annual memberships available. AE, MC, V accepted in Museum gift shop only.

Take a spin on the "Momentum Machine," yell into the "Echo Tube," and visit an active beehive. Within the museum, there are 125 exhibits that focus on the ecology of South Florida, the structure and function of the human body, the patterns of light and sound, and natural history. Children will enjoy participating first-hand in these exhibits by pushing buttons, pulling strings, or turning dials, and then watching what happens. They'll also want to visit the exciting special exhibitions that are presented several times during the year.

The Collection Gallery is also interesting to kids. They can see petrified wood, butterfly species, ostrich eggs, and the skull of a killer whale. Open one of the "pull-out" drawers to find a surprise!

The Wildlife Center, on an acre of land outside the museum, focuses on wildlife rehabilitation and environmental issues. There are 13 exhibits to study, including some that feature owls, eagles, lizards, snakes, and tortoises. Question-and-answer signs are posted throughout the area, making this a fun and educational adventure.

The Planetarium is a 65-foot dome where learning about the night sky and space science is fun. View the heavens in 3-D and learn about the moon, planets, star clusters, and nebulae. Star-gazing on Thursday nights is free at the Planetarium.

There are plenty of reasons to visit the museum, so you may want to consider a family membership. Classes are available for children from preschool to high school ages, ranging from computer labs to holiday, summer, and overnight camps. **Tips:** Hot dog stand, vending machines, and picnic tables available. Gift shop sells film and unique science-related toys and games. Best times to visit are afternoons and holidays. For party information, see listing in "Celebrate in Sytle."

☐ **National Hurricane Center**
1320 South Dixie Highway, Coral Gables 33146. (305) 666-4612. Call Monday through Friday, 8 A.M.–4:30 P.M., to schedule tours. Free admission.

Learn how to track hurricanes and see a film about these devastating storms at the National Hurricane Center. Recommended for children in grades 6 and up, a standard tour includes a film or slide show about hurricanes, and a view of the operational area and satellite equipment. Tours usually last an hour and are geared for groups of 35 or less. Please note that tours may be cancelled at the last minute due to inclement weather conditions.

□ **Naturalist Services**
Dade County Park and Recreation Department, A.D. Barnes Park, 3701 SW 70th Avenue, Miami 33155. (305) 662-4124.

There are many opportunities for children to learn about nature and wildlife through the parks system. Call for information packets that tell about classes, workshops, nature walks, and more. Topics often include Florida's natural history, Indian culture, ecosystems, and marine life.

□ **Preston B. Bird and Mary Heinlein Fruit and Spice Park**
14801 SW 187th Avenue, Homestead 33031. (Thirty-five miles south of Miami; take Florida Turnpike or U.S. 1 to SW 248th Street and head west.) (305) 247-5727. Daily, 10 A.M.–5 P.M. Free admission. Tours on Saturdays and Sundays, 1 and 3 P.M.: adults, $1; children under 12, 50¢; minimum charge of $12 for weekday tours. Group tours are available by reservation only. Guidebook, $1.50.

The only park of its kind in the United States, the Fruit and Spice Park abounds with over 500 varieties of fruits, spices, herbs, vegetables, and nuts from around the world. Some of the more unusual fruits to look for include the Panama Candle Tree and the Star Fruit.

Fruit cannot be removed from the park; however if you'd like to identify and eat a fallen sample, ask park personnel to help. Adults can make special arrangements for collecting seeds and cuttings, or get advice on what to plant in the family garden.

Visit the Redland Fruit Store on your way into the park for interesting tips, or browse for a unique gift for Grandma, like canned fruits, jams and jellies, spices, or a unique cookbook. While there, pick up a copy of *A Pioneer History of the Fruit and Spice Park,* which gives a detailed account of how this park came into existence. It is part of the Redland Historic District.

Tours of the 20-acre park are held on weekends or by special request during the week. School tours are available for preschoolers and older, and can be specifically designed to coordinate with the students' courses. All tours include taste samples, as well as touching and smelling when appropriate. There is a nominal fee, so call for reservations and detailed information. Classes and workshops are also available.

*A tour of the Fruit and Spice Park gives
children a chance to touch and smell
native tropical trees and their fruit.*

Each January you will want to visit the park during the Redlands Natural Arts Festival held here; it's fun for the entire family. **Tips:** Children should wear closed-toed shoes. Although there is an abundance of shade, remember the sunscreen. Visit any time of year, as there's always something "fruiting." Drinking fountains, picnic area, and gift shop with souvenirs are available. For more information on special events, see listing in "Mark Your Calendar."

☐ Southern Cross Astronomical Society, Inc.
(305) 661-1375. Student membership, $20; Family, $32.

The Southern Cross Astronomical Society, founded in 1922, is one of the largest amateur astronomical organizations in the U.S. This society has free public telescope observations most Saturday evenings from 8 to 10 P.M. at the Old Cutler Hammock Nature Center (SW 176th Street and 79th Avenue.) The hammock area provides the darkest observing sky closest to downtown Miami, so you will be able to catch a glimpse of planets, constellations, and galaxies (weather permitting). Although telescopes are provided, you may want to bring your own, along with binoculars, lawn chairs, protective clothing, and bug repellant.

On Sundays from 11 A.M. to 2 P.M. meet at the Metrozoo (12400 SW 152nd Street) to get a view of activity on the sun's surface. (You will be protected by special filters which filter out dangerous rays.)

Call for more information about meetings, classes, and special events for children and adults. Southern Cross is a nonprofit organization. For more information and directions to the Old Cutler Hammock, see listing in "Under the Sun."

☐ Trade-In Sam's Recycling Center
8500 SW 107th Avenue (just north of Kendall Indian Hammocks Park), Miami. (305) 279-4890. Tuesday through Saturday, 9 A.M.–5 P.M.

Did you know that recycling one ton of paper will save 17 trees? That plastic milk containers can be made into sleeping bags? New Florida state legislation includes a 1994 deadline for the recycling of 30 percent of municipal trash, so let's all pitch in now. A trip to Sam's is a nice way to introduce recycling to children, and the people working here are always full of interesting facts about the recycling process. Sam's will accept newspapers, aluminum cans, plastic beverage bottles, glass containers, and cardboard.

For more information on recycling call the Dade County Solid Waste Management Department, (305) 375-3997; Broward County Office of Environmental Services, (305) 978-1135; or Solid Waste Authority of Palm Beach County, (407) 471-5770.

☐ Tropical Audubon Society
5530 Sunset Drive, Miami 33143. (305) 666-5111. Open weekdays, 9 A.M.–2 P.M.

For many years the Audubon Society has given us an opportunity to learn about and appreciate the world around us by taking a closer look at nature and wildlife. Headquartered in the historic Arden Hayes "Doc" Thomas House in South Miami, this environmental education center has been designated a wildlife sanctuary. Presentations are offered periodically to bring the natural environment to the public. Some of the "stars" of their programs include a great horned owl, an American crocodile, a red-tailed hawk, and a gopher tortoise.

Included in the center is an outdoor amphitheater for environmental programs, a campfire circle, a specialized library, an Indian chickee hut with picnic tables, a kitchen, barbecue facilities, and a restroom area. During the week the grounds are open to the public for picnicking, birdwatching, or touring the building. The wildlife area is closed. For more information, see listing in "Celebrate in Style" and "Mark Your Calendar."

Broward County

□ Buehler Planetarium
Broward Community College, Central Campus, 3501 SW Davie Road, Davie 33314. (305) 475-6680. Call for times and prices of shows.

Buehler Planetarium was built in 1966, but has recently been renovated and now contains a modern star projector and a sophisticated computerized automation system. Located at Broward Community College, the planetarium uses its state-of-the-art equipment to explore outer space, and offers shows and astronomy programs to children and adults.

In addition to six public shows each week, the planetarium has programs geared for children ages 4 to 11, and school shows during the week for children in grades 3 and up. A mobile astronomy program that travels to schools and organizations provides young audiences (pre-kindergarten through second grade) a look at our universe. Reservations are a must, so call for details and cost information.

The public can also visit the observatory and use telescopes on Friday and Saturday evenings to gaze at the moon, stars, planets, galaxies, and other celestial objects. Be sure to stop by the Sky Theatre as well, where short multimedia presentations give you insight into astronomy and space-science topics. **Tips:** Shows last approximately one hour. Stroller and wheelchair access provided.

□ The Discovery Center
231 SW Second Avenue, Fort Lauderdale 33301. (Located on the New River

*in downtown area. From I-95 go east on Broward Boulevard. Turn south on
SW 2nd Avenue, go two blocks.) (305) 462-4115. September through May:
Tuesday through Friday, noon–5 P.M.; June through August: Tuesday
through Friday, 10 A.M.–5 P.M.; Saturday, 10 A.M.–5 P.M.; Sunday, noon–5
P.M. Adults and children over age 3, $3; children under 3, free; seniors,
$2.50. AE, MC, V accepted for memberships and in museum store.*

The Discovery Center is located in one of the area's historic buildings and
offers kids of all ages, as well as their parents, hands-on educational
experiences in science, art, and history, the specialties of this three-story
museum. Try your hand at laser games and visit a computer lab. Study
beehives and anthills, baffle your mind with optical illusions, and try
tackling some mathematical puzzlers. Ask about classes while you're here,
and stop by the museum's Explore Store for a souvenir (a museum-related
book, game, star chart, science kit, or puzzle). **Tips:** Stroller and wheelchair
access on first floor only. Public park outside. Parking is available on SW
2nd Avenue and in the city parking garage nearby. For party information,
see listing in "Celebrate in Style."

□ Spyke's Grove and Tropical Gardens
*7250 Griffin Road (west of Davie Road), Davie 33314. (Two miles west of
US 441, 1/2 mile east of University Drive.) (800) 327-9713. Daily (October
through July), 9 A.M.–5:30 P.M. Closed August and September. Tours
available. Admission is free.*

Take a tram through working citrus groves and see such favorites as orange,
grapefruit, tangelo, tangerine, lemon, and lime trees. Visit a small zoo on
the grounds, which is home to a raccoon, a skunk, alligators, goats,
peacocks, and a Himalayan black bear. Spyke's, in business since 1945,
ships fruit and gifts all over the country, so check out the gift shop for
special things like jellies and candies. Free samples of fruits and drinks are
also available. For 25 cents you can drink all the fresh-squeezed OJ you
want. Then take a seat in the garden for a nice rest! **Tip:** Plan to spend one
hour to tour. Call ahead for tram schedule.

Palm Beach County

□ Arthur R. Marshall Loxahatchee National Wildlife Refuge
*State Route 7, Boynton Beach. (U.S. 441 between Boynton Boulevard and
Atlantic Avenue—central entrance is approximately 13 miles north of Palm
Beach/Broward county line, 14 miles from the Atlantic and on the fringe of
the Everglades.) Mailing address is Route 1, Box 278, Boynton Beach 33437.
(407) 734-8303; concessionaire, 426-2474. Refuge: daily, 6 A.M.–sundown;*

Visitors' Center: weekdays, 9 A.M.–4 P.M.; weekends, 9 A.M.–4:30 P.M. Closed on Mondays and Tuesdays during the summer. Cars, $3; pedestrians, $1.

Loxahatchee Wildlife Refuge is a 146,000-acre segment of the Everglades. The park's boundaries create a haven for rare and endangered species, such as the Florida panther and the bald eagle. Over 250 species of birds have been identified here as well.

If you stop by the visitors' center you can request to see a short slide show about the area. There's also a display of animals, birds, and Everglades trivia.

The concessions area offers boat and fishing rentals and airboat rides. Note that picnicking is not encouraged on the refuge grounds.

□ **Blood's Hammock Groves, Inc.**
4549 Linton Boulevard (one mile west of I-95 on Old Germantown Road), Delray Beach 33447-2106. (407) 498-3400 or (800) 255-5188. Open November to May, Monday through Saturday, 8:30 A.M.–5 P.M.; closed Sunday.

Blood's has been in the fruit business since 1949. Whether you're in the mood for some freshly squeezed OJ or want to impress your northern friends by sending them some of the best Florida citrus, Blood's is always a fun stop.

Walk beyond the display room to an observation deck and watch the fruits come in from the field; they're washed, waxed, dried, polished, and graded here. See some of the orchard and sample some of the fresh varieties of fruit. There's also a vegetable and flower stand on the premises.

□ **Children's Museum of Juno Beach**
1200 U.S. Highway 1 (in Loggerhead Park), Juno Beach 33408. (407) 627-8280. Tuesday through Saturday, 10 A.M.–3 P.M. Closed Sunday and Monday. Free admission, but donations are appreciated.

What a great find! This museum, inspired by Eleanor M. Fletcher (the Turtle Lady of Juno Beach), is devoted to the conservation of Florida nature and wildlife. The focus of the museum's work is on rehabilitating endangered sea turtles.

The museum, located in Loggerhead Park, has a few exhibit rooms that house marine aquariums and hands-on table displays—an especially interesting exhibit shows the life stages of seashells! But perhaps the most unique feature of the museum is outside, where you can observe sea turtles

The Children's Museum of Juno Beach helps children to appreciate the plight of the endangered Loggerhead sea turtles.

of various sizes and ages as they swim in huge touch tanks. The baby turtles are fun to watch as they swim around the tanks, while the older and larger ones show off their interesting shell and head features.

A nice resource library is found within the museum. Field trips are popular, and "Turtle Watches" in the summer allow visitors to observe nesting habits. An underground tunnel goes to the beach—just a short walk from the museum. For park information, see listing in "Under the Sun."

□ Gumbo Limbo Nature Center
1801 North Ocean Boulevard (one mile north of Palmetto Park Road on Route A1A), Boca Raton 33432. (407) 338-1473. Monday through Saturday, 9 A.M.–4 P.M.; closed Sunday. Free tours on Saturdays at 10 A.M. and 2 P.M. Free admission. Memberships available.

Named after a red, peeling-barked tree found in this area, the Gumbo Limbo Nature Center consists of 15 acres of well-preserved woods located in Red Reef Park on a barrier island between the Atlantic Ocean and the Intracoastal waterway. The land is similar to what the first pioneers encountered when they settled on the southeastern shores of Florida. A number of mammals, reptiles, birds, and fish can be found within the area's boundaries. Be on the lookout for sea turtles, osprey, manatees, and brown pelicans.

The nature center houses a display of sea turtles, snakes, birds, and other creatures. You'll also find a collection of shells, sponges, corals, and sea beans that can be found on southern beaches. **Tips:** Plan to spend one hour to tour. Drinking fountains, gift shop, and restrooms available.

□ **Mounts Botanical Gardens**
531 North Military Trail (between Southern Boulevard and Belvedere), West Palm Beach 33415-1395. (407) 233-1749. Monday through Saturday, 8:30 A.M.–5 P.M.; Sunday, 1–5 P.M. Guided tours on Sundays at 2:30 P.M. Free admission.

A picturesque 14-acre botanical garden, Mounts features tropical and subtropical plants, a fern house, and a rain forest. Take a self-guided tour at your leisure, or join the staff for a Sunday afternoon walk. The poisonous plant area and herb garden will be interesting to young children. Please note that this is not a park facility. **Tips:** Stroller and wheelchair accessible. Picnic tables, drinking fountains, and restrooms available. Located across the street from an airport, so children will enjoy watching airplanes fly above them.

□ **South Florida Science Museum and Planetarium**
4801 Dreher Trail North, West Palm Beach 33405. (407) 832-1988. Daily, 10 A.M.-5 P.M.; Planetarium show: weekdays, 3 P.M.; weekends, 1 and 3 P.M. Adults, $4; seniors, $2.50; children, $1.50; children under 4, free. Planetarium: $1; children under 4, free. Annual memberships available.

This museum contains permanent and temporary exhibits on natural history. Kids can participate in hands-on activities that give insight into the world of space and motion, study a South Florida aquarium, adventure through a snake room, or try to outsmart a computer in a computer arcade. An Everglades display is popular and includes a small alligator, an aquatic-creature touch tank, and a native-plant learning center. The laser shows at the planetarium are always fun! **Tips:** Best times to come for this 90-minute tour are in the afternoons, Friday evenings, or weekends. Be prompt for the planetarium shows. Picnic facilities available.

Monroe County

□ Key West Aquarium
One Whitehead Street, Mallory Square, Key West. (305) 296-2051. Daily, 10 A.M.–7 P.M.; tours at 11 A.M., noon, 1, 2, 3, and 4:30 P.M. Adults, $5; children ages 8 to 15, $2.50; children ages 7 and under, free. Private and group tours available.

Big and little kids will be able to get up-close to view sea creatures in over 40 aquariums of different sizes and shapes. There's a 30,000-gallon aquarium that contains barracuda, grouper, snapper, tarpin, and sea turtles. The touch tank has new creatures daily; children are always interested in the starfish, conchs, snails, and horseshore crabs. Watch as the aquarium staff feed the stingrays, sea turtles, and sharks. If you dare, they'll let you pet a baby shark!

□ Key West Hurricane Museum
201 William Street (at corner of Caroline Street, 3 blocks east of Duval), Key West 33040. (305) 294-7522. Daily, 10 A.M.–6 P.M. Adults, $3.50; children under 12, free.

Learn about hurricanes and weather by seeing photos and documents of the history of storms (the first recorded hurricane was the 1935 "Labor Day Hurricane"). Discover the difference between a hurricane and a tornado; learn how hurricanes get named, and how they are tracked. See photos and a videotape taken from the Yucatan Peninsula of the devastating Hurricane Gilbert of 1988. Take a hurricane quiz, and create your own tornado with sand.

□ Lignumvitae State Botanical Site
Mailing address is P.O. Box 1052, Islamorada 33036. (Site is off U.S. Highway 1 near Islamorada.) (305) 664-4815. Tour boat leaves daily (except Tuesday and Wednesday) at 1:30 P.M. from the Indian Key Fill (Mile Marker 78.5) on U.S. Highway 1. Boat tours: adults, $5; children under 12, $2.50. Walking tours: adults, $1; children under 6, free.

Sit back and relax on this 30-minute boat ride to Lignumvitae. Thousands of years ago this island started out as a living coral reef; now you can walk through tropical hammocks and mangroves and learn about the island's vegetation and formation. Once on the island, you will take a two-hour walking tour, so be sure to wear proper shoes and bring insect repellant. **Tip:** No wheelchair access provided.

□ Looe Key National Marine Sanctuary
Mile Marker 30, Big Pine Key. Mailing address is Route 1, Box 782, Big Pine Key 33043. (305) 872-4039.

In 1981, Looe Key, located five miles offshore, was declared a National Marine Sanctuary. Fishing, snorkeling, and swimming are popular here, with water being extremely clear and very shallow in areas. Brightly colored fish and coral reefs can be easily seen, and snorkeling equipment is available for rent.

□ National Key Deer Refuge
Mile Marker 31.5 (take Key Deer Boulevard to Watson Boulevard), Big Pine Key. (305) 872-2239.

Key deer, the smallest species of white-tailed deer in existence, make their home within the refuge. Only 250 of these deer, all living here, exist in the world; they are considered an endangered species. When fully grown, the deer stand about two feet high at the shoulder, and weigh about 65 to 75 pounds.

A man-made fresh-water lake and nature trail are open to the public and allow a unique opportunity to view the deer and other wildlife that live here, such as the alligators and the great white heron.

□ Riggs Wildlife Refuge
Near International Airport and South Roosevelt Boulevard, Key West. (305) 294-2116.

Birdwatchers will find a variety of heron, egrets, ibis, and osprey to observe here, as well as many types of fish in Salt Pond. An 80-foot observation deck offers a good view of the refuge area. **Tip:** If the gate is locked, please call the above phone number for the combination.

Everglades National Park

There's no place like it in the world. It has a mixture of 1.4 million acres of land and water, and is the second largest national park in the United States, outside of Alaska. It is made up of pine forests, dense subtropical hammocks, tree islands, mangroves, sawgrass prairies, and swamp. It is the Everglades, with a subtropical beauty all its own, that is home to 11 endangered wildlife species and more mosquitoes than possibly anywhere else in the world.

Twenty-five native mammals, over 300 bird species, and 60 reptiles (including 23 snake varieties) live within the Everglades' boundaries. They roam here naturally and freely. Feeding them is dangerous and is prohibited by law. Possibly the most noted creature of this part of Florida is the alligator, a quick and unpredictable fellow. He can move with amazing speed, so remind your children to keep their distance.

From mid-December to mid-April all the activity centers are busy and crowded. In the summer, when it's hot, humid, and full of mosquitoes, weather is very unpredictable, with heavy rains and lightning storms popping up out of nowhere. Come with a full tank of gas, drinks, and suitable wading clothes (loose-fitting, long-sleeved shirts and long pants) that will also protect you from the biting bugs.

Swimming in the Everglades is not encouraged. Fresh water ponds have alligators and poisonous snakes living in them, while saltwater areas are often shallow, muddy, and home to many sharks and barracudas.

Always call ahead when planning your trip. If you call weeks in advance, ask for a newsletter or park brochure. There's some very good information at the park's offices. Also, remember to verify the centers' hours before coming—they may vary during the tourist season.

Main Park Visitor Center

Mailing address is P.O. Box 279, Homestead 33030. (Located approximately 10 miles southwest of Florida City on State Road 9336.) (305) 247-6211. Daily, 8 A.M.–5 P.M. Private motor vehicles (car, van, motorcycle), $5; commercial vehicles (bus), pedestrians or bikes, $2 (for ages 16 or older). Golden Access, Golden Age, and Golden Eagle passes accepted. Admission is good for seven days.

Stop by this visitor center for an orientation film, displays, and a schedule

No trip to South Florida would be complete without a chat with one of the local natives.

of activities and events. There's a nice bookstore here with excellent reference material for children and adults.

Royal Palm

Inside park, take first left at State Road 9336 Extension. Visitors center, (305) 247-6211, ext. 246. Open daily, 8 A.M.–4:30 P.M.

□ **Hikes**
Wet or dry hikes, three-hour walking tours that take you through the various land personalities of the Everglades, are planned periodically. The popular Anhinga Trail lets you see alligators, snakes, birds, and fish below in the Taylor Slough from a boardwalk. Wear shoes, long pants, and mosquito repellant! Call ahead—there's a limit to the number of people who can participate.

□ **Campfire Program**
This 45-minute session with a park ranger is fun for everyone. Meet at the Long Pine Key Campground Amphitheater at 7:30 P.M., Tuesdays through Sundays, for a discussion under the stars. Topics include wildlife, plants, and ecology.

Flamingo

Thirty-eight miles southwest of the main entrance. Mailing address for Flamingo Lodge, Marina, and Outpost Resort is Box 428, Flamingo 33030. (305) 253-2241.

This is the southernmost point of the park that is accessible by car. A motel, swimming pool, restaurant, gift shop, store, cruises, tram tours, campsites, canoe rentals, fishing boats, and houseboats are all available.

□ Visitors Center

Here you'll find exhibits of the flora, fauna, and natural history of the area. Check the bulletin board for special weekly naturalist programs.

□ Camping

One of only two camping places in the Everglades (the other is at Long Key), Flamingo has 300 sites for trailers and tents, and an additional four sites for large groups. There is a shower facility, marina store, and amphitheater meeting place. Star-gazing at night might interest your youngsters, as there is no light pollution here—you are definitely in the wilderness! Bring your binoculars and celestial maps, and search for Orion, Scorpio, and the other constellations.

□ Walking Tour

At 7:30 A.M. on Saturdays, Sundays, and Wednesdays, a walking tour, led by a ranger, leaves from Eco Pond. You'll see ibis, alligators, and roseate spoonbills.

□ Canoeing

A half-day wilderness canoe trip leaves Fridays at 8:30 A.M. The trip is for children ages 6 and older, and previous canoeing experience is required. Please bring a packed lunch and beverage, as well as insect repellant. Reservations are needed; call (813) 695-3101. A shorter canoeing adventure is held on Sunday and Tuesday afternoons. The same rules apply as for the half-day trip.

Shark Valley

Tamiami Trail, about 40 miles west of Miami. (305) 221-8776; tram tours, 221-8455. Visitors' center open daily, 8:30 A.M.–5:15 P.M. Cars, $3; admission is good for seven days. Tram rides: adults, $5; children, $2.50.

A tram tour of the area, a two-hour trip that takes you to the heart of the Everglades, is available daily; times vary throughout the year, however, so call ahead for a schedule and weather conditions. You'll get off to stretch your legs at a 65-foot observation tower, where you'll be provided with a spectacular view.

☐ **Bike Tour**

On weekends Shark Valley rangers sponsor a 3½ hour, 15-mile bike tour through sawgrass prairies and hammocks that may be okay for durable children! Bring your own bikes and drinks, along with your own baby carrier if needed. Rental bikes are available on a first-come, first-serve basis. Don't forget your binoculars!

☐ **Nature Walk**

Meet a park ranger for a stroll along the Bobcat Trail—it lasts about a half-hour and you never know what you'll see! There is a taped cassette trail guide available. Ask at the information center for times.

☐ **Interpretive Center**

West of Shark Valley (23 miles) you'll be glad you found the Loop Road Interpretive Center. The drive is scenic and the reward is great! Children will enjoy a library set up just for them and learn lots from the displays about the Everglades. There's a nature trail through a hardwood hammock here, too.

Everglades City

Across U.S. 41 and 5 miles south on State Road 29; 80 miles west of Miami. (813) 695-2591.

□ **Boating**
Daily tours through the Ten Thousand Islands let you see wildlife deep in the Everglades. Canoe rentals, two cruises are available daily.

□ **Visitors Center**
Displays, maps, and information available.

Celebrate in Style

Whether you are planning a very special birthday celebration, an end-of-school party, a religious event, or just a special day, sometimes it's fun to go all out. This chapter will give you a few ideas of places to go and people who can to help plan your special occasion. Family parties at home give children wonderful memories, but sometimes a bit of a splash is more appropriate, so here goes!

Please keep in mind that some small children are afraid of costumed characters—be wise in your selection. Remember to call well in advance to get the date you want and to confirm package information and prices.

Dade County

☐ Actors' Playhouse Children's Theatre
SW 107th Avenue and Kendall Drive (in Kendall Mall), Miami 33183. (305) 595-0010. Cost starts at $5 per child; groups of 15 or more, $3.50 per child.

Throughout the year, the Actors' Playhouse performs delightful plays for children. There is no party room here, because the stage is where the action is. All guests will get preferred seating and the birthday child will be asked to come on stage to receive a T-shirt. There's a "no food" policy at the playhouse, but parents can make party plans at one of the restaurants in the mall. For more information about the playhouse, see listing in "Adventures in the Arts."

☐ The Ancient Spanish Monastery
16711 West Dixie Highway, North Miami Beach 33160. (305) 945-1461. Rentals start at $75.

This ancient building (the oldest in the Western Hemisphere) is a perfect backdrop for special occasions. You must see this facility to appreciate its beauty—it may be particularly nice for religious celebrations. You can rent a particular part of the monastery, such as the garden or chapel. For more information about the monastery, see listing in "Tracing the Past."

□ **Arch Creek Park**
1855 NE 135th Street, North Miami 33181. (305) 944-6111. $35 for chickee rental.

Parks are great places to have parties—this one is a bit more unusual than the average neighborhood park, as it contains artifacts that date back to prehistoric times. Have a scavenger hunt and nature tour in the woods here, then picnic (no grills, please) in a chickee hut that you can decorate with colorful balloons. Partygivers must provide food and beverages, but staff personnel are on hand to help hide your goodies for the scavenger hunt. If you'd like, have an Indian-theme party; children can make clay pottery similar to those made by the Tequesta Indians that inhabited the area thousands of years ago. Clay can be provided by the park, if requested, for an additional fee. For more information on the park, see listing in "Under the Sun."

□ **Beam Me Up**
Mailing address is P.O. Box 600442, North Miami Beach 33160-0442. (305) 940-7503.

Music and parties go hand in hand, so this idea is a natural for children ages 5 and up. Jill Ayn Schneider (a former educator) and Ricky Hitchcock (a British performer) bring their musical talents together to form a musical comedy duo that performs today's music for children. Styles include rock, blues, folk, and contemporary, for "when your children graduate from Raffi." Some of their original songs include "I've Got the Giggles," "Homework Blues," "Bubblegum Rap," and "I Am an Astronaut." Performances last approximately 30 to 45 minutes.

□ **ChildRead**
13629 South Dixie Highway, Suite 129 (in Colonial Palms Plaza), Miami 33176. (305) 378-8503. $25 per child, $5 per adult; 15-child minimum.

This quality book store for children hosts fun and educational parties. The setup, decorations, partyware, food, entertainment, and cleanup are all provided by the staff. (Invitations are included in the package, but parents have to mail them!) Just come and have a celebration you'll never forget. A hands-on activity appropriate for the birthday child's age, and a visit by a clown who paints faces, sings songs, reads stories, plays games, and provides balloons for the group are on the party schedule. The menu includes a pizza (by Roma's Italian Restaurant), a yogurt birthday pie (by I Can't Believe It's Yogurt!), and fruit juice. Remember to call at least two weeks in advance to make a reservation. For more store information, see "Bytes, Kites, and Toy Delights."

☐ Cowlicks and Curls Family Hairstyling Salon

Snapper Creek Plaza, 7166 SW 117th Avenue, Miami 33183, (305) 274-6695; Country Walk Plaza, 13709 SW 152nd Street, Miami 33186, (305) 253-7111. Cost starts at $15 per guest.

Plan a unique shampoo and style party for your child and his or her friends (recommended for children ages 5 and up). For $15 each, guests will have their hair shampooed, styled (the French braid is a popular one), and color-sprayed or gelled. Girls can also have their nails polished and receive a makeup lesson; boys may opt for a colored gel style. Children can roam around and watch as their friends are glamorized. A birthday banner is given to the birthday child, and Mom or Dad can come set up cake and goodies in a designated area.

☐ Dodge City

16330 SW 147th Avenue, Miami 33187. (305) 233-3500. Open daily. Call for prices.

In operation since 1965, Dodge City hosts parties and picnics on a four-acre ranch or at your home. Pony rides, mechanical rides, food, music, games, and hayrides are provided.

☐ Don Carter's Kendall Lanes

13600 North Kendall Drive, Miami 33186. (Other locations in Tamarac, Lantana, Sunrise, Okeechobee, and Boca Raton.) (305) 385-6160. Parties can be scheduled on Saturdays and Sundays, 1–3 P.M. Cost starts at $5 per child.

Parties include one hour of bowling and one hour of table time (eating). Food packages are available at the concession stand, or you can bring your own. For more information about the lanes, see listing in "On Your Mark, Get Set, Go!"

☐ Douglas Park

2755 SW 37th Avenue, Miami 33134. (305) 442-0374. Call for costs and rental information.

If your birthday child likes to play make-believe, he or she will love this park, as it has an extra-special feature—a wooden castle where princesses and princes have been seen on occasion! This is a very popular park, so make reservations at least one month in advance. For a description of the park, see listing in "Under the Sun."

☐ **Florida Gold Coast Railroad Museum**
12450 SW 152nd Street, Miami 33177. (305) 253-0063. $10 reservation and setup fee; $4.25 per adult; $2.25 per child (25% discount for groups of 20 or more).

All aboard! For a railroad theme, try this attraction for your next party. Kids get a 30-minute ride on a diesel locomotive and a tour of the museum. Tables are available, but parents need to provide the refreshments. For more information, see listing in "Tracing the Past."

☐ **Gymboree**
914 Alfonso Avenue, Coral Gables 33146. (This is the main office; additional locations in Miami and other counties.) (305) 284-8295. $125 for 90 minutes.

Gymboree, known around the world for its parent-child exercise programs, offers children 40 pieces of "tyke-sized" equipment to jump, climb, slide, and crawl on. A trained teacher is on hand to supervise and organize the party, which also includes singing and playing games. Parties are limited to 20 guests under the age of 5. For an additional charge, "Gymbo the Clown" will come for picture-taking and a puppet show. Moms and dads must supply refreshments and cake.

☐ **HMS *Bounty***
401 Biscayne Boulevard (docked at south end of Bayside Marketplace), Miami 33132. (305) 375-0486. Boat rental begins at $265.

For a pirate theme, try this on for size! You can get exclusive use of this famous boat for 90 minutes. Begin with a tour that gives the young guests some hands-on experience (raise the anchors, mate!). Food time is next, with mom or dad bringing aboard the pizza or cake and other refreshments. Then it's on to the upper deck for a real pirate show, a sword fight, and a magic demonstration. For more information about the ship, see listing in "On Safari in South Florida."

☐ **Hot Wheels**
12265 SW 112th Street (Devon-Aire Shopping Center), Miami. (305) 595-3200. $6–$7 for minimum of 10 children.

Youngsters will enjoy a pirate theme
birthday party aboard the HMS Bounty.

If roller skating is your child's delight, he or she will love this fun idea. Choose from Standard and Deluxe party packages: both parties come with printed invitations, admission and skate rental, food and beverages, decorations, party favors, a personal party hostess, and a gift for the birthday child. The Deluxe package offers a choice of foods, popcorn, tokens for the video arcade, and a deluxe gift for the birthday child. Birthday cakes are also available upon request. For more information, see listing in "On Your Mark, Get Set, Go!"

☐ **Kids Haircut Station II**
11276 SW 137th Avenue (Calusa Crossing Shopping Center), Miami. (305) 382-6504. $13 for girls, $12 for boys.

This hair-styling party package also includes manicures, make-up and hair glitter, balloons, photographs of the group (12 are provided), lollipops, and a gift to each child. Tables and chairs are supplied, so be sure to bring the birthday cake!

☐ Kids on Board
10201 Hammocks Boulevard, Miami 33196. (305) 386-0155. Cost starts at $150 for 12 children; call for information.

The creators of the "Sweet Shop" game provide entertainment at parties for children ages 3 to 8. Children become playing pieces on a life-sized board game in which everyone wins. Kids on Board also provides invitations, balloons, goody bags, games, and a T-shirt for the birthday child.

☐ The Little Farm
16630 SW 234th Street, Homestead 33031. (305) 245-0588. Cost is based on distance traveled and duration of party.

This hands-on traveling farm will come to your home with their goats, ducks, chickens, sheep, pigs, rabbits, turkeys, and geese. Children may hold and touch these friendly animals. **Tip:** Animal pens are wheelchair accessible.

☐ Locomotion Children's Theatre
Mailing address is P.O. Box 161392, Miami 33116-1392. (305) 382-3246.

Dubbed the "Fantastic Fun Traveling Show," this children's theater is a treat for any special occasion. The theater's main mission is to entertain your children and stimulate their imaginations through songs, dances, stories, and games in which children themselves can participate. All performances are done on a "Magic Gameboard"—a large (14 feet square), colorful gameboard that creates a stage or focal point for the audience. The show can be performed indoors or outdoors at your home, school, park, or actually *anywhere!* The birthday child will receive a special T-shirt in addition to lots of fond memories. Performances run 20 to 60 minutes and are appropriate for children ages 3 to 10.

"Kiddie-Grams," in which a singing messenger entertains your child for approximately 20 minutes, are also available through Locomotion Children's Theatre. Again, stories, songs, and games are presented in a way that encourages your young one's participation (recommended for children ages 3 to 6.) For more information, see listing in "Adventures in the Arts."

☐ Malibu Grand Prix
7775 NW Eighth Street, Miami 33126. (West of the Palmetto Expressway, just north of the Mall of the Americas.) (305) 266-2100. Cost starts at $5.95 per child.

This castle fun-house was remodeled in 1989 and has plenty of amusements for kids of all ages. Birthday packages include lots of food, games and entertainment, plus paper goods, and balloons. Kiddie rides (for ages 6 and older), miniature golf, nine batting cages, 160 video games, and two new go-kart racetracks can be found here. Call for updated hours and reservations.

□ **Mark Twain's Riverboat Playhouse**
Kendale Lakes Mall, 8700 SW 137th Avenue, Miami 33183. (Take Kendall Drive/SW 88th Street exit off Florida Turnpike and go west 1½ miles.) (305) 382-1000. Cost starts at $4.75 per child with a 10-child minimum; $15 deposit is required.

Larger-than-life animated singing country animals entertain your guests. A game room is also a highlight and features skeeball, basketball, video games, and kiddie rides. Decorated tables, pizza, drinks, game tokens, and cake are included in the package.

□ **Metro Parks and Recreation Department**
(305) 666-5885.

The department that knows Dade County parks inside and out can help you select the right outdoor site for your party or picnic. Looking for just the right playground? The best beach? A not-so-crowded picnic area? Call for information and ideas. Packages include food, drinks, music, kiddie entertainment, and activities for children and adults. Within four working days of your request, they will give you three ideas to choose from and cost estimates for each idea.

□ **Miami Metrozoo**
12400 SW 152nd Street, Miami. (305) 233-8389. Cost starts at $10 per child.

Party with the animals at the Metrozoo. Packages include zoo admission, food, room rental, party supplies, tables, and chairs. For a complete description of Metrozoo, see listing in "On Safari in South Florida."

□ **Miami Museum of Science and Space Transit Planetarium**
3280 South Miami Avenue, Miami 33129. (305) 854-4245. Cost starts at $5 per child.

This hands-on museum makes a wonderful party spot for inquisitive, active children. There are three party packages available. The Basic Birthday ($5 per child) provides free, full-day admission to the museum, plus the use of a classroom. Parents must bring decorations, food, and games. The Birthday Bash ($10 per child) includes free admission, use of a classroom, a gift certificate from the museum store, a science demonstration, and an activity. The Birthday Bonanza ($20 per child) is loaded with extras. The museum provides invitations, admission, a decorated classroom, party and paper goods, a cake, juice, balloons, a science demonstration, an activity, and cleanup. **Tip:** Reserve your party one month in advance. For more information, see listing in "Exploring Science and Nature."

☐ **Miami Seaquarium**
4400 Rickenbacker Causeway, Key Biscayne 33149. (305) 361-5705. Cost starts at $265 for 15 people.

Packages include a Flipper birthday cake, kisses from Salty the Sea Lion, handshakes from Dolph the dolphin, a special birthday gift, use of the children's playground, and admission to all shows. For more information, see listing in "On Safari in South Florida."

☐ **Miami Youth Museum**
Bakery Centre, Third Floor, 5701 Sunset Drive, Miami 33143. (305) 661-ARTS. Costs start at $56.25.

Children love this museum that was made just for them, and a birthday party here is always a delight. Choose from two party packages for different age groups. Each includes invitations, a guided tour of the museum, use of the party room for 30 minutes, hands-on play with the exhibits, and a special gift for the birthday child. Party A (minimum charge $56.25) is 90 minutes in length and is recommended for children ages 3 and older. Party B (minimum charge $86.25) is a two-hour event that includes a 30-minute art project taught by a staff member, and is recommended for children ages 5 and older. **Tips:** Charges are based on a 15-child minimum. Museum members will receive a 10% discount. Parents of the birthday child are included in package price—additional adults are $3 each. Refreshments and cleanup must be supplied by the party givers. For more information, see listing in "Adventures in the Arts."

☐ **Omnibirthday**
1601 Biscayne Boulevard (in Omni International Mall), Miami 33132. (305) 374-6664. Basic package is free; food prices vary.

**Birthday parties at the Miami Youth
Museum offer children lots of hands-on
activities, with help from volunteers.**

Balloons, hats, placemats, and two free carousel rides per person are a part of the package; tables and chairs in the Food Court area are provided. You can choose a caterer from the restaurants in the court. For more information, see Omni International Mall listing in "Bytes, Kites, and Toy Delights."

☐ Parrot Jungle and Gardens
11000 SW 57th Avenue, Miami 33156. (305) 666-7834. Cost starts at $85.

A tour of the "Jungle," plus lunch, party favors, and special recognition for the birthday child are the treats in this birthday package. For more information, see listing in "On Safari in South Florida."

☐ Pirates Family Entertainment Center
7090 Coral Way, Miami 33155. (305) 262-2232. Cost starts at $4.95 per child, with a 10-child minimum.

Over 100 activities, including video games, a merry-go-round, and pony rides, are available here to help entertain your youngsters. Birthday parties include invitations, pizza, balloons, live shows, tokens for rides and games, and a gift certificate for a portrait of the birthday child.

☐ Red Berry's Baseball World
7455 SW 125th Avenue, Miami 33183. (305) 279-2668. Cost starts at $125; additional charge for pool rental.

For sports-minded boys and girls, check out this top-notch facility for your next party. A one-hour baseball theme mini-clinic offers tips for better playing, including throwing and catching instruction, and is followed by an exciting game and awards ceremony. You'll have your choice of menus, and a cake can also be provided. For more information, see listing in "On Your Mark, Get Set, Go!"

☐ Roxy Sound and Light Show
325 NW 99th Street, Miami 33150. (305) 541-7699. Cost starts at $300.

A disc jockey can be yours for four hours of music and games. Sack races and games like tug-of-war are organized, and all equipment for the games is provided, but Mom and Dad will have to supply the prizes.

☐ **Sparkles the Clown/Moondancer Productions**
*Mailing address is P.O. Box 331661, Miami 33233-1661. (305) 856-3400.
Cost starts at $85.*

Sparkles the Clown is a delight to children of all ages. She can also come to your party as Mother Goose, Cinderella, or a dinosaur. Her cast of muppet-style puppets are also a big hit for birthdays as well as holiday theme parties. Entertainment lasts from 30 minutes to three hours.

☐ **Tony's Traveling Zoo**
(305) 258-8943. Cost starts at $125.

Your little Tarzan or Jane will really like this "safari" theme party! Tony's Traveling Zoo will delight your guests with an exotic animal show that includes a song and dance routine done by very personable parrots. Have the children listen carefully, because some of these birds will sing "Happy Birthday!" Skunks, hedgehogs, and monkeys will make their way into your backyard or outdoor facility. And by the way, at the end of the show there's a very special visitor!

☐ **Tropical Audubon Society**
5530 Sunset Drive, Miami 33143. (305) 665-5111. Call for prices.

Rent the facilities at this unique, peaceful place in the middle of a busy section of South Miami. The Audubon staff provide an entertaining and educational party for your youngsters. An amphitheater provides the backdrop for a wildlife program, during which guests will see such animals as the American eagle, the crocodile, the great horned owl, and more. If they're brave enough, they may pet the baby crocodile featured in the shows. There's a chickee hut available for picnicking, complete with grill and tables. For more information, see listing in "Exploring Science and Nature."

☐ **Venetian Pool**
2701 DeSoto Boulevard, Coral Gables 33134. (305) 442-6483. $375 for Coral Gables residents; $550 for nonresidents.

Entertain your young party-goers at this famous and historic watering hole. The beautiful coral rock formations will make a beautiful backdrop for your party movies and photographs. The rental fee entitles you to exclusive use of the pool area for five hours and a lifeguard will be on hand during this time. Parents must bring refreshments and provide other entertainment. For more pool information, see listing in "On Your Mark, Get Set, Go!"

Broward County

☐ **All Sweets**
8612 NW 44th Street (Forum Plaza), Sunrise 33351. (305) 748-4988. Cost starts at $7 per child, with a 10-child minimum.

Enter into the kitchen of the "Chocolate Lady" and create your take-home favors: lollipops, peanut butter cups, marshmallow cones with sprinkles, cookies, and pretzels. It's messy, but is it fun! Yogurt, ice cream, soda, and juice are on the party menu; the things you make are to take home. An extra treat is the chocolate face-painting; boys get mustaches and beards, girls get beauty marks! Recommended for children ages 4 and up.

☐ **Bright Ideas**
8698 Griffin Road (Timberlake Plaza), Cooper City 33328. (305) 434-8801. Cost starts at $75.

Leave the setup, cleanup, and catering to Bright Ideas. All you need to do is supply the kids and the theme. Popular ideas are dinosaurs, fantasy/fairy tales, circus show, Double Dare, Mickey Mouse, and '50s rock'n'roll. Games will be played according to the theme you choose. They supply the cake, party goods, beverages, and balloons. Recommended for children ages 2 and up. For a complete description of the store, see listing in "Bytes, Kites, and Toy Delights."

☐ **Butterfly World**
3600 West Sample Road (Tradewinds Park), Coconut Creek 33073. (305) 977-4400. Cost starts at $40.

Packages include a 60-minute tour of Butterfly World, party favors, and use of picnic tables. Children should be at least 3 years old to participate. For more information, see listing in "Under the Sun."

☐ **Chuckles the Clown**
(305) 731-6974.

Chuckles travels anywhere from the Jupiter area to the Keys to provide entertainment at parties. His 45-minute, one-on-one magic shows and balloon sculptures have delighted children for over 25 years. Children are encouraged to participate in the show.

□ Circus Playhouse
420 South State Road 7, Hollywood 33023. (305) 966-5500. Cost starts at $4.75 per child, with an 11-child minimum.

Packages include an animated character show, video games, rides, pizza, soda, game tokens, party goods, and balloons. Cake is provided for an additional charge or parents can supply their own.

□ The Discovery Center
231 SW Second Avenue, Fort Lauderdale 33301. (305) 462-8803. Cost starts at $35, with a maximum of 12 children.

Imagine having reptiles, rainbows, and Seminole Indians at your child's next party! It's all possible if you're a member of the Discovery Center. A special room is available to you for serving refreshments, and the party guests can tour this hands-on museum or participate in a science workshop. **Tips:** Recommended for children ages 4 and up. For more information, see listing in "Exploring Science and Nature."

□ The Gentle Farm
4930 SW 199th Avenue, Fort Lauderdale 33332. (305) 680-FARM. Cost determined by distance traveled to party and by number of children.

Here's a real-life farm that comes to you. Children can touch, pet, and handle the small farm animals (chickens, pigs, rabbits, goats, and sheep). The animals are friendly and clean. **Tip:** Staff accommodate special needs.

□ Giggles the Clown
Mailing address is P.O. Box 7065, Hollywood 33081. (305) 963-0400. Call for prices.

Giggles' one-hour shows include clowning and magic, using rabbits and doves and complete audience participation. Face-painting and balloon art round out the entertainment.

□ Hobby Box
945 University Drive (Esplanade Plaza), Coral Springs 33071. (305) 341-9307. Cost starts at $8 per child.

Have a racing theme party and use the slot car track for fun races. The store provides prizes and a party table in the back of the store to serve the food you bring. Each child receives a helium balloon and a glider as gifts. The party runs for about 90 minutes, with 40 minutes use of the slot car track.

☐ **Hot Shot**
8510 NW 44th Street (Forum Plaza), Sunrise. (305) 749-PUTT. Cost starts at $3 per child; extra charge for hot dogs.

This two-hour party includes a round of miniature golf, plus chips and beverages. Parents can bring a cake and use the patio area for singing and eating!

☐ **Lighthouse Point Ice Skating Arena**
4601 North Federal Highway, Pompano Beach 33064. (305) 943-1437. Cost starts at $5.75 per child.

Tell your guests to dress warmly for this party on the ice. Skate to the tunes, then be treated to a birthday meal in a decorated party room. For more information, see listing in "On Your Mark, Get Set, Go!"

☐ **Ocean World**
1701 SE 17th Street, Fort Lauderdale 33316. (305) 525-6612. Cost starts at $11 per person.

The party package includes all-day admission to Ocean World, a personalized cake, a reserved decorated picnic area, and a kiddie basket filled with lunch. For more information, see listing in "On Safari in South Florida."

☐ **One-Way Puppets**
Mailing address is P.O. Box 5346, Fort Lauderdale 33310. (305) 491-4221. Cost starts at $125.

This musical variety show is appropriate for children ages 2 to 10, but the entire family will enjoy the performance. A cast of 18 marionnettes dance and sing in short musical numbers. Entertainment lasts 35 to 40 minutes.

☐ **Plaster Carousel**
7542 West Commercial Boulevard, Lauderhill, (305) 748-4724; 9865 West Sample Road, Coral Springs, (305) 753-5354. Cost starts at $3.75 per child.

Here's a great idea for young artists. The kids pick out their own plastercraft mold and colors, and paint masterpieces to bring home. The package also includes use of the already-decorated birthday party room. You will need to provide the cake, beverages, and paperware. Recommended for children ages 5 and up.

□ **Roller Skating Center of Coral Springs**
2100 University Drive, Coral Springs 33071. (305) 755-0011. Cost starts at $50 for 15 children.

Be sure to book your party well in advance at this popular skating rink. The party package includes skate rental, food, party room for 45 minutes, invitations, balloons, skate car ride, special birthday song, and the birthday child's name on a giant T.V. screen. Call for a brochure. **Tip:** No ice cream cakes allowed.

Palm Beach County

□ **Children's Gym**
337 First Street (Indiantown Road, west of Military Trail), Jupiter 33458. (407) 747-3646. Cost starts at $95.

Recommended for children ages 3 and up, party ideas include gymnastics, fairy tale theater, circus, karate, and creative dramatics. You can reserve a weekend afternoon, with parents responsible for food, drinks, and paper goods. The gym's coaches will set up the table, supervise the children, and clean up. Parents can take advantage of the freedom to take photos or movies, or (eek!) relax. A full line of either preschool or Olympic equipment will be used according to age group.

□ **Clowning Around**
7651 Overlook Drive, Lake Worth 33467. (407) 969-0174. Cost starts at $75.

Clowning Around will customize your party, or come up with their own theme, like a "Decorate-a-Cake" party, where kids decorate an already-baked cake with the help of Cinderella or a clown. Puppets, unicyclists, jugglers, and, of course, clowns are available to perform magic shows, paint faces, and create animal balloons.

Face-painting draws children into the magical world of clowns.

☐ Little Palm Theatre for Young People (Florida Academy of Dramatic Arts)

Mailing address is P.O. Box 1682, Royal Palm Dinner Theatre, 303 Golfview Drive, Boca Raton 33429. (407) 394-0206.

See a play at 9 A.M., then have a party on the patio. The performers from the play will mingle with the children. Parents provide party refreshments. For more information, see listing in "Adventures in the Arts."

☐ The Palace

6016 Old Congress Road, Lantana (one mile west of I-95). (407) 967-0311.

Packages include admission, skate rental, a special party room, food, and beverages. For more information, see listing in "On Your Mark, Get Set, Go!"

☐ Scoops Ice Cream Parlor and Restaurant

9919 Glades Road (Shadowood Square, corner of 441 and Glades Road), Boca Raton 33434. (407) 487-3155. Cost starts at $2.75 per child (plus tax and gratuity); costumed characters start at $65; magic show starts at $80.

Balloons, a birthday letter, bells, sirens and singing, lunch, and a sundae make for a fun and delicious party. A "Make Your Own Sundae" party is a fun idea for an additional charge. For more information, see listing in "Come and Get It!"

□ **South Florida Science Museum and Planetarium**
4801 Dreher Trail North, West Palm Beach 33405. (407) 832-1988. Cost starts at $45 for 15 children.

Frozen shadows and huge bubbles are part of the entertainment for your child's party at this museum. Parents can decorate a private room and bring cake and other refreshments to serve the birthday group. There are plenty of hands-on activities here and a special demonstration at the marine-life touch tank is always a winner! For more information on the museum and planetarium, see listing in "Exploring Science and Nature."

□ **Studio Kids**
Shoppes of Loggers Run, 11435H West Palmetto Park Road, Boca Raton 33428. (407) 479-3273. Cost starts at $75.

Children always enjoy arts and crafts, and with that as their theme, let Studio Kids host your next party. Choose from a variety of projects ranging from papier-mâché characters to three-dimensional mask designs. T-shirt art is also a popular theme. **Tips:** Parents must supply food and beverages. Parties are held on weekends only. Parents may bring balloons and a banner, but no other decorating is needed. A limit of 35 children.

Monroe County

□ **Bert Lee/Children's World Theatre**
(305) 294-0322. Cost starts at $200.

This professional close-up magic and comedy show is recommended for children ages 6 to 10. Bert's performances last about 30 minutes and include pantomime geared especially to his young audience.

□ **Coral Bowl**
Mile Marker 83.5, Islamorada 33036. (305) 664-9357. $12 per lane.

On weekend afternoons you can have a "Lease-a-Lane" party at this bowling alley. Two hours of bowling and shoe rental are included in the package. The hostess can decorate the area behind the lanes with balloons and crepe paper. A snack bar is available, but you should plan on bringing your own cake and party goods.

☐ Pinwheel Puppet Theatre
1015 Flagler Avenue, Key West 33040. (305) 296-8983. Cost starts at $40 ("cheaper than a sheet cake").

"The Puppet Lady" offers a delightful puppet show for boys and girls at birthday celebrations and holiday parties. Parties have two formats: a very personal 30-minute puppet show that tells a story about your child's party, or a "workshop party," where the theme of the party can come alive in a hands-on activity. A member of the Puppeteers of America, the Puppet Lady will perform outdoors in a park or come to your own home.

☐ Theater of the Sea
Mile Marker 84.5, Islamorada. Mailing address is P.O. Box 407, Islamorada 33036. (305) 664-2431. Cost starts at $4.40 per child; $7.60 per adult.

Packages include admission to the attraction and a ride on a dolphin-pulled boat for the birthday child and eight friends. There are picnic tables outside of the park if you want to serve refreshments (provided by parents) before you go into the attraction. For more information, see listing in "On Safari in South Florida."

Appendices

Appendix A
Mark Your Calendar

Festivals, arts and crafts fairs, annual cultural and sporting events, and musical, historical, and holiday happenings can be opportunities for families to get out and get to know South Florida and each other. This listing is by no means exhaustive; investigate on your own and you'll find that something is happening near you this week. Note that not all listings include addresses, phone numbers, or admission prices. Check your local newspapers for details.

Dade County

January

☐ **Art Deco Weekend Festival**
(305) 672-2014. Free admission.

Relive the '20s and '30s in the historic Art Deco district in Miami Beach. Here you'll find period artwork, memorabilia, and collectibles, along with music from the Big Band era and other entertainment. The festival is very crowded, and maneuvering with strollers is difficult. For more information about the Art Deco District, see listing in "Tracing the Past."

☐ **Homestead Frontier Days and Rodeo**
(305) 247-2332 or 372-9966. Admission charged.

This is the biggest event of its kind in South Florida, with rodeo events, parade, arts and crafts, and food.

□ **Our Lady of Lebanon Lebanese Festival**
(305) 856-7449. Admission charged.

As the name implies, you'll find Lebanese foods, live music, dancing, gifts, and an indoor game room. Parking is free.

□ **Pig Bowl**
Admission charged.

This is the annual police football competition between Metro-Dade/Miami Police and a visiting out-of-state team, held at the Orange Bowl. Watch local newspapers for details. No strollers allowed.

□ **Redlands Natural Arts Festival**
(305) 247-5727. Admission charged.

Held at the Preston B. Bird and Mary Heinlein Fruit and Spice Park in Homestead, this festival's theme represents the Pioneer Spirit of the region, with craft demonstrations, foods, clowns, pony rides, and Indian and Pioneer exhibits. For more information, see listing in "Exploring Science and Nature."

□ **Ringling Brothers/Barnum and Bailey Circus**
(305) 673-7300. Admission charged.

The famed circus comes to town at the Miami Beach Convention Center. Try to get downtown for their annual Elephant Walk.

□ **Three Kings Parade**
(305) 856-6653. Free admission.

This parade takes its path down the famous SW Eighth Street as part of the Latin Festival. Enjoy Latin rhythms and colorful floats and costumes. Don't forget to taste the food in Little Havana.

February

□ **Around the World Fair**
(305) 854-4247. Admission charged.

Tropical Park hosts this juried art exhibition, along with entertainment, international foods, rides, and a flea market. The Small World children's area includes pony rides, puppets, and face-painting. The fair is sponsored by the Patrons of the Miami Museum of Science.

☐ **Black Heritage Celebration**
(305) 347-3003 or 347-3007.

Events showcase the history and contributions of African Americans and take place all month at schools, libraries, festivals, and other locations. Check your local newspapers for event information.

☐ **Buskerfest: The Celebration of Street People at Bayside**
(305) 577-3344. Free admission.

Magicians, musicians, mimes, sword swallowers, slapsticks, storytellers, and clowns perform at this festival. Check out the balloon animal workshop.

☐ **Coconut Grove Art Festival**
(305) 447-0401. Free admission.

Each year this event gets bigger and better, but harder to get around with children, especially with strollers.

☐ **Country Day at the USDA**
(305) 235-6212. Free admission.

Held at the U.S. Department of Agriculture Subtropical Research Station, the Country Day offers free tram rides, animal exhibits, food, country music, a flower show, and educational displays.

☐ **Doral/Ryder Open PGA Golf Tournament**
(305) 477-GOLF or (305) 592-0570. Admission charged.

Here's one of the best known PGA golf tournaments, held annually at the "Blue Monster" course at the Doral Hotel and Country Club. Older children will probably enjoy seeing the pros and celebrities. Usually the first few rounds are free to the public; after that tickets are needed.

☐ **Hialeah Spring Festival**
(305) 888-8686.

Enjoy ten days of entertainment at Hialeah Race Track, with ethnic foods, games, rides, and fireworks.

☐ **Ryder Pitch, Putt, and Drive**
(305) 665-8292. Free admission.

*Libraries offer free storytelling, art
exhibitions, and other cultural events
during Black Heritage Month.*

This junior golf competition is for boys and girls ages 17 and under and is located throughout Dade County. Golf clubs are available if needed.

☐ Scottish Festival and Games
(305) 757-6730. Admission charged.

At Crandon Gardens, Key Biscayne, the events include Highland dance, bagpipe competition, and traditional foods and crafts.

☐ Superstars
(305) 579-2676. Free admission.

Watch sports celebrities compete in various events.

March

☐ Arti Gras
(305) 893-6511. Free admission.

Theater, opera, ballet, dance, jazz, puppets, and other children's shows make this a very popular arts event.

☐ Beaux Arts Festival
(305) 284-3536. Free admission.

Beaux Arts is the longest running outdoor arts festival in Greater Miami. Look for art classes in the children's area. For more information, see Lowe Art Museum listing in "Adventures in the Arts."

☐ Carnaval Miami
(305) 324-7349. Admission charged to some events.

Carnaval Miami offers an excellent way to taste the city's Latin flavor. Almost two weeks of events, with 60 stages for music and over 500 food vendors, culminate with "Calle Ocho," the world's largest and most famous block party. Look for entertainment and activities for kids. Events become quite crowded, so use discretion with children.

☐ Dade County Youth Fair
(305) 223-7060. Admission charged.

Dade County hosts the largest youth fair in the country; you'll find a showcase of student projects, plus entertainment, rides, and science and agriculture exhibits at Tamiami Park. Can be crowded at times.

□ **Italian Renaissance Festival**
(305) 759-6651. Admission charged.

A 16th-century marketplace is recreated at Vizcaya with crafts, merchants, and food. Entertainment includes jugglers, jesters, madrigal groups, troubadors, and a living chess tournament (the players are people!), all in period costumes.

□ **Lipton International Players Championships**
Admission charged.

The best tennis players in the world compete on the courts during this two-week tournament at picturesque Key Biscayne.

□ **Miami Grand Prix**
(305) 662-5660. Admission charged.

Downtown Miami becomes a race course for the many drivers and spectators from around the world who come for this event. Crowd size makes it difficult to bring young children.

□ **St. Patrick's Day Parade and Festival**
(305) 949-8400. Free admission.

This parade down Flagler Street will give you an even bigger excuse to wear green! Enjoy foods, live entertainment, and more.

April

□ **American Traditions Festival**
(305) 347-2582. Free admission.

At Miami-Dade Community College's South Campus, you'll find two days of music, hot-air balloons, ethnic foods, children's games and theater, helicopter rides, and fireworks.

□ **Dade Heritage Days**
(305) 358-9572. Admission to some events.

Get to know all there is to know about the place we call home by participating in this month-long celebration of Miami's history. Historic neighborhoods take part with festivals, tours, and parades. Events for kids include storytelling, workshops, and some hands-on activities.

□ Oceans Miami/Bounty of the Sea
(305) 361-5786. Free admission.

The Bounty of the Sea Festival offers a month-long celebration with exhibits and demonstrations that help us better understand our ocean, as well as a full lineup of music, children's activities, and arts and crafts.

□ River Cities Festival
(305) 887-1515. Free admission.

This three-day, five-community event includes bike shows, a dog show, a "Chili Cookoff," a torchlight parade, a beauty contest, and arts and crafts activities.

□ Tropifest
(305) 887-8838. Free admission.

Tropical Park comes alive for everyone during this annual sports and arts festival, featuring area celebrities and sponsored by SCLAD (Spinal Cord Living-Assistance Development, Inc.).

May

□ Great Sunrise Balloon Race and Festival
(305) 245-6204. Admission charged for some events.

This event takes place at Harris Field in Homestead, with hot-air balloon races, country and western music performances, and arts and crafts demonstrations.

June

□ Diabetic Children's Camp
Diabetic Children's Camp, Coral Gables Youth Center, Coral Gables.
(305) 285-2930.

Sports, exercises, movies, and arts and crafts are supervised by trained nurses and counselors.

□ Goombay Festival
(305) 445-8292. Free admission.

The Goombay Festival is one of the largest black heritage festivals in the U.S. This weekend event features Bahamian arts, foods, a colorful parade, and musical entertainment in Coconut Grove. Several blocks of the neighborhood are closed to traffic during the festival.

☐ **Royal Poinciana Fiesta**
(305) 371-2723. Admission charged to some events.

For over 50 years, this fiesta has celebrated the blooming of the breathtaking Poinciana trees. A week of events includes a folkloric variety show featuring music and dance from 12 nations, an art exhibition, and a bus tour of areas rich with the red, yellow, and orange blooms of the Poinciana.

July

☐ **Bayside's Fourth of July Celebration**
(305) 577-3344. Free admission.

Biscayne Bay is the backdrop for this celebration and fireworks display. It's at the popular Bayside Marketplace, where food and fun go hand in hand.

☐ **International Music and Crafts Festival**
(305) 223-8388 (weekends), 223-8380 (weekdays). Admission charged.

Musicians and craftspeople from many countries around the world share their art, crafts, music, dance, and foods. Held at the covered amphitheatre at the Miccosukee Indian Village. For more information, see listing for Miccosukee Indian Village in "On Safari in South Florida."

☐ **Hacienda Mardenpaz**
12240 SW 72nd Street, Miami. Free admission.

Several days of events for the whole family, topped off by a fireworks display. Hacienda owner and Cuban immigrant Eduardo Martínez invites the public to this event as an act of thanksgiving for his new life in the United States.

☐ **PACE/Hammocks July Fourth Festival**
(305) 382-3377. Free admission.

The area adjacent to Hammocks Junior High School becomes the site of a petting zoo, a children's corner with face-painting and games, dance performances, and plenty of music. This is a great way for the entire family to celebrate our nation's birthday. The event is sponsored by PACE, a nonprofit organization that supports the work of South Florida performing artists. Traditional fireworks and a special concert are the highlights.

☐ **Pops by the Bay**
(305) 361-6730. Admission charged.

Enjoy this summer concert series at Miami Marine Stadium. It's fun to see the people on the boats who are watching the concert on the barge.

August

☐ **Lee Evans Bowling Tournament of the Americas**
(305) 652-4197. Free admission.

Amateurs compete from 24 countries. This spectator event may only interest older children.

September

☐ **Catch-a-Cure**
(305) 477-3437.

Families and children alike can compete in this benefit fishing tournament for diabetes research.

☐ **Festival Miami**
(305) 284-3941. Admission charged.

Jazz, opera, chamber music, and piano pieces are showcased in this two-week celebration of performing and visual arts, with concerts by University of Miami and international performers. No stroller access.

☐ **Preschool Children's Health Fair**
(305) 375-5416.

Kids are weighed, measured, and fingerprinted at this fun health fair just for youngsters. Local doctors and therapists are on hand to give brief check-ups, and answer questions. Clowns, puppet characters, and refreshments make this a fun way to introduce health care to children. Sponsored by the Metro-Dade Department of Human Resources.

□ Oktoberfest
(305) 255-4579.

In Homestead you'll find a celebration with folk dancing, bands, and German oom-pah-pahs.

October

□ Baynanza
(305) 662-4124.

Over a week of celebration and salute to Biscayne Bay. Enjoy music, arts and crafts, seafood dishes, and boating events.

□ Campus Life Haunted House
(305) 271-2442. Admission charged.

This carnival features shows, magic, and rides, along with a Haunted House at Miami Metrozoo/Gold Coast Railroad Museum. Not recommended for young children.

□ Electric Island Run
(305) 477-3437.

This 15K race held on Miami Beach is a benefit for diabetes research. Moms and dads can walk with strollers.

□ Friends of Germany Oktoberfest
(305) 374-7610. Free admission.

Enjoy this German street festival that features music, food, and drink.

□ Hispanic Heritage Festival
(305) 541-5023. Admission charged for some events.

Celebrate Miami's Hispanic roots with this month-long series of cultural events, which includes a re-enactment at Bayfront Park of Columbus's discovery of America.

☐ **Miami Air Show**
(305) 685-7025. Admission charged.

Runways become exhibit and display areas, with special entertainment by the U.S. Navy's Blue Angels.

☐ **Museum of Science Fine Arts Show**
(305) 667-0500. Free admission.

There's a new theme each year at this popular and educational museum. Not recommended for young children.

☐ **Paella Festival**
(305) 347-3205. Admission charged.

This is a part of the Hispanic Heritage Festival, held at the Wolfson Campus of Miami-Dade Community College. Enjoy Latin food at its best, prepared in the largest *paella* pans you've ever seen. For a list of Spanish food terms, see Glossary at the end of "Come and Get It!"

☐ **South Florida Auto Show**
(305) 758-2643. Admission charged.

See the latest trends in cars at the Miami Beach Convention Center. The show floor is often too crowded for strollers.

☐ **Sunday in the Park with Art**
(305) 238-4575.

This family-oriented fine arts show is held at the Charles Deering Estate. Look for the kids' tent, which holds all-day activities and art competitions. For more information on the Charles Deering Estate, see listings in "Tracing the Past" and "Under the Sun."

November

☐ **Asiafest**
(305) 577-3378. Free admission.

You'll be delighted by the Far East treasures at Bayfront Park, from countries such as Japan, India, China, Korea, Thailand, and Singapore. Highlights include performing arts, cultural and craft pavillions, and distinctive cuisine from each of the countries represented.

□ **Cornucopia of the Arts**
(305) 579-2680. Admission charged.

Young artists and performers are featured in this art show on the grounds of Vizcaya. Enjoy artworks and performances by dancers, actors, youth symphonies, sculptors, and more.

□ **Fall Festival at Cauley Square**
(305) 258-0011. Free admission.

Fall Festival features over 125 arts and crafts booths and a variety of foods and music. Can get a bit crowded at times. For more information on Cauley Square, see listing in "Tracing the Past."

□ **The Harvest**
(305) 375-1492. Free admission.

Experience this weekend celebration of South Florida's folk culture. Events include demonstrations of various handmade crafts such as woodcarving, roping, and piñata-making, and antique car and engine displays. There's lots of music and other forms of entertainment at Tamiami Park.

□ **Junior Orange Bowl Festival**
(305) 662-1210. Admission charged for some events.

Young athletes from around the world participate and compete in this largest sports and cultural festival for children and teens. The eight-week-long event includes golf, tennis, racquetball, gymnastics, cheerleading, football, running, writing, photography, and fine arts competitions, as well as Sports Ability Games for the physically challenged. The Junior Orange Bowl Parade concludes the event through the streets of Coral Gables on the Thursday before New Year's Day.

□ **Miami Book Fair International**
(305) 347-3258. Free admission.

Major publishers and authors lecture, exhibit, and market their works at the Miami-Dade Community College Wolfson campus. This week-long event hosts children's storytellers, puppeteers, and performing jugglers. For more information, see listing in "Adventures in the Arts."

□ **St. Sophia Greek Festival**
(305) 854-2922. Admission charged.

Join this celebration of Greek heritage at St. Sophia's Greek Orthodox Cathedral, complete with food, entertainment, and dancing.

☐ **Wildlife Weekend**
(305) 666-5111. Admission charged for concerts.

This environmental festival with display booths and wildlife benefit concerts takes place at the Tropical Audubon Society.

December

☐ **Christmas at the Biltmore**
(305) 445-1926. Free admission.

Celebrate the holidays with a festive flair at Miami's famous Biltmore Hotel. Children will love seeing Miami's largest gingerbread house, which weighs 1,150 pounds. For more information on the Biltmore, see listing in "Tracing the Past."

☐ **Christmas Lights at Vizcaya**
(305) 579-4626. Free admission.

Holiday lights trim the trees and gardens around Vizcaya—a magical and simply gorgeous celebration of Christmas.

☐ **Fairchild Tropical Gardens Ramble**
(305) 667-1651. Admission charged.

Highlights include exhibits by plant societies, sales of rare plants, and foods and crafts relating to plants. Some exhibits and hands-on activities for children are offered. For more information on the Gardens, see listing in "Exploring Science and Nature."

☐ **Garden Christmas at Vizcaya**
(305) 854-6559. Admission charged.

Punch and cookies add a special touch to this great holiday event for kids. Costumed characters and choral groups perform. Stroller access is difficult. For more information about Vizcaya, see listing in "Tracing the Past."

☐ **Hometown Tree Lighting**
(305) 667-5511. Free admission.

A 30-foot high Christmas tree lights up South Miami. Caroling, candy canes, and a reading of the Nativity story delight children.

☐ Miccosukee Annual Indian Arts Festival
(305) 223-8380 (weekdays), 223-8388 (weekends). Admission charged.

Representatives from nearly 20 tribes gather at the Indian Village for song, dance, and performances. For more information, see Miccosukee Indian Village listing in "On Safari in South Florida."

☐ Orange Bowl Festival
(305) 642-1515 or 642-5211 or 1-800-634-6740.
Admission charged for some events.

Greater Miami's largest festival, which begins midmonth with the Orange Bowl/Rolex International Tennis Championships and the Junior Orange Bowl Festival and Parade, also includes the Orange Bowl Regatta Series and the world's largest nighttime parade (the King Orange Jamboree Parade). Then follows the Fiesta By The Bay, with music, fireworks, and food. The Orange Bowl Stadium is the site for (you guessed it!) the Orange Bowl Football Classic, where two of the nation's top-rated college teams fight it out on the turf!

☐ Santa's Enchanted Forest
(305) 226-8315. Admission charged.

Over one million lights cover Tropical Park and convert it into a magical forest. See a laser show, visit a petting zoo, and take your child's picture with a 50-foot snowman.

☐ Winter Reflections on the Bay
(305) 947-3525. Free; parking fee charged.

Boats decked in holiday lights make their way down the Intracoastal Waterway, taking off from Bayfront Park. Fireworks and live music top off the evening.

Broward County

January

□ **Gulfstream Park Annual Family Day**
(305) 454-7000, in Broward; (305) 944-1242, in Dade. Admission charged.

Youngsters get a chance to saddle up for the day and even try on jockey silks. Watch the horses work out and meet famous jockeys.

February

□ **Orange Blossom Festival and Pro Rodeo**
(305) 581-0790. Free admission.

One of the oldest cultural events in South Florida provides fun for the entire family with a pro rodeo, country fair, parade, street dance, and hot-air balloon race in Davie.

□ **Seminole Tribal Fair and Rodeo**
(305) 583-0244. Admission charged.

Alligator wrestling, snake shows, Indian dancers, and craftspeople make up this cultural event. A rodeo features barrel racing, bull riding, calf roping, and steer wrestling. Find wonderful handmade items like patchwork jackets, palmetto fiber dolls, and sweetgrass baskets.

□ **Sistrunk Historical Festival**
(305) 765-4663.

Join in the celebration of the ethnic black community in commemoration of Dr. James Sistrunk, Broward County's first black physician. Festival includes art exhibits and cultural arts contributions from the African American and Caribbean communities.

March

□ **Art in the Sun Festival**
(305) 941-2940. Free admission.

Features work from over 250 artists, plus live entertainment and children's attractions, all in Pompano Beach.

□ **Flamingo Gardens Easter Egg Hunt and Spring Arts Festival**
(305) 473-2955. Admission charged.

Children, divided by age groups, hunt for traditional Easter eggs. Arts and crafts are also on display. For more information, see listing in "On Safari in South Florida."

□ **Florida Derby**
(305) 454-7000, in Broward; (305) 944-1242, in Dade. Admission charged.

This horse race is held at Gulfstream Park. Activities for children include a petting zoo, a wild animal race, jousting, and music. For more information, see listing in "On Your Mark, Get Set, Go!"

□ **Riverwalk Art Festival**
(305) 764-2005. Free admission.

Bubier Park on the New River is the setting for this arts festival with a special "Kids' Art Korner," where even the tiniest of visitors can participate in art activities.

□ **St. Patrick's Parade and Festival**
(305) 764-4393.

Wear your green and attend this festive parade in downtown Fort Lauderdale.

□ **South Florida Irish Festival**
(305) 429-1542. Admission charged.

Highlights of the festival include traditional Irish foods, a shoppers' bazaar, a carnival, and arts and crafts activities. Continuous children's entertainment consists of puppet shows, clowns, magic, and sports. Contests are held to determine who has the most freckles or the reddest hair.

April

□ Fort Lauderdale Downtown Festival of the Arts
(305) 761-5388.

There are lots of things here for children to enjoy, such as hands-on booths and communal arts projects. Mimes and clowns provide entertainment.

□ Week of the Ocean
(305) 462-5573.

In conjunction with National Week of the Ocean, this event is held in various educational settings, with contests, exhibits, and ecology-focused events that children will enjoy.

May

□ Festival of Nations
(305) 667-1905. Free admission.

Memorial Day weekend is when this family-oriented festival takes place. On the campus of Broward Community College, you will find international foods and performances of all kinds. Over 40 ethnic groups are represented. Children can listen to storytellers, make flags from around the world, and enjoy kiddie rides.

□ Kite Flight
(305) 477-3437. Admission charged.

On Dania Beach you'll find lots of kites, as children gather for demonstrations and give-aways.

□ Pompano Beach Seafood Fest
(305) 941-2940. Free admission.

Great way to introduce new food to the children. Sample shrimp, chowders, conch, and other kinds of seafood!

June

□ Automania
(305) 921-3404. Free admission.

Here's a chance to see classic cars from yesteryear, displayed at Young Circle Park. Entertainment and food booths can be found here as well.

July

□ City of Fort Lauderdale July 4th Sandblast
(305) 761-5388. Admission charged.

For nearly 40 years young and old have enjoyed the sand sculptures of "Sandblast." Contests have categories—and winners!—for all ages.

□ Hollywood Hoe Down
(305) 921-3404. Free admission.

Here you'll find down-home country western fun with hayrides, a petting farm, amusements, and a children's stage area.

October

□ Fort Lauderdale Oktoberfest
(305) 761-5388. Free admission.

Traditional Bavarian and German food, authentic dancers, and music are all on tap, along with a petting zoo and performances by a children's theatrical group.

November

□ Broward County Fair
(305) 923-3248. Admission charged.

This traditional county fair at Gulfstream Park has a midway, student exhibits, and lots of music and food.

□ Florida Championship Rodeo
(305) 797-1145. Admission charged.

In addition to the professional cowboys, watch for pony rides, clogging demonstrations, and even Santa!

December

□ Candy Cane Parade
(305) 921-3404. Free admission.

Here's a beachside parade that children participate in—and so does Santa!

□ Christmas in Old Fort Lauderdale
(305) 761-5388. Free admission.

As the holidays approach, this downtown historical district lights up with Christmas trees and menorahs. Horsedrawn carriages wend their way around the area, while carols are sung. Activities to interest children include hands-on art projects, crafts, displays of Christmas scenes from years gone by, and a special puppet show.

□ Festival of Trees
(305) 525-5500. Admission charged.

Join the Museum of Art for a holiday display of designer Christmas trees. Serenades, tours, and refreshments (including a "Teddy Bear Tea") are offered. For more information, see Museum of Art listing in "Adventures in the Arts."

□ Holiday Enchantment at Flamingo Gardens
(305) 473-2955. Admission charged.

At this time of year, the Gardens are transformed into an enchanted forest! Take a tram ride for a closer look. For more information, see listing in "On Safari in South Florida."

□ Pompano Beach Holiday Boat Parade
(305) 941-2940. Free admission.

See the oldest holiday boat parade in the nation. Over 250,000 spectators watch each year as decorated boats take a five-mile parade route along the Intracoastal Waterway.

☐ Fort Lauderdale Winterfest
(305) 522-3983. Admission charged for some events.

This month-long festival is a mix of holiday activities and beach parties. The seven-mile boat parade down the Intracoastal Waterway tops off the festival—a night of fun and fireworks!

Palm Beach County

January

☐ South Florida Fair and Exposition Showcase
(407) 793-0333 or 1-800-527-FAIR. Admission charged.

This showcase of agricultural, industrial, and educational progress features rides, shows, contests, livestock, 4-H exhibits, and handmade crafts.

February

☐ Flagler Museum Anniversary Day
(407) 655-2833. Free admission.

This popular open house has taken place here yearly since the late '50s. The program includes shows, exhibits, mimes, clowns, refreshments, and fireworks. Arrive early to find convenient parking. For more information, see listing of Henry Morrison Flagler Museum in "Tracing the Past."

☐ *Hatsume* Fair
(407) 495-0233. Admission charged.

This festival celebrates the "first bud of spring" with ethnic foods and entertainment. There are demonstrations to interest children and adults of all ages. The fair gets quite crowded, and stroller access can be difficult. For more information, see listing of The Morikami Museum and Japanese Gardens in "Tracing the Past."

☐ Winter Equestrian Festival
(407) 798-7040. Admission charged.

Over 300 riders from around the world compete in three grand prix events at the Palm Beach Polo and Country Club. For more information, see listing in "On Your Mark, Get Set, Go!"

May

□ Sunfest
(407) 659-5980. Admission charged.

West Palm Beach hosts this four-day event, with jazz performances by big-name entertainers, power boat races, a "For Kid's Sake Park" art show, and fireworks! This street fair is Florida's largest outdoor jazz festival.

June

□ Kite Flying Festival
(407) 627-2000.

One of the PGA Sheraton Resort's golf courses provides the backdrop for this annual kite-flying extravaganza. Entertainment, food, and games are also on tap.

August

□ *Bon* Festival at The Morikami
(407) 495-0233. Free admission.

Don't miss this unique street festival that features Japanese dancing, drum music, fireworks, and a lantern-floating ceremony! For more information, see listing of The Morikami Museum and Japanese Gardens in "Tracing the Past."

□ Boca's Festival Days
(407) 395-4433. Free admission.

This month-long celebration has activities geared for everyone. The schedule changes yearly, so be sure to watch the newspaper for detailed information. Past events have included sand sculpting, concerts, art shows, and fun parades.

December

□ Lake Worth Christmas Parade
(407) 582-4401. Free admission.

This charming parade, along with fun holiday arts, crafts, and food festival, makes for an enjoyable outing.

□ *Osho Gatsu* (Japanese New Year) at The Morikami
(407) 495-0233. Free admission.

The Morikami Museum and Japanese Gardens is the stage for a series of Japanese cultural demonstrations and workshops in celebration of the New Year. Activities may include kite making and kite flying, and designing and making holiday ornaments, decorations, and New Year's greeting cards. For more information, see The Morikami Museum and Japanese Gardens listing in "Tracing the Past."

Monroe County

January

□ Florida Keys Renaissance Faire
Marathon hosts this festival of arts and crafts, jousters, jesters, and "kingly feasts."

February

□ Old Island Days
(305) 294-2587.

Celebrate Key West's unique history and architecture through festivals, tours, and contests. There's a little here for everyone.

April

☐ **Conch Republic Days**
(305) 294-4440.

A salute to island living! Enjoy the annual Kite Festival, fishing tournaments, and other traditional festival activities.

☐ **Indian Key Festival**
(305) 664-4815. Free admission.

This event focuses on the 1830s when this key was the Dade County seat, and offers free boat rides, island tours, archaeological displays, and native foods.

May

☐ **Sand Castle Building Contest**
(305) 664-2321.

Islamorada is the host for this fun family event, usually held on a weekend just before school is out. Come celebrate the beginning of summer!

August

☐ **World Cup Jet-Ski Races**
(305) 664-2321.

Top jet-skiers from around the world compete and entertain the entire family!

November

☐ **Festival of the Continents**
(305) 296-5882. Admission charged.

In Key West, this performing arts celebration focuses on dance, musicals, symphony, folklore, drama, opera, and pops. Events run continuously through April.

December

☐ **Arts Explo**
(305) 292-7832.

This festival runs 105 miles from Key Largo to Key West! Painting, dance, music, and literature are the main highlights.

Appendix B
By Land, Sea, and Air

Discover the treasures of South Florida by land, sea, and air. The following list will give you a brief overview of the endless possibilities for touring; choose from gondolas, seaplanes, bicycles, trolleys, airboats, balloons, and more.

Dade County

☐ **Agricultural Guided Tour**
Farmer's Market, 300 Krome Avenue, Florida City 33034. Mailing address is 101 Gateway Estates, Florida City 33034. (305) 248-6798. Tours leave at 9 A.M. and 1:30 P.M. Adults, $8; children, $4 (or, as the tour guide said, "Oh, about half price!"). Group rates available.

Visit the southernmost farming area of the United States during the winter production months from December 1 to April 1. Since 1977, this 2½-hour lecture bus tour (popular with tourists and local residents alike) looks at the reasons why Dade County is among the top five counties in the United States for winter vegetable production, and is the leading county for producing tropical fruit crops. Children over the age of 10 may get off the buses to get a closer look at wells, machinery, and banana groves, or to pick a sample of vegetables in season. **Tips:** The bus is not easily accessible for wheelchairs or strollers. Florida State Law prohibits children under the age of 10 from entering produce fields.

☐ **Carnival Cruise Lines**
Departs from Ports of Miami and Fort Lauderdale. Mailing address is 5225 NW 87th Avenue, Miami 33178-2193. (305) 599-2600 in Dade County, (800) 325-1214 in Florida, (800) 377-7373 nationwide.

"Junior Cruises" and "Fun Ship" programs, for children ages 4 to 12, are available on several of Carnival Cruise Lines' ships. Activities include scavenger hunts, kite flying, Italian lessons, drawing contests, and games. Some ships have children's pools and game rooms; counselors and staff have teaching experience and know how to plan fun and educational activities for children. **Tip:** Not all cruises are appropriate for children. Call for information and recommendations for your family's particular needs.

□ Catamaran Rides

Docked near Dockside Terrace Restaurant at Bayside Marketplace. Rides leave Friday through Sunday, 5, 7, and 9 P.M. Adults, $10; children, $5.

The 55-foot, 49 passenger *Pau Hana* takes you for rides on Biscayne Bay.

□ Celebration

Departs from Bayside Marketplace at Miamarina. Mailing address is Celebration Excursions, Inc., 3239 West Trade Avenue, Suite 9, Coconut Grove 33133. (305) 445-8456 or (800) 545-7874. Adults, $10 plus tax; children admitted free with adult.

A cruise in this new 90-foot, air-conditioned luxury yacht will take you through Biscayne Bay and Millionaire's Row.

□ Dade Helicopter Jet Services

950 MacArthur Causeway, Miami Beach. (305) 374-3737. Daily, 9 A.M.– 6 P.M. Adults, $39 to $109 per person; children accompanied by two adults pay half price. MC, V accepted.

Fly over Miami Beach, Port of Miami, Virginia Key, and Bal Harbor for a bird's eye view of the city and an experience you'll never forget! There is no age restriction on these flights.

□ Everglades Airboat Tours

40351 SW 192nd Avenue, Homestead. (305) 247-2628. Continuous tours run daily, 9 A.M.–5 P.M. Adults, $7.50; children, $3.50; children under 4, free. Cash payment only.

Whiz through the "sea of grass" for half an hour. Watch out for alligators, fish, turtles, birds, and other wildlife. A walk through an alligator farm is also included. Note that airboat rides are very noisy, and may frighten young children.

□ Gold Coast Helicopters

15101 Biscayne Boulevard, Miami. (305) 940-1009. Daily, 9:30 A.M.– 5 P.M. $45–$170 for 7 to 60 minutes. AE, MC, V accepted.

Routes can take you above the Miami Beach coastline, over the Everglades, or above the homes of stars. Maximum of two children allowed per group.

☐ **Gondola Rides**
Depart from center of Bayside Marketplace. (305) 529-7278. $5 per person ($20 minimum).

Glide along the bay in an Italian-style gondola.

☐ **Heritage of Miami**
Docked at Bayside Marketplace, Miamarina. (305) 858-6264. Departs three times daily from September to May. Call to check daily schedule. Adults, $10; children under 12, $5. Personal checks accepted.

If a trip on a tall ship sounds exciting, you might try this 85-foot steel topsail schooner. Up to 49 passengers at a time can enjoy the two-hour cruise on Biscayne Bay. Bring your own food if you wish; snacks, soft drinks, and ice are available on ship. **Tip:** Birthday parties can be held on board for a minimum of $120; you bring the party supplies, they supply the boat and the bay.

☐ **Horse-Drawn Carriage Rides**
Depart daily from south end of Bayside. $5 per person for short rides; $10 for long rides. Children, $3.

Children always enjoy horses, and this is a novel way to see them in action, and see Miami as well.

☐ **Metrorail**
There are 20 stations along the 21-mile track that extends from Dadeland in Kendall to Opalocka. Schedule and transfer information, (305) 638-6700; Maps-by-Mail, (305) 638-6137. Weekdays, 6 A.M.–9 P.M.; weekends, 6:30 A.M.–6:30 P.M. Extended service for some special events. Full fare, $1; reduced fare, 50¢. (Reduced fare available for seniors, children, and handicapped persons.) Permit and I.D. required—call for qualifications. Change machines are available at the stations.

Local residents and tourists alike can get an overview of the Miami area, or get to places such as the South Florida Historical Museum, the Center for Fine Arts, Vizcaya, the Museum of Science and Space Transit Planetarium, and the Hialeah Racetrack by taking Metrorail. Children enjoy seeing the cars, buses, boats, houses, and more from above, and everyone will appreciate the air-conditioned and comfortable ride.

Strollers can be used on Metrorail, but they should be folded up during peak periods. Elevators are available to get to the platforms.

Transit Agency personnel suggest always holding the hands of small children when entering and leaving the vehicles. Step on and off together. Please remember that the platform is a dangerous area; keep your children behind the lines painted on the floor and away from the tracks at all times.

□ Metromover

Nine downtown stations along a 1.9-mile loop track. Connects with Metrorail at Government Center station. Monday through Friday, 6:30 A.M.–9 P.M.; Saturday, 8:30 A.M.–11 P.M.; Sunday, 8:30 A.M.–6:30 P.M. Extended service for special events. Full fare, 25¢; reduced fare, 10¢. Transfers available.

Ride 25 feet above the ground for a quick tour of downtown Miami, or to get to such places as Bayside Marketplace, Gusman Center for the Performing Arts, and other downtown destinations.

□ Metro-Dade Aviation Department

Mailing address is Miami International Airport, P.O. Box 592075, Miami 33159. Marketing and Communications, (305) 871-7017. Monday through Friday, 9:15 and 10:30 A.M. Free public service of Aviation Department.

Miami International Airport is one of the world's largest and busiest airports, with air services provided by over 85 airlines. Over 1,000 daily flights come and go from Miami. With all this activity, a trip around the airport is sure to be exciting for children. This 90-minute tour takes kids onto the air field to watch takeoffs and landings, fueling of the planes, and cargo and baggage loading. They will also tour the fire rescue area and the terminal building, where they will stay in the international area in hopes of entering a major airline's plane. Children touring this facility are expected to behave responsibly and respectfully, as they will enter restricted areas of operation.

Tours are geared toward the children's particular age group. For preschoolers or groups wishing to avoid the hustle and bustle of the airport, the Aviation Department will bring slide presentations to groups upon request. **Tips:** Tours are only for groups of around 10 to 40 children. Make reservations well in advance. Recommended for children ages 5 and up.

☐ Miccosukee Indian Village and Airboat Tours

Miccosukee Reservation, U.S. Highway 41 (Tamiami Trail). (305) 223-8380. Continuous tours daily, 9 A.M.–5 P.M. $5 for 15 minutes; $6 for 30 minutes. Children under 3, free. Cash payment only.

Both the short (15-minute) and long (30-minute) tours include a fast trip through the canals and over the "sea of grass," where alligators, wading birds, and other wildlife can be seen. The long tour makes a 10-minute stop at an Indian camp on an island in the Everglades. **Tips:** Rides are very noisy and may bother small children; cotton ear plugs are provided. Be sure to call in advance to confirm that the rides are being offered, as they are suspended when the water level in the Everglades gets too low.

☐ Nikko Gold Coast Cruises

Haulover Park Marina, 10800 Collins Avenue (one mile south of 163rd Street), Miami Beach. (305) 945-5461; (305) 921-1193 in Broward County. Daily, 8:30 A.M.–7 P.M. Cost varies according to tour. Rainchecks available. Major credit cards accepted.

Three 150-passenger boats travel down the Intracoastal to Biscayne Bay to give you a peek at such sights as Millionaire's Row, Bayside Marketplace, Seaquarium, Vizcaya, Fort Lauderdale, and the Everglades. Tours are fully narrated. The seven-hour tour package may include stops at Seaquarium, Bayside, or Vizcaya. The trip from Fort Lauderdale includes a stop at an Indian Village. **Tip:** Arrive a half hour before the departure time. Snack bars and restrooms are available on board. Stroller and wheelchair access provided.

☐ Old Town Trolley Tours of Miami

Bayside Marketplace, 650 NW Eighth Street, Miami 33136. (305) 374-TOUR. Departs daily every 30 minutes, beginning at 9 A.M., from 14 convenient locations. Adults, $11; discounts available for children.

You'll have seen it all—or almost—after taking this tour which visits over 100 points of interest, including Vizcaya, Parrot Jungle, and Calle Ocho. Your driver will point out the history of Dade County in buildings, streets, and even trees. And by the time you're back to your point of origin you and your child will be ready for a game of "Dade Trivia."

The Trolley leaves every half hour from Bayside and takes about 90 minutes to complete the loop. You will stop at 12 different locations, where you can hop off, look around, and catch the next trolley that comes by to continue your tour.

□ **Port of Miami**
1015 North America Way, Miami 33132. (305) 371-7678.

Known as the "cruise capital of the world," the Port of Miami hosts over one-third of the free world's fleet of cruise ships. All the well-known cruise lines can be seen here.

□ **Tropical Balloons**
4790 SW 72nd Avenue, Miami. (305) 666-6645. By appointment. $110 per person.

Up, up, and away . . . this one-hour balloon ride lets you see the upper keys, Everglades National Park, Biscayne Bay, and downtown Miami.

Broward County

□ **Hibiscus Tours**
1848 SW 24th Avenue, Fort Lauderdale 33312. (305) 792-5518. Daily, 8:30 A.M.–1 P.M. Adults, $22; children under 12, $20. Cash payment only.

The tour bus picks up passengers from several hotels along Fort Lauderdale Beach, and includes a 45-minute airboat ride, an animal and alligator show, a trip to a working orange grove, and a stop at Everglades Holiday Park. Make reservations at your hotel, or call for information. Snacks and restrooms are available at most tour stops.

□ **Las Olas Horse and Carriage Rides**
Catch them at corner of East Las Olas Boulevard and SE Eighth Avenue or wherever you see them along their route in downtown Fort Lauderdale. (305) 763-7393. Tuesday through Sunday, 7–11:30 P.M. Twenty-minute New River ride: adults, $8; children, half price. Thirty-minute ride through Colee-Hammock Park (old residential area): adults; $12, children ages 4 to 10, half price. Cash payment only.

Children and adults will enjoy this novel way to see Fort Lauderdale. If you come without the kids, bring your own champagne—they'll provide the glasses. Doors on the carriage provide extra saftey for children on board.

☐ Port Everglades
Take I-95 to State Road 84/Port Everglades exit and follow signs east.
(305) 523-3404.

The second busiest cruise port in the world, next to the Port of Miami.
Nearly 2 million passengers a year sail from this 2,100-acre seaport on over
23 major cruise lines.

☐ Pro Diver II
Bahia Mar Yacht Basin on A1A (just south of Las Olas Boulevard), Fort
Lauderdale. (305) 467-6030. Departs daily, 9:30 A.M., plus 2 P.M. Sunday,
and 8 P.M. Saturday. Adults, $12; children under age 12, $6; under 5, free.
Adult snorkelers (equipment included), $18; children under 12, $12.

A daily glass-bottom boat trip to Fort Lauderdale's Twin Ledges coral reef
(off the beach near the Sheraton Yankee Trader) gives adults and children a
chance to view the underwater world through the boat's glass bottom, or
"up-close and personal" with the use of snorkeling equipment. The two-
hour trip will give passengers a look at the Intracoastal Waterway, Port
Everglades, and the reefs and fish of the Atlantic Ocean a half-mile offshore.
Tip: Parking available in the Bahia Mar parking lot. Pro Dive shop will
stamp parking ticket for discount.

☐ Rickshaw Express
Downtown Fort Lauderdale. (305) 522-4640. Weekends only: Friday,
6 P.M.–midnight; Saturday, noon–midnight; Sunday, noon–9 P.M. Twelve-
minute ride: adults, $3; children, $1.50. Twenty-five-minute ride: adults, $6;
children, $3. Cash payment only.

This is fun way to see the sights of downtown Fort Lauderdale. And part of
the fun is in walking downtown and waiting for the rickshaws to come by.

☐ Sawgrass Recreational Park Tour
Pruitt Tour Service, Sawgrass Recreational Park, 5400 U.S. Highway 27,
Fort Lauderdale. (305) 389-0202. Daily, 9 A.M.–5 P.M. Adults, $9; children
ages 2 to 12, $5; children under 2, free. Cash payment only.

The 35-minute airboat ride includes an alligator show and a bird show. Row
boats and canoes can be rented, and island camping facilities can be
reserved. Snack and soft drinks are available at the bait and tackle shop.

□ **Trolley Tours, Inc.**

832 South Military Trail, Deerfield Beach 33442. (305) 426-3044 in Broward County, (305) 948-8823 in Dade County, (800) 32-LOLLY elsewhere. Daily, 10 A.M., noon, 2, and 4 P.M. Adults, $10; children under 12 free when accompanied by adult. Tickets are valid all day. Call about charters, tours, and birthday party arrangements. Cash payment only.

The trolleys pick you up at Fort Lauderdale's major beach hotels and take you on fully-narrated historical tours, where you'll see sights such as the International Swimming Hall of Fame, the Galleria, and Las Olas Boulevard. You may get off at any stop to see sights on your own, and then hop back on the next trolley that comes by. This is a good idea if you want to get to Ocean World or the Jungle Queen. **Tip:** Restroom stops can be made at several places along the tour; let the guide know when you need to go!

□ **Voyager Tram Services**

Travels from Diplomat Mall to nearby residential areas. (305) 458-6576. Monday through Saturday, 9 A.M.–4:30 P.M. 25¢.

□ **Voyager Sightseeing Tram Services**

600 Seabreeze Boulevard, Fort Lauderdale 33316. (305) 463-0401 in Broward County; (305) 944-4699 in Dade County. 10 A.M., noon, 2, and 4 P.M. Adults, $6.50; children ages 3 to 12, $3; children under 3, free. Group rates available. Cash payment only.

An open-air coach pulled by a jeep takes you for a 1½-hour, 18-mile historical tour of 60 points of interest in Fort Lauderdale. See Port Everglades, Las Olas Boulevard, fishing fleets and military vessels, manatees, and tropical fish. Tours can be arranged for groups of 15 or more. Special stops can be arranged for children's tours.

□ **Water Taxi**

VHF Channel 68. 14 South New River Drive East, Fort Lauderdale 33301. (305) 565-5507. $2.50 per person; charters are available for $50 per hour (26 people maximum).

Call from any waterside location along the Intracoastal Waterway between Commercial Boulevard and Port Everglades, or from the New River to downtown, and this bright yellow taxi with a surrey on top will take you to your destination. Any place with a dock will do. Kids might enjoy taking a ride from the dock behind Discovery Center to a dock at a local park. **Tip:**

Allow about 30 minutes for the taxi to pick you up, and remember that water conditions may affect travel time.

Palm Beach County

□ **"A Familly Affair" Bicycle Tour**
Meet at Patch Reef Park, 2000 NW 51st Street (Yamato Road, just west of Military Trail), Boca Raton 33431. (407) 391-0800. Call for dates and times. $1.50 per rider; $5 maximum per family.

This tour takes you through eight of Boca Raton's most spectacular parks. This is an 18-mile ride, and refreshments are served at one of the parks along the route. **Tips:** Riders should be at least 8 years old. Be sure to wear helmets and bring water bottles. Bicycles should be in good working condition.

Monroe County

□ **Captain Buddy's Family Fun Trips**
Mile Marker 28, P.O. Box 1488, Big Pine Key 33043. (305) USA-3572. Open daily at various times. Cost for adults starts at $29; first child age 5 or under free with adult; additional children pay half price. MC, V accepted.

This customized four-hour tour explores the coral reef and out islands. Snorkeling equipment is available.

□ **Conch Classic Air Tours, Inc.**
(305) 296-0727. $40-$120; children under 2, free. AE, DIN, MC, V accepted.

Put on your helmet, goggles, and complimentary scarf to take a flight in a 1987 WACO open-cockpit plane. Fly over Key West to the coral reefs and out islands. You'll get a great view of the sea life below. Flights last 20 to 40 minutes. Call for reservations and directions.

□ **Conch Tour Trains**
601 Duval Street, Key West 33040. Departs from Mallory Square and

Roosevelt Depot. (305) 294-5161. Daily, 9 A.M.–5 P.M. Adults, $10; children, $3. Group rates for 20 or more available with reservations.

This 1½-hour narrated ride highlights over 60 historical and unusual sights. Along the 14-mile route you will see such points of interest as the Hemingway House, the Audubon House, Mel Fisher's Treasure Exhibit, Truman's Little White House, and the Southernmost Point. Some of the most interesting stories capture the days of pirates, conquistadors, and Old Key West.

□ Fireball Glass-Bottom Boat

Departs from north end of Duval Street. Mailing address is 2 Duval Street, Key West 33040. (305) 296-6293 or (305) 294-8704. Open year round, 8 A.M.–sunset. Boats leave daily, 9:30 and 11:30 A.M., and 2 P.M. Prices vary. Group rates and rainchecks available. MC, V accepted.

Don't forget your camera on this one! During this two-hour trip you'll get a narrated history lesson as you pass by Fort Zachary Taylor, live coral reefs, and shrimp boats. Children can feed the fish off the deck of this 65-foot boat. **Tips:** A water cooler is brought on board and film is available, just in case you forget it when you pack the camera! There are also two restrooms on board. Strollers may be brought on board. Sunscreen is advisable.

□ Key Largo Princess Glass Bottom Boat

Mile Marker 100, Holiday Inn, Key Largo. (305) 451-4655. Departs at 10 A.M., and 1 and 4 P.M. Adults, $12; children under 12, $6.

This company has been touring the coral reefs since 1953.

□ Key West Seaplane Service

5603 Jr. College Road, Key West 33040. (Between Mile Markers 5 and 6. Turn west to bay side and drive past landfill [highest point in Keys].) (305) 294-6978. Departs daily, 8 A.M. and noon. Extra flights on Sunday if necessary. Adults, $99; children ages 6 and under, $50. AE, MC, V accepted.

This 40-minute, low-flying flight gives you a view of shipwrecks and marine life as it takes you to Fort Jefferson. You can spend two hours swimming around and exploring the island. A cooler with soft drinks is provided, but take a picnic along. For more information about Fort Jefferson, see "Tracing the Past."

☐ **Old Town Trolley**
Old Town Trolley Car Barn, 1910 North Roosevelt Boulevard, Key West 33040. (305) 296-6688. Departs from Mallory Square in Old Town every half hour beginning at 8:45 A.M., with the last tour at 4:30 P.M. Adults, $10; children ages 4 to 15, $4; children under 4, free. MC, V accepted.

Narrated tours last 90 minutes, but you can get off at any point and rejoin a tour at 30-minute intervals. Over 100 points of interest are covered, and all-weather transportation is provided. Foreign language tours are available. Free parking is also available at the Key West Welcome Center, 3840 North Roosevelt.

Photo Credits

Index